The Teachings of Acumana

Coming In On A Ray of Love

Volume I

William P. Kinney

Back Cover Artwork:
The Blessing, Rosalie Heacock, ©2001

The Forum Light Publishing
PO Box 5915
Santa Fe, NM 87502

ISBN#0-9678047-0-1
Library of Congress Control Number: 2001097265

Contents

Preface

Acumana appeared out of nowhere on a clear winter evening and spoke through Bill in broken English. In my vision Bill was gone and in his place sat this little Oriental man with a sweet smile. His first words were: "Acumana greet you, daughter of light." "Who are you?" I asked.

"Acumana be teacher," he replied. "Will teach this way for many times, for many people." Bill and I didn't know many people. We lived a very reclusive life, based on survival and the care of our three little children.

Acumana's appearance would change our lives totally. He gave us solace and hope. After getting over the shock of the event of his arrival, we started looking forward to our evening appointments with him. Shortly after his first appearance, he said, "Must go now, so William may return. Tell him is all right, is all right to leave and come back and let Acumana speak with his voice. Tell him this."

Acumana left and Bill returned. "Sorry I fell asleep, Carol," he said. "I had the strangest dream. I dreamed I was going up a hill through a woods, and as I was walking up the path, this little Oriental man was coming down. He had his hands in his sleeves and he bowed to me. I found a grassy spot up on the knoll, laid down and went to sleep. When I woke up and came down the path, this little man was going up the path, and he bowed to me again. I felt like I knew him somehow. What a strange dream."

"He was here, Bill," I said. "You left and he was there where you are sitting. He spoke through your voice. He said he will come again this way. He said to tell you not to be concerned."

Our evenings were lovely. We all had a nice dinner together, played with the children until sunset, read story books to them, put on a music tape, and tucked them into their beds. We were happy with our routines.

Bill prepared our dinette table with votive candles, flowers from our garden, and a crystal bowl of water. He didn't know why he wanted the bowl of water on the table, but it seemed important.

We started our prayer time by saying the Lord's Prayer together. After which, each of us spoke a personal prayer, then became quiet to pray silently. After several weeks of this dedication to prayer, our lives greatly improved. Then Acumana came, and our lives were changed forever.

Acumana told us that his origins were Oriental. "From the land of the great wall," he said, "From land of Zoroaster, too, from Persia, understand? Long time ago from Persia."

Acumana came as a teacher, he became a friend, a confidant, a spokesperson for a group of spiritual teachers from the Higher Dimensions. Indeed, he did teach many people over a period of many years. He told us of his own teacher, Djwhal Khul. He stated the purpose of the Masters in communicating in this special way.

"Our purpose is to help the student to find Truth. We, the Elder Ones of the Race, Teachers of a Higher Realm, wish to provide you with help on the Path of Spiritual Enlightenment. It is our desire to assist you in this mighty undertaking, for we have been where you are. We remember how difficult life seemed before we let go of struggling and allowed our outer selves to surrender to that within which is beautiful and holy.

"You are in the forefront, with many others, leading the way into the Golden Age of Spiritual Freedom, an age in which men and women of Good Will have the ability to reach as far as their dreams can take them. The world that you see with your eyes and hear with your ears is a momentary illusion, created by your thoughts and the thoughts of other inhabitants of your world. When you have a glimpse of what your planet is to become, what you are to become, you want to be a part of it all. There is so much more you have not seen, beauty that cannot be described, love that envelops all. When you come to see the so-called future, you will be inspired.

"Come, walk with us down one of the many paths that lead to the Luminous Lake of Holy Spirit. You are welcome."

—CAROL B. KNIGHT, SCRIBE

CHAPTER I

Self Mastery

As you see with the inner sense your truer nature, your higher soul-self, you will cease striving toward petty accomplishments. The truer you, the soul-self, the I-am-ness, which is personified in you by the great laws of your Father, is so grand and dynamic that it makes your physical body very small, inconsequential, in comparison with that which is the real you.

Students need to maintain equipoise and balance from within. To do this, begin to rely upon your own higher intuitive faculty. Your desires and your goals are for more Light and more wisdom. If you desire and maintain continuous personal reference, you only deter your own growth. That which is round and about you in the world of materiality is of your own making, which you shall soon discover as we proceed into some of the deeper teachings. You will discover that which is reflected about you, in every degree and there is no exception, is a reflection of the law "As above, so below."

Look upon each other as fellow members upon the ladder of wisdom. There is no distinction between one who has acquired more knowledge than another, for not one of you is able to perceive the inner nature of the other person. Therefore you have not the authority nor the power to predetermine who is worthy of such teachings and who is not worthy.

You must accept the precept that all who seek wisdom and have the ears to hear and the eyes to read must be deserving.

You have all journeyed different roads, different avenues. The ancient Romans, in all their pagan understandings, in the latter days of their history, coined a most adequate expression, "All roads lead to Rome," Rome at that time being the hub and center of the world. By equal measure, each of you in your journey from life to life have chosen an avenue, a spoke on the wheel of evolution, which brings you to the hub of wisdom. Wherever you are upon that spoke is your determined goal.

There is a word familiar to each of you in your everyday affairs. It is called ALL. *A-L-L.* This word is important in the philosophy which we are endeavoring to convey to you. Certain key words must be given so that the flow of teaching may be carried on consistently from generation to generation.

What is the All? Do not try to define the All, for it is undefinable, Unexplainable. It is a law. It is a fact. It is that essence which is the ever-expanding O. The All is Omnipotence. It is the infinite ever-expanding being of the universe. It is the Supreme Emanation of wisdom.

The three aspects of Infinite Supreme Being are Power, Word and Motion. These are the aspects of the Supreme Infinite Being. Acumana has not said "God." God is related to your universe. Now you must consider what is beyond your universe. So the All contains these three aspects: Power, Word and Motion.

The third aspect, Motion, only comes through the law brought about by the first two aspects, Power and Word. When Power and Word are brought together they produce Motion. It is a chain reaction. There is no inner law which determines the All to function accordingly. It does because It is that law.

In man, for example, the desire to appease his appetite is brought about, for want of another word, by instinct—the instinct to eat for survival. What produces this instinct within man? Mind. Which mind, Divine Mind or mortal mind, corporeal mind? Both. The Master said to you: "Know ye not that ye are gods?" This means that the potential is within you for godhood. Since this potential is within you for godhood, then contained within you must be this aspect of mind. Your mortal mind is brought about by the law of Divine Mind. You are gods, yet you are not gods. For if you were a god, would you be sitting in the limitation of this vibration? Would you be limited by having to scratch words on a tablet to remember? You would not, if you were gods, be limited to such a motivation; however, an aspect within you, brought about by the three aspects of the Supreme Infinite Being (Power, Word and Motion), is endowed with that inner nature called Spirit. It is God.

What is Spirit? It is the All. Man is a reflection of certain vibrations lowered according to physical law, brought about through density, to reflect an aspect of the Supreme Infinite Being whose goal is to achieve godhood. Note, The Master did not say, "Know ye not that ye are Infinite Supreme Beings," He said, "Know ye not that ye are gods?" Therefore, being as a god is your goal.

How do you achieve godhood? By self-mastery. And you achieve self-mastery through recognizing, becoming cognizant of, discerning, contemplating, growing, and striving to achieve a degree of understanding of yourself, the spirit within you and the body. The flesh and the blood.

The blood is a vibration of spiritual energy. The body is a vibration of physical energy brought about through certain definite chemical laws. You learn that love is a rate of vibration of great intensity. Love produces harmonious chords throughout the universe. It produces and reproduces and multiplies.

The great chain reaction in the universe is called the Hierarchy. For your edification, Acumana shall briefly explain this to you, so that you may grasp a glimmering of what is meant by the All, on the seven higher cosmic planes.

The first cosmic plane is Supreme Infinite Being—Power, Word and Motion—the great ever-expanding O. It has no beginning, no origin, no conclusion. It is the ALL.

The second cosmic plane is where the great Logoi dwell. There are forty-nine hierarchies on the second cosmic plane. Each of these has a septenary division of seven, which would therefore lead to the third cosmic plane, which has three hundred forty-three hierarchies. And if you multiply each by seven and then by another seven and then by another seven, by the time you proceed down the ladder of the cosmic planes to the seventh cosmic plane where your solar system dwells, you will find an infinite dimension and number of hierarchies.

It is all part of the All, all within the mind of Supreme Infinite Intelligence. You cannot even yet conceive of God.

The three aspects of God are Will, Wisdom and Activity. It is likened unto a pyramid. Make a pyramid on a piece of paper. At the peak of the pyramid put "Power." At the side of it write "Word," and at the other side write "Motion." Make another pyramid, that is God. Put God in the center of the Pyramid. Above it write the first aspect which is Will, then write Wisdom and then Activity.

Note the difference in the intensity between the two. First is Supreme Infinite Intelligence. The second pyramid is God. That is your goal. That is what you strive for—God awareness.

Each hierarchy, the number of which you cannot measure, has charge of a solar system, a galaxy. And in your solar system on your seventh cosmic plane you find the Seven Spirits before the throne. The Seven Spirits before the throne are your seven major planets of evolution. There is a Lord in charge of each. Each Lord, in turn, has three aspects. These we will consider at another time. It is beyond this purpose now. Only know that each Lord of a solar system has three aspects. He, in turn, (using the word "He" only as a point of reference; it is neither masculine nor feminine, to connote only Power and Will) has divisions and subdivisions beyond calculation. Your seven planets of evolution contained within your solar system are guided and governed by the Supreme Intelligences of the seventh cosmic plane—the Hierarchy.

What has Acumana said of the sun to you? It is the closest symbol you have to God. Though Christian man calls the ancient Grecians and Romans pagans, for they worshipped the sun, yet were they so wrong?

The seven planets in order are: Uranus, Saturn, Jupiter, Mars, Earth, Venus and Mercury. The seven cosmic planes are beyond your powers of comprehension. It is only for you to contemplate and know they exist. They are not your immediate goal. Your immediate goal is to transcend the seven spiritual planes. When you have done this, you have reached God. This is your degree of mastery.

Now we will come back to the All. Contained within the All is all that is, and the All is mind. The All is the aspect of the Supreme Infinite Intelligence which is Word, Power and Motion. The All is contained within the three aspects of God, which are Will, Wisdom, Activity. It embraces the endless depths of the universe. It is all things. It is energy. It is matter. It is vibration. It is substance. It is the will factor of the universe.

Where is the universe? It is around and about you. Your seven spiritual planes, as Acumana has said recently, are not above you in space that you must climb to. They interpenetrate one another. They are inter-blended within one another. They are a part of the All, which is the mind of the Supreme Infinite Intelligence.

What is said in the Bible of this? "In Him we live and move and have our being." Is this not true? Spirit is not above you millions and millions of miles. The spiritual planes are all about you in different rates of vibration.

Be not ever deceived that it is far removed from you. It is not. For if it were, mark you, Acumana could no more converse with you than you could converse with the proverbial man in the moon. "In Him we live and move and have our being." All the seven dimensions of the spiritual world inter-blend, interpenetrate one another in your ethers.

There are seven dimensions of ether. Those seven dimensions of ether are the seven spiritual vibrations or planes of man. Not the seven cosmic planes. They are different.

Now, let us consider another aspect of the All. The All moves within you, yes? What is the quote Acumana has given you?

"In Him we live and move and have our being." Does this not say to you vividly that Mind, the All, is within you? It does, indeed. It says that you have within you awareness, power. It says, "Know ye not that ye are gods?" As above, so below. As above in the seven cosmic planes, so below, in the seven spiritual planes, and as below in the seven sub-planes.

See a cross extended before you. You can never find the end of the cross. The cross is continued upward and downward. Which is up? Which is down? Which is right? Which is left? Which is north? Which is east, west and south in direction? In space and dimension there is no such thing.

These things are only limited to a physical rate of vibration. And this you must transcend, you must transmute. Daily discipline your mind. If you have in your corporal mind, which is the lower dimension, a feeling called envy, what is the opposite of envy? Charity. You cannot substitute, for example, love as an opposite of heroism. Fear and heroism parallel. Love and fear are not on the same pole.

Now let us consider the base nature of man. You have, let us say, envy, to overcome. Here is a key for you. What you want is love, so how do you transmute envy to love? First you must find the opposite of envy, which would be charity. Then substitute charity in place of envy.

If you have a thought of greed, what is the opposite of greed? Unselfishness. Transmute greed, a base metal, for a higher alloy, silver or gold. Transmute greed, by the moment, by the second, to unselfishness. Change each thought as it comes. You are the guardians, my children! Only you are the guardians. No one in the universe can do this for you, only you. You know your thoughts. You know your meanings. You know your being. If you have a feeling of anxiety or fear, hatred, envy, greed, lust—whatever they be on the bottom of the scale, substitute it immediately with its opposite. That is transmutation. Transmute the thought.

Each thought that you project has a reaction on something in the universe, some matter in the universe. Some degree of matter is affected by your thought.

"Know ye not that ye are gods?" If this is true then you must have power, latent dormant power, within you. Do not be foolish enough to declare yourselves gods. Only know that the potential exists within you.

Nothing is omitted from the universe. Each thought that you project affects your universe, your being, your body, because you have projected it. Therefore, what causes bodily decay, disease, frustration anxiety, is whatever you will. If you will these things, they are yours. The law works to perfection. If you envy, if you dislike, if you are frustrated, if you have any of these base conditions in life, you are the recipient, no one else. Your world begins to disintegrate. It is why man today experiences many diseases and breakdowns. He is daily committing suicide with his thoughts. He is literally committing suicide.

It is an advantage to live long years in good health. Do not think you must hurry through life to return to spirit. It is better you handle all you can here. The more you are able to handle and stay in life, the greater you are benefited on your scale of evolution. Each of you should live two to three hundred years. You are equipped to live this long, or longer, depending upon your mental discipline. Why live only to seventy or eighty years?

You can learn to transmute your thoughts, through mental discipline, to rise above conditions. If there is fear about you, courage is what you strive for. How do you accomplish this? Do you proclaim words which will give you courage? Do you read prayers which will give you courage? These are only symbols. If you feel you must use them, do it. But the best way to approach it without any affirmation or prayers—for not a one of you know how to pray yet—is this way:

Say to yourself, "I am filled with fear. The opposite of fear is courage. In the face of God, what is there to fear? What is there to fear in the All? What can I lose? What can harm me?" No harm can come to you. Nothing can harm you. You can lose nothing. You may lose material goods, but what do they matter to you when you know that, through the law of mind, you may have them replaced immediately? But if you possess and cling, you assuredly will lose them. If you use them because they are gifts of God, for your enjoyment, and pleasure, you will always have them.

You may walk out of your home on the morrow without any goods, and on the following day you may walk into another home with twice as many goods to use. But that is not your goal. Never seek after goods. Come to practice what is called the everyday metaphysical approach to abundance. Why frustrate yourselves? You are beyond it. That is worshiping the golden calf.

First search after the kingdom of God, the kingdom of heaven. Maybe then you will find, that in the kingdom of heaven there is gold, there is beauty. If it happens to be in materiality, fine. If it does not, it matters not to you. Cease to worry. Cease to be confused by what tomorrow will bring. Tomorrow will bring the fruits of your thoughts of today. Each day you build for tomorrow. According to the seeds of your planting, abundance comes. If you say, "I desire certain material conditions, you will begin to understand that if you have a want—the opposite of want is fulfillment—then you contemplate fulfillment. If you are gods as a potential, then you live within the All. Does the All not know what you need? It is so!

So if you have a want, you take the opposite of want, which is fulfillment, and you rise above want. Fill your consciousness with fulfillment. Think of fulfillment. Think of flowers as a symbol. There is no greater symbol of fulfillment than the profusion of flowers around and about you at all times. The more flowers and growth you have around you, the more you have coming to you through the ethers of fulfillment.

What Acumana has given you is a summation, that you may grasp a concept of the mind, which is the striving toward self-mastery every day.

First you must become unselfish. You must become honest. Take your measure by yourself alone, honestly. If you have to, stand before a mirror. Look into the mirror at your reflection. That is the image that you project. Just as you are the image that God projects, God is the image the Hierarchies project. And the Hierarchies are the images which Infinite Supreme Intelligence, the All, projects. As you look in the mirror take your measure and say, "Who and what are you?" Go to both poles, the positive and the negative. Take each aspect on the negative pole within you, and start on the morrow, one at a time, to eliminate your bad habits, your bad qualities, your bad thoughts. Purge your heart and your soul of them through mental discipline. Transmute them, as the alchemists did. Be your own alchemist!

Take every impure thought and deed, find its opposite, and strive to fill your consciousness with it. Only by constant repetition is this achieved.

Each time you have a thought recur, stop the thought, transmute it, rise above it. Whatever anyone says to you, if they hurl negation at you—and the world will try always to pull you to its level—rise above it. You know the laws, the world at large does not. Who then is the bigger, you or the multitudes?

Now you may ask Acumana questions of this.

Student: **Acumana, in the transmuting from the negative to the positive, is it strictly a mental process? Could you please give us an example?**

Say you desire more patience. What is the opposite of impatience? Patience. You are impatient. How do you approach this? You recognize first of all that characteristic which is undesirable. You recognize it. Each time the circumstance presents itself for impatience, you discipline the mind and force patience upon yourself. No matter what inconvenience it causes you, you force yourself to be patient, tolerant, until you learn the lesson. But you do not say, "I must be patient, must be patient," for then you will become angry and add one more negative. Do not force yourself to be patient under every extreme condition. Look at the conditions around you with objectivity so that you will know what the Law of Flexibility is. You will say, "Such and such a condition exists because—", but find fault with nothing.

Find the reason for the impatience. You will find that the world functions differently for different people. All cannot fit into a perfect little corner. So each time a condition presents itself to cause you impatience and anguish, live through it and create yourself to be patient, radiant and happy.

Do not become passive. Passivity is only reached at a higher state of consciousness. You must learn to fight now. Each of you must become a spiritual warrior in the great army of mastery. And when you have reached mastery then you reach a point of peace where you have blended and perfected both natures within you. Now you must stand firm because you will find that every base tendency within you will come to the surface. Satan will unloosen all of its power. All of its forces will come against you to beat upon you.

Student: **From outside as well as from within?**

Yes, from the outside, but not to the extent that you will suffer consequences mentally. We are speaking of a mental conquest. This is your higher nature. Your higher nature is striving for light and recognition. It is reaching out. The giant within you is growing. So the opposite of your god self, which is darkness, wants to hold on to the corporal nature. It enjoys harboring thoughts of negation, impatience, desire, envy. The seven cardinal sins are most pleased in gratifying themselves.

They will strive to hold their position, but you must become strong and outflank them, completely outflank them, by knowing that ye are gods. And in Him you live and move and have your being by mentally disciplining each thought.

You will find yourself each day having a different thought than you have had before. You will say to yourself, "Strange that such a thought should come into my mind." You will say, "Is this opposed to the teaching I've been given?" It is Satan loosening within you all those conditions to oppose you. But remember, it is likened unto a tempest in a teapot. For you all have the ability to transmute every base quality within you.

Student: Is it important, when you recognize this lesser thought, to identify clearly the opposite, which is the positive thought?

Yes, and if you do not find the correct opposite, you are on another pole, and you will not succeed. It is like field maneuvers in a battle. If the general knows his enemy is entrenched on a certain hill and he desires to surround them, if he has not studied the topography of the land, and he takes his ranks all the way down the river to cross the bridge, by the time he arrives there the enemy will have slipped away, and perhaps the enemy will have sneaked up behind them and outflanked them. So you must study the topography. You must study the opposites, to know which one to call upon. Each one has a power unto itself.

Student: I would like to clarify a point of balance on the subject of abundance. Somewhere between dismissing the thought and saying "I have all that I need," there is a balance. Where is the balance, how much energy do we give the thought and when do we quit?

Acumana has given you the balance. It ceases to be important for any of you now for that to be your goal. Your goal is what? What does it say, "Seek ye first the kingdom of God, and all these things shall be added unto you." Forget your need. You are living in the old self if you constantly become aware of your need and project it. The All knows your need. The All is your need.

If ye are god, therefore, and are a part of the All then the All knows your need. And if you seek first the kingdom of God, then the All must be part of that kingdom of God.

Student: Then the attention need not be focused consciously from this point on?

It need not. Dismiss it in the full sense. For you know you are the law. You know there is a need. What is the opposite of need? Fulfillment.

Fulfillment, not prosperity. That is the physical. That must be eradicated from your consciousness. Prosperity is not your goal. Abundance of wisdom is your goal. Abundance of God-awareness is your goal not prosperity. Prosperity perhaps is an aspect of that. That is only determined by the individual destiny. Do not be concerned with prosperity. You must be part of the law of fulfillment.

***Student:* Acumana, in Power, Word and Motion, what is the definition of "Word"?**

Word is that which produces Motion. Motion produces the universe. The universe produces the aspects. The Word is life. Power is the ability to conceive. Power is mind. Can you conceive of this, my students?

Power is mind. It is the first aspect of Supreme Infinite Intelligence. Power. That is the spiritual inner nature, and it produces the Word. The Word produces Motion. Acumana speaks the Word. Is that not motion? It is vibratory motion, as well as its physical counterpart of motion being the movement of the lips. Motion. Acumana says to you, walk. You walk. Acumana says breathe. You breathe. So Word is the sustaining of life through the Power, which produces Motion. The three together are the harmonies of the universe.

***Student:* I was thinking about it in relation to, "In the beginning was the Word, and the Word was of God, and then it was God."**

Yes, in the beginning was the Word. What did the Word produce? Movement, Motion, Activity. The Word is the beginning of movement in chaos. It is energy. It is substance, and it produces Motion.

***Student:* As it is above, so it is below—are those who have "passed over" who are "in spirit" at the same stage of evolvement as we may be here?**

It is not the same. It is a different dimension. They are in spirit for to be "in spirit" is to be in energy. But you also may live both in spirit and in flesh. To be living in spirit in the flesh is to be living in the knowingness of the laws, that every moment you are aware of the law, and that your every thought is a productive thought. That is living in spirit. It is knowing that every thought in your being must be a positive productive thought for the world, your world. That is spirit.

You are doing your Father's work. And what is the work of the Father? What does Jesus say? I am about my Father's work. Never is there an idle moment in His daily affairs, nor should there be in yours. Let even your moments of contemplation be filled with creative thoughts.

You all live, according to the infinite understanding of life, very lazy lives. You get about conveniently. You do not walk enough. You do not breathe enough. You do not enjoy enough. Each of you should walk every day at least two miles. Why do you think your fore-fathers lived to be so old? Why do you think they were so healthy? They walked. Their bodies were built as your bodies are built. Man has life too convenient today. If you cannot walk two miles, walk at least a mile, every day.

How can your bodies circulate? How can your energies, your universe within you, build, when you sit constantly day by day? Each of you need to eliminate obesity from your natures. It is contrary to the law of positivity. You must enjoy the out-of-doors more, the breath of the air, flowers, nature.

> ***Student:*** **You spoke of praying, you said that most of us didn't pray correctly. Should we eliminate some of this and think more in a positive manner, instead of more or less praying for things?**

It would be a more adequate approach, Yes. In those hours you have set aside for prayer, instead of repeating words, discipline your mind, concentrate, and think of God. Think of the universe. Think of the radiant Christ, His deeds.

Think not of self, but of the universe. Discipline the mind in prayer. Pray for others. Offer up numerous prayers for those in need. Pray for the world.

Now, may the great radiant Light descend upon you all, surround and envelop you in your daily journey. May you be endowed with the power of the universe to assist you in your disciplines. Know that you walk in the presence of God. Know that you are that potential. Trust it. Believe it. Know it to be. A part of the All, the All of the I AM within.

THE PATH

In Truth and in Light,
The path is never long,
But is always strong
And always pleasant,
If we but view it
With the eyes of Truth and Light.
We walk upon this great path
In search of perfection and Godhood.
I seek perfection and light.
All men seek perfection and light,
Even while struggling in darkness.
May I always understand this truth.
May I never condemn another.
May I walk uprightly on the path,
Giving forth Truth and Light
That others may see and believe
That in Truth and in Light
The path is never long.

CHAPTER II

Spirituality

Acumana would like you to consider the word spirituality. What is spirituality? It is a word greatly misinterpreted, misrepresented, and above all misunderstood by the populace of Truth students. For are not Truth students a populace unto themselves?

Spirituality is an element, a power, a substance. It is neither one individuality, but all collectively. Spirit is energy. Spirit is substance. Spirit is power. It is the dimension, height, width, depth, breath and full scope of the cosmos. That is spirit.

What is spirituality in comparison to spirit? Spirituality is the effect of the knowledge of Truth or the knowledge of spirit acting upon a conscious individual.

Let Acumana paraphrase this for you. Spirituality is a degree of conscious Truth within you whereby it enables you to be conscious of spirit and conscious of the cosmic substance around you. That is spirituality.

Spirituality is not assuming humility. Spirituality is not assuming reverence. Spirituality is not assuming compassion, kindness, meekness, dedication, service or any of these other fine qualities. Spirituality is a motivating power or energy within a man which reflects in his daily life.

You speak of service. So many times Acumana hears you say, "I want to serve." It is good, grand and noble that you should serve your fellow man, for that is your mission, your goal here in this, your boarding house, your world.

But what does it mean to serve? To serve is to know Truth and understand it. Mind you, Acumana did not say to be Truth, for that comes later. To know Truth is to serve Truth. To attempt to practice Truth is to serve Truth. When a person recognizes the depth of his own spirituality, there is no force in the universe to hold him back from service. His every moment, his every second, his whole motivation, will be directed to a point of specific service. This does not mean you can go blindly about things. You must use discernment. First, know and understand Truth to the best of your ability. Coordinate this with the desire to serve. There is a balance. The more you are exposed to Truth and allow it to flow through you, the more you begin to serve. You need not say, "I must serve," with a fever and a passion. Then you are not in Truth, for the desire is too great for you. When the desire to serve is too great, then the purpose of your service is lost.

So, what do you do? You open your consciousness to Truth, so that your own spirituality, your own energy, your own godhead, will shine and flow through you. Then you cannot help but serve.

Now, let us consider the Christ consciousness. Herein is a principle, the principle of evolvement, Christ, the Christed state, Christ consciousness. It also represents, symbolically as well as literally, a race of consciousness within a being of great height and dimension who has journeyed upon the same mundane plane that you are journeying upon, in another cycle. It is one who has transcended all physical, karmic lessons and who has become fully integrated within the cosmic law of the human being. It is one who is in full rapport with his spirituality, with his great I AM, with his great God-consciousness, and has served. How could he help but serve under such terms? He could not, for when one has reached such a point of consciousness he cannot help but serve. To become aware of who and what you are is what is important.

Spring represents the birth of Christ consciousness. In this time of year there are more babies born than any other time. In this time of year man's consciousness is more open to gaiety than at any other time, for the spirit of Christ consciousness as a universal principle—mind you, as a principle—is regeneration and rebirth. Is it not, therefore, significant that in the spring, in the rejuvenating cycle, that one who gave substance and blood to the Earth of a man called Jesus of Nazareth, should rise and ascend? He ascended in the spring, as a visible, physical, concrete example of the cosmic law of ascension, which nature performs annually without effort.

Is a tree conscious of practicing the law of positiveness? Is the tree worried and bothered over the feeding on the morrow? Is the tree concerned with who will provide it with water? It knows, because it is. The law feeds it, according to law. The tree grows, according to law. It is spirit in consciousness. But it is of another cycle of evolvement.

Man is the only creature who worries. The tree does not worry. The rock does not worry, and the dog does not worry. Who worries? Only man. However, he must learn now, because of his freedom of expression, his free will, to transcend all lower thoughts, one of which is to worry. He must rise above these thoughts.

The spring of the year, therefore, is symbolic of resurrection. You, in turn, must daily resurrect your thoughts and rise above the race consciousness, the world consciousness. You must apply these principles which Acumana gives to you, over and over. The more Acumana gives them the more they will begin to seep into your inner consciousness. Just as the blotter will hold only as much as it is capable of holding, when that point is reached another consciousness will open within you. It is impossible to measure the depth of a person's spirituality. That is the inner chamber that no man knows, only the Father.

The principle of Christ ascending, the ascension, gives the lesson that there is a purpose to each season. In the spring it is ascension. To ascend to the great spiritual heights, that you may be maintained and sustained throughout the next three seasons. Each season brings a perfection. Spring is the season of procreation, repopulation, regrowth, rejuvenation, whereby it expresses its beauty. Observe nature daily in this season. As it reaches completion and its cycle is over and done, it returns back to the dormant state. Fall and winter are like your transitory periods after the transition called death, where you rebuild, reaccumulate, regather your inner substance. You go within in dormancy. Spring and summer you produce, you work, and show your labors, as nature does.

You are not above nature. Which of you has stepped upon this plane other than through natural cause? Not one. Each of you must therefore, be subject to natural law. What applies to natural law applies to you.

Since you are of nature, nature is of you. You are all of the same source. The Lord Jesus has proven this to you. There is a harmony between all things throughout the universe. Correspondence is the law whereby all things, all energies, originate from the same source, work together, blend together in a symphony, a harmony.

Nature is part of you. You are part of nature. Each of you is born of the substance of the Earth. Within your body is every substance contained below you.

Only now the substance turns to energy that exists in your ethers. Then you must have also within you energy weaknesses, energy attractions, which subject you towards certain planetary influences. As above, so below.

Now, since you are the perfect blend of nature and heaven, what do you do? Do you ignore one and heed the other, or heed the one and ignore the other? You do not. You balance them. To balance them is to recognize them, to rise above them. In the study of astrology or numerology one knows certain conditions will exist. As a student of Light, it is your prime obligation of life to rise above those conditions, to transcend the conditions.

The masses will not rise above conditions. They must be subject to various conditions for their growth. Just as a child in school must learn with other children. Unless he is so gifted and outstanding that he learns alone, as a few do, he must become one with the herd. He must share the herd vibration, share the community expression and the benefit that each of his brothers has to offer him. Each one is different, but each lends a power unto the other. Though he is taught collectively, he assimilates the knowledge individually. And as the individual within the collective group, he learns to rise above the group. He ascends, and soon he becomes a master unto himself. Then he need not be one of the group, for he becomes above the group. Are you not part of the mass? You are, but yet you are not the mass. Where are you, then? You are in between, and between is the balance point, the apex, the middle, whereby you could become subject to man's laws or you could become subject to Divine Law. You are at the crossroads. Is not your neighbor down the way subject to the same things you are subject to? According to his degree and condition of evolution, he, just as you, is at the crossroads.

You speak of the masses, as Acumana speaks of the masses, and yet is not the neighbor across the way part of a mass? Are you not including him as one of the masses? You must, for how can you ignore him or yourself? Yet he, in his own room, would speak of the masses and he is speaking of you, and those about him. It is a point of view. He, in his place, is at the crossroads, as you are at a crossroad. The one subtle difference is that you are conscious of the All. He may not be. He is conscious of God, but you are conscious of the All.

Therein is your mark of distinction. You are aware of the Truth. Your eyes are opened. You have come to the well. You have looked at the water, felt its cool, tingling sensation about your bodies. You have sipped of it, and now you thirst for more.

Your neighbor is still down the road. He sees the well, but he is not thirsty yet. Therein is the difference. He is no less a part of you than you are a part of him. Are you not both from the same source? You are from the same, identical source. You are from the hub of the wheel, as he is from the hub of the wheel. You are one spoke, he is another. You are both journeying to the rim.

There is an interblending of all the worlds, all the vibrations. All things work together in harmony. Sound and color work in harmony. What you have in sound is a vibration. What you have in color is a vibration. All things are vibration. What you cannot see in color, beyond your octave of sight, is a vibration. It, in turn, is also a sound. Your senses are limited. You are limited to five senses. You cannot conceive of a color beyond any color that is mentioned in your spectrum or its combination. How could you? If Acumana says to you, "There is the most glorious, brilliant, luminous pink around you," what do you think of? Pink. Pink is what? Red and white. They are in your spectrum. So how can you conceive of the pink Acumana tells you of? It is not in your spectrum. This limits Acumana because it is beyond your understanding. But the mind can conceive of it, can see it. The mind works in the blending of all planes, of all Truths.

You have two minds. You have your divine, God-given mind, and you have the human, mundane, mortal mind. Where shall you dwell? In the middle, with mastery over all! If you have limitation, cease to consider limitation. It does not exist as a word in your vocabulary. Strike it from the records.

Be aware, however, that confusion can exist. If confusion exists, then the opposite of confusion also exists. For you, confusion must not exist, but do not be blind to the fact that there is a state of confusion existing in the world. You will not be a part of that confusion because you have stricken it from your God-given power.

Be harmonious at all times. If you cannot be in harmony, then go off alone for a few minutes, an hour. Gather your faculties together. Reason with your lower mind. Allow your divine mind to come into you, and talk to you, bringing you back to your center.

Have your divine mind say, "Now, I must live within you. You are my shell. You are the physical expression of my consciousness. However, I AM divine. Understand? I AM divine. You are not. You are substance, physical substance expressed on this physical plane. You have shape, size and dimension. The I AM does not. Its shape, size and dimension is the universe. It is not limited to your expression. I am your master. You obey my will. You say to me, confusion, fear, limitation. I say to you, it exists not in my realm."

And then, strangely, what will happen, as you look within yourself, your physical mind and your emotions will begin to become fearful, they will say, "But...but...but..." Your physical mind will find excuses to hold you from the Truth.

Then you say, "Silence! By the power of the universe!" And then say to it, "Be not fearful." Then you must give it peace, and reassurance. For it is an animal, with animal desires, to eat, to sleep, to drink and to reproduce. Those are animal desires. Spirit needs not those things. Spirit needs not sleep, food, drink and to reproduce. It is all those things.

So the animal part of you must be reassured, like a dog or a cat or a horse. You create confidence, and it then becomes subject to your will, your higher will, the divine consciousness. You reassure it. Say to it, "Be peaceful. Allow me to handle and manage you. I shall not lead you astray. I shall, if you behave, bring you to ascension."

You say to it, "I will bring you to the ascension. I will teach you, my little universe, my little world, how to purify your whole being, that you may not be a part of the multitude, that each cell, each organ, each atom of your being, shall be repolarized out of fear and limitation into positiveness and Light. And we will work together as a harmonious unit."

Talk with yourself this way. Do whatever needs to be done to convince the animal part of your nature to stop expressing animalistically. Otherwise it holds you back.

Within the fifth root race which you are in there are many round and about you who have not progressed. They are the laggards from the fourth root race. Do not be among those. In time you will be part of the sixth root race. Truth gives you the key to liberty. This your Lord proved, for He said to you, "All that I have done ye also may do." Would He deceive you? Never! Would Truth deceive you? Never! Truth is what it is, consistently, throughout the ages. It is only for man to recognize it.

You shall see, after you begin to master yourselves, that that part of you which functions at the opposite end of the pole is the animal, and you are the divine. Together you work for self-mastery.

These philosophies sometimes are for some a lifetime of study and endeavor, and the sooner you sit down to the work at hand and apply yourself to the study, to the opening of your mind, being aware of what is around you, the better.

You live in a world of blindness. You arise in the morning and accept the sun. You do not once think of it. Man is not aware of what the sun is, why it shines, what it does.

What does that radiant light shining upon the tree do to the tree? Who stops to think of these things?

What of the bird? What of the robin, the bluebird? What of the vibrations around and about you? What of the air you breathe? What of your neighbor? What of your thoughts, your desires? Who stops to think? Acumana will tell you what man stops to think of. He thinks how he may produce more money. He thinks of the benefits of producing money. Money, money, money. That is all he thinks. Let him so think. For, mark you, he will be the one that shall sink when the great purging comes. Those who cling to the manna will be those who have not the fruit from the honey tree.

It is fine to appreciate and express that which you have, but if your goals are only to manifest material goods, money, then you will not be in Truth. That is not the cause and purpose of Truth, contrary to many teachings. Many teachings say, open your mind to the power that is within. Do they say God? No. They say, open yourself to the power within your mind. You hold within your hand the power to master others, power to have whatever you will. That is negative occult teaching. Whenever a teacher teaches metaphysics without the power of God once mentioned, without the deeper philosophy, he is in black magic. Stay away from him. Have no part of it.

It is not your soul's purpose here to produce material goods. Your purpose here is to learn. If in the course of learning you are able to produce, fine. If not, it matters not. There are other things. Trust the law, as the tree does. You will be fed, you will be clothed, and your needs will be taken care of. But you must work, you must produce and put forth an effort. Do not lie back and say, "He will care for me." Who is "He"? Are you taking from another, or are you putting forth your individual effort, mentally, physically, and spiritually, the trinity to bring about whatever your wish is? Ask yourself.

What, therefore, is the purpose of Truth? The key is to become as the microcosm that which is in the macrocosm, the reflected image, and know that you are the reflected image. All things reflect the image of the Father, but many do not know it. Those in Truth must become conscious that they are the reflected image.

Now you may ask Acumana questions.

***Student:* I'd like to clarify one question relative to the ascension of Jesus. Many, or some, metaphysicians, state that He did not elevate the body or ascend in the flesh, but that that was symbolic.**

They are on a different path. Pray that they may learn the law of ascension. Be assured, it did so happen. Any teacher who teaches contrary to this is not on the Christward path. They are leaning toward the negative expression. Have no patience with it. Shake the dust and go your way. The ascension is symbolic and it is literal. That is the beauty and the glory of Truth. You cannot say it is only one and not the other, for if you say it is only one and not the other you are not on the true path.

Acumana will give you another comment. Truth is the quality which consistently has proven its value by the age and the time. When all things blend in perfect harmony, then it is Truth. When all recognize that God, Father, Jehovah are the same principle, that is Truth. Truth is that which is consistent throughout the ages. Truth is likened unto the wheel. It starts at a given point, goes the full circumference, and returns. It returns to the same spot.

Student: **How do you know that you know?**

You know by trusting your higher instinct. You know you know when you know. How do you know that you do not know? Answer it that way. If you keep asking whether it is so, then you do not know. Each individual must arrive at the point where he knows he knows, and then when he knows he finds that he does not know it all, but he knows he does not know it all!

Student: **Don't we need to retreat from the world to learn to practice these things?**

Acumana is trying to teach you to be in communion with your own higher self while in the world, how to balance the spiritual and the material. You rise above the material by handling it through the balancing and the perfection of the spiritual. There are times of retreat most essential in certain areas of study, where students are told by teachers specifically you must have time away from the world at large.

There you are in a specific retreat for a specific purpose, that you must fully rechemicalize, revitalize and reenergize your entire physical orbit. Then you are quickened in your process to handle your spiritual teachings.

Student: **Acumana, when you refer to the Father are you speaking of the Supreme Being? And when you speak of God you only use the word, God.**

When Acumana speaks of the All, we are considering what? The God, the Father, and the Son, the great ever-expanding O, Supreme Infinite Being. God is your pinnacle, on your seven spiritual planes. The All would be the spirit of the Father.

Now is the time of great awakening in the world. Heed to the call of nature by awakening your consciousness. Shed from yourselves all negative aspects. Ascend in your mind and your soul to the great glorious heights of Christ awareness. May your thoughts always be positive and pure, and your actions and deeds maintain equilibrium. Just as nature awakens to the call, you, as a part of this law and principle, must awaken to its call for lofty ideals, pure thoughts, noble deeds. Peace be unto you, in the name of the Father, Son and Holy Spirit.

Blessings of Ahura Mazda.

APPEAL FOR ILLUMINATION

Oh God, my Father, I come before Thee
In need of release.
My path and road of awareness
To the great Olympian heights
Is steep and treacherous.
Oh God, my Father, when I turn to the right,
And to the left,
I see the myriad faces of distraction,
Faces of the world,
Faces of materiality,
To deter me on my path.
I beseech Thee, oh God,
To take from me the self,
That I may stand before Thee
Selfless within myself,
That the flame of awareness
Shall burn brightly on the altar
Of illumination,
That my one spark of divinity
May blend with the greater light of awareness,
And shed illumination to the many.
This is my fervent prayer, my Father:
Keep my eyes straight forward,
Keep my goal bright before me!

CHAPTER III

The Voyage

Likened unto the great sea and the voyage, in life there are tempests, there are storms. Acumana observes often one of the crew members frantically rushing to the railing! These are the inner disturbances in the course of life. Once you have spewed them from your consciousness, they no longer exist.

Once you become accustomed to the voyage, you become a hardy seaman. So you will find the sea and the land have many things in common in Truth, in the absolute. Many lessons are to be learned from the great deep.

All things in the great, mighty, expanding universe are in a constant state of revolution, perpetual movement. Nothing is at rest. All things move, expand, evolve, and grow. No matter how far into the great depth of the universe you explore in the course of your evolution, you will never find a condition of total rest. You will always find motion and movement.

Though your bodies remain now in a motionless position, nevertheless there exists a great field of energy round and about you. Your own molecular structure vibrates at varying rates of vibration. Those rates of vibration are, in accordance with universal law, to hold your body together. If each of your atom structures were of a greater degree of power and energy, there would be a disintegration of your matter, and your vehicle would be scattered into dust. Your rate of vibration is condensed, so to say. It is of a grosser nature.

Imagine in the various levels of vibration, the great spiritual planes, going on and on, vibrating at greater and greater rates and degrees. They appear motionless. At the extreme depth of the pole, the lesser degrees of vibration also appear to be motionless.What is in between? Millions and millions of varying degrees of vibration.

From the higher spiritual vibratory rate you descend downward to slower and slower degrees. Then you meet what is called the intermediate.

But you cannot discern where one begins and another ceases, for they are all the same, except that in degree their vibration is different. And you descend to the lowest. Or you may ascend from the lowest to the highest. It matters not. They are the same. One is to rise and one is to lower. Thought is a manifestation of vibration on your plane. On the physical and mental plane there are varying degrees of manifestation. On the plane of human mind there are many subdivisions. The human vehicle is the sum total of those divisions, as manifestations via the projection of thought—mind and thought—wherein is the difference? One is the operator and the other is the operation, the transmission. Mind is the house wherein the thought is projected. Mind is the vehicle.

Ethereal substance is the vital link between all planes, all manifestations, all means of communication, to whatever degree it is communicated, be it energy, be it matter, be it mind. For mind, according to your mental understanding, is the head of the individual. Mind transcends the physical appearance of the head of man. It is energy and power. If it is energy and power, it must, therefore, be vibration. Each mind has a degree and rate of vibration different than another. Each one is distinct unto itself, that is, in its operation.

There are two facets of mind—material mind and spiritual mind. They are two extremes of the same pole. Material and spiritual. Now, if a man functions in the vibration of the spiritual pole, that which he projects from his mind as a vibratory degree of consciousness can attract only positivity. If he is vibrating on the material plane, he can, therefore, attract only its degree of polarization, the material. To be balanced is to be in the intermediate whereby, through discernment, you are able to become aware of both degrees, and to utilize the law as the perfect balance. To separate the material vibration from the spiritual vibration, you are able, through your own spiritual discernment, to distinguish the two distinct degrees of vibration, the material and the spiritual, remembering that within each degree there are subdivisions.

On a graph for temperature (thermometer) there are many degrees, are there not? Five is considered the halfway mark. Are there not equally the same number of degrees from fifty to one hundred as there are from one to fifty?

What is the difference between heat and cold? They are two extremes of the same condition. Their vibration is different, that is all. According to the vibration is manifested that degree on that particular plane.

Your mind, that which operates your body, vibrates at a given rate of vibration. It manifests on a plane of the same nature, according to that manifestation that it is best fitted for, which is the physical plane, because of the grosser degrees of vibration which are still within its consciousness.

Let Acumana further explain, as it is complex in nature. In order to learn you must evolve, so you must go through various degrees of vibration. Consider evolvement like the thermometer, rising from frigid cold, at its lowest point, solidation, which is man evolving. Can ice become more frozen after it reaches one point? Man rises on different planes of understanding like unto to the thermometer rising to different levels. And as man ascends there are conditions to be learned. Herein karma is involved.

If, for example, you are vibrating at the tenth point, reaching for the eleventh point and you have not learned the lessons on the tenth, you must take them with you to the eleventh, and if on the eleventh you have not learned the lessons, you must take the tenth and the eleventh with you to the twelfth. And as you ascend to the thirteenth, if you have not learned the other three you must take the tenth, eleventh and twelfth with you to the thirteenth. Each grade you go to you must take the same lessons. Now you have four times as much to learn, because of your own free will.

Each life gives you one basic lesson. Sometimes it takes a whole lifetime, in its varying degrees, for it to unfold. If you have not learned the lesson, that is, applied all the principles that you know, and you have committed more sins, as it is said, then you must learn twice the number of lessons through evolvement, slowly, ever so slowly.

Fallen angels must become the ascended illuminations. Your spiritual self is pure in its origin. It is pure, untainted, untinged by any other shade or hue. It is pure power and energy. Why, therefore, can it not separate from the material plane and ascend into the great spiritual realm? It is incomplete in its vibratory nature, though its potential is for the great vibratory realm. Potentially, you are all ninety years in age, are you not, potentially? But which one of you is ninety? Since you are not ninety you cannot say you are not ninety in potential.

The same thing applies in vibration. You are potentially the whole scale of vibration. Potentially, not in actuality. Not in reality, not in what is called substantial reality. So you must evolve through growth, that your soul may become more and more broad in its power. Potentially, the full power is there, but it must experience in order to expand, to fill in the gaps of all the vibrations.

The only way this is possible is through a manifestation on a plane. And as Acumana has said to you before, that which you take on this plane you must pay back on this plane. It has to manifest on the plane on which it started originally because of the vibratory nature of that plane. It is fulfilling the need of the incompletion within the vibratory nature of the potential spiritual nature.

What of thought? This is most important. Your thought carries with it great potential power of vibration. Each thought you speak and project vibrates. The ethers round and about you teem with millions upon millions of degrees of vibration, ethereal substance. It is the medium of transmission, the intermediary plane. It conveys all things.

It is from ethereal substance whereby the embryo is conceived. The embryo draws unto it from the ethereal substance all the vital elements essential for its growth and development in the womb of the woman. It is the medium. Ethereal substance conveys. We shall endeavor to explain more of ethereal substance to you under another lesson, for it is important for your understanding.

In vibration, therefore, if you project anxiety, if you project fear, doubt, any of the varying degrees on the negative end of the pole, then what must you manifest according to the law? Only similar conditions, similar moods, because the ethereal substance is nonpartisan. It cares not what you feed it. It is objective. It is neither for one man nor for the other.

It is unbiased—impartial. So you, being a divine center of awareness, have power behind you and when you project, according to the pole of vibration, negative aspects, you can only expect negative results. It is a law. It happens because it happens. There is no other way.

However, if you are aware that you are projecting those varying degrees of negation, you who are in Truth have this to your advantage. You have the power to repolarize your vibration. When you learn how to repolarize your vibration, you may stop, in a moment, any condition which exists and redirect it at will.

Equally you may do this with others. If they are projecting negative attitudes toward you, with your own mental power you may stop their vibration and divert it into a positive channel of repolarization. This is the law that all the great masters work with, vibration on the ethereal substance plane.

They are not only able to control, manipulate and master all phenomena and substance of nature, they can as well, at will, do the same throughout the universe, as well as on the physical plane. They have learned this law.

The first law for you to learn is how to mentally control yourself. When you have learned the mental control of vibration, then perhaps you may proceed into some of the other phenomena whereby you could control certain physical conditions. The physical conditions which come about through your daily lives only come as manifestation of your own mental vibratory projection.

Any event, any sequence of events, is a physical manifestation on the physical plane, under the law of vibration, coming to you because of the power you have put behind it. There is no way to escape this, absolutely no possible way.

What shall you do with it? Ignore it? Chase it from your consciousness and say, "Tomorrow I shall think of this?" Or shall you become master of it and say, "I know this to exist. It is paramount that the negative aspect be eliminated." Or will you become wishy-washy in your approach and say, "I am being negative but I enjoy being negative for the time being, because it satisfies my feelings."

Many of you do this. You are negative because it satisfies your desire. Remember, desire is of the mundane plane. On the spiritual plane there is no desire. All that you could desire already exists. Desire only manifests on the physical lower level.

As an example, take your electric fan as it is motionless, then let it spin. Let it spin faster and faster. Do the vibrations not change as its revolutions increase? The vibration must change, therefore, the substance, the energy pattern, which is emitting through that vibration in the ethers around it, equally must change.

Sound issues forth from this vibration and it begins to set forth as a humming sound. Faster and faster the hum increases. Soon what happens is that as the speed and revolutions increase you go through the whole musical scale. When the last note is reached in the musical scale, the high octave, there ceases to be sound to the physical ear. It is the sound of the universe then.

Sound and vibration take on a different dimension. What happens as the speed increases more and more? What phenomenon is produced then? Color. Color, which is another degree of sound on a different plane. First in the spectrum is red. As it increases its vibratory rate, brighter and brighter, it becomes orange, then yellow. Then through the full scale of color it goes, to blue and indigo, through all the infra-reds and the ultraviolets.

Then when its speed is increased at such a degree of vibration as it revolves, it burns itself out of physical manifestation and scatters into the universe. It burns itself up into energy.

For you cannot go beyond the physical phenomenon of pure white in vibration. It disintegrates. But that does not make it non-existent. It goes into a finer energy.

When it reaches the zenith of the phenomenon on the physical plane, which is the heat and vibration of the greatest intensity, it melts, it dissolves. Where is it then? Its degree of vibration has become greater and it cannot withstand the grosser nature of vibration in the physical plane, so it ascends. This process is what happens in the state of ascension, the state of transmutation.

You control through the conscious will. You direct with your will the rapidity of motion. You know the rate of vibration of the atomic structure of your element, your substance, and you quicken that rate of vibration.

Take a coin. You wish to bring a coin from one place to another.

You know the ratio of the coin and its structure. You know the degree of vibration of the molecular structure manifested in a coin. Every object has a different degree of vibration. And you know its degree of vibration manifested as a coin, you know its ratio. You then, with the conscious will of vibration, quicken the ratio of vibration in its atomic structure. That is, each molecule and electron is vibrating in its own universe and you quicken its revolution. Each structure is quickened in its revolution until it disintegrates the matter that it adheres to as a coin. But it is adhered together in ethereal substance. That is, it does not scatter about. It remains as a solid substance in ether, but is not tangible. It is still adhered together by cohesion, but is invisible. Its rate of vibration has been quickened.

If you held such a coin, it would be very warm to your hand, even hot. for its structure would be revolving, rotating, at a rapid degree. Then with your conscious will in ethereal substance (ethereal substance transcends all matter), you place it wherever you desire. You consciously lower it then, let it lapse back to its normal rate. That is all you do, and it recomposes itself as a coin. It is simple. Now go try it!

This is the essence, only the essence of how you transmute. The same law applies to the mental approach for transmuting conditions. Disintegrate them out of existence! Bring in the opposite. The greater the degree of vibration, the less it appears to exist, the more motionless it seems. That is why, when you look about you into the universe above you, you see stillness. You do not see motion and yet you know motion does exist. You know your Earth is revolving. Can you see it revolve? You cannot. You cannot gaze at a fixed object in the sky, another star, and watch your Earth revolve.

You know you are revolving, you know you see the object here, and at a later time you see it there, but you cannot discern the motion because it is so rapid. Your world and its galaxies spin through the universe at great rates of speed, yet they are motionless in appearance, so high is the degree and rate. The rate of vibration of your planet Earth is so rapid for its bulk and size that it appears motionless.

Now, the difference between physical vibration and the vibration of the elemental kingdom is only the degree. There is no higher, no lower. For example, if you say, "Well, the animal kingdom is lower in vibration and I am higher," how do you know? Since you are here and they are there, then perhaps they are higher and you are lower! What is up? What is down? You cannot make a comparison. You can only say, "It is only in degree that they are different. In many ways their degree is more pure than your degree, as in other ways your degree is greater than their degree. Each in its own area of manifestation is perfect because of that degree of vibration for that area of manifestation.

The benefit, the most essential point of the whole teaching, is for the purpose that you may be enlightened about life around you. That you may be better equipped and handle yourselves so that you will not beseech your guardians in prayer for more assistance. You will then become the guardians, and others will come to you for assistance. To know the life about you, you must observe, study, contemplate, meditate. Open your inner eye, your inner mind, your inner ear, to the greater realities which are around and about you.

Man wastes so much time in idleness. This does not mean that every moment of his existence must be to study, study, study. There are certain social amenities you must abide by, but they should be productive. Do not waste your breath, your time, in purposeless discussion, gossips, worries, anxieties. What does it profit you or your neighbor to discuss your worries and your anxieties, unless by such discussion you can bring about a concrete inner example and repolarize the condition. Then it is a positive discussion.

Simply to discuss it for the sake of discussion is a waste of precious time. If you have a problem, it is fine to discuss it with another, for perhaps together you can resolve the problem by repolarizing its condition. But if you only waste time for the sake of time, it is gone forever. So make your discussions purposeful. Desire a resolution for each thing you discuss and in your discussion search for a resolution.

Now, you may ask Acumana a few questions.

***Student:* I have heard of the law of vibration as being referred to as the Scepter of Power. Is this because if we learn to apply it properly we can convert through mind—convert vibrations?**

Yes. When you have learned the significance of mind then you have the Scepter of Power of destiny in your hand. Remember, good and evil are only opposite in degree. The laws can be worked for wrong as well as for right. But woe and pity unto the man who uses the laws for self-gain, self-aggrandizement, any purpose for negation and for evil, for vengeance. For vengeance particularly, or for the power of mastery over another. Woe unto the man for when he has spiritual discernment and does this, great is the suffering.

It is up to the individual to choose which road he takes. To the teachers it matters not. They give you Truth. What you do with it is your concern. Always they hope, they pray, in their innermost beings, that you direct it positively toward education, toward betterment, toward advancement, toward enlightenment.

***Student:* Acumana, when you raise the degree of vibration of your mind, what actually happens?**

You become warm, for one thing. You will feel a great surging of warmth flood your body. You have all had an experience of this nature. When you have prayed, when you have concentrated, or had great inner elation, have you not had great floods of warmth come over your body? You feel warmth all over your head, shoulders and whole being. You have elevated your vibration. When the consciousness is re-vibrated or elevated, the first noticeable change is the rise in your temperature. The higher you raise your vibration, the more it reaches a state where your body could not withstand the heat. It reaches as far as it can in that vibration, then its nature takes on more power and energy and it elevates, it levitates. Your structure is held together, for you cannot disintegrate your structure, but it is vibrating at such a degree it levitates. Its revolutions are more rapid than the revolutions of gravitation, and it transcends the law of gravity. It neutralizes with the law of gravity.

***Student:* If it neutralized so completely, then—it could be the ascending…**

Yes, but that takes great inner consciousness. That is only brought about through inner growth, through evolvement.

***Student:* But a student through the application of this law could levitate?**

Most assuredly. Each of you have the capacity to go into profound meditation and levitate. Not a one of you does not have that capacity. But you are all too lazy to do it, too undisciplined. You give too many excuses not to try it. You are too tired, too busy. You have too many other things to call upon you. If you only took ten minutes a day to practice mental control, to quiet your thoughts and your body, you would at least be in the process of beginning. It is up to you.

***Student:* When you speak of a person taking a law and using it in the negative sense, would there be necessarily less power in using it negatively than if you used it positively? Or would it be equal?**

It would be the same degree of power. The only difference is from where you are directing it. If you are directing it positively, then that is one degree of the pole. If you are directing it negatively, that is another degree of the pole. Zero being the middle, fifty is one way and fifty the other way, how can you distinguish whether one is better, higher or lower? The only difference is in the direction. And that cannot be contested, because which is up and which is down? They are only opposites, that is all. As above, so below.

***Student:* I keep finding myself led back to the great laws which govern the universe. For example, we keep running into the Law of Relativity, if such exists as a law.**

Yes. Within the seven planes of consciousness of man there are many laws. Relativity exists as a degree of consciousness with the plane of human mind. There are various degrees of comprehension, and according to the various degrees of comprehension you find the various laws governing those degrees of comprehension.

Assimilation is another law in the mental plane. Coordination, mental coordination, is another law of mental consciousness.

They relate to the degrees of mental consciousness brought about by spiritual discernment, spirituality. As you evolve, so you change from one mental plane to another, and as you change from one mental plane to another you open up another degree, another law, on that mental plane.

***Student:* Do you then leave the Law of Relativity?**

You never leave one law for another. You are always within the full scope of all the laws.

***Student:* When do you then go into the Absolute?**

When you have completely transcended the full cycle of material law, the human mind and its degrees of evolvement. When you have reached complete self-mastery. Then you have reached the state of masterhood, and you may leave the Law of Relativity in this plane. Then you become aware of Substantial Reality.

***Student:* Acumana, I was thinking of physical healers. Would they raise the vibration of the patient to cure an ill?**

In effect, it is likened unto that, yes. Those who have true healing power are in resonance with the healing vibration which exists in the etheric substance, etheric substance being the medium for all things. So there is a vibratory degree of cosmic healing energy which is always flowing through ethereal substance. Those who have true healing power are in resonance with that degree of vibration. Then they transmit that degree of vibration to the patient, raising his vibration, in a sense, or raising the vibration of the afflicted condition, rebuilding the molecular structure.

***Student:* Then, as the vibration rises in the body the heat rises. What about a fever?**

Oh, this is different. Remember, there are differing degrees. There is positive and there is negative. The physical condition is only of the physical nature. You have the same degree of temperature on spiritual ascension or meditation that you can have when you are physically ill, but it is different in intensity and is directed differently.

***Student:* Isn't that so-called vibration of healing what we apply when we treat the individual in prayer? Isn't this in effect what we're actually doing?**

In effect you are trying to quicken the vibratory rate of your own power of mind to direct it specifically through ethereal substance to its goal, and revibrate, yes, the recipient.

***Student:* Trying to trace the genealogy of vibration, would this be the aspect of Word from the Supreme Being given forth as the great OM and down into what we know as the law of vibration?**

It is so, yes, remembering that vibration equally has its poles, higher and lower; as above, so below. The physical manifestation of vibration is the spoken word. That which Acumana projects as a word is in reality a vibration. Each word is a combination of a number of vibrations, each at a varying rate or degree, and as they break the ethers they form energy patterns. Those energy patterns are received by your antenna, your intelligence, as word forms. The word forms each represent a picture or an image.

If Acumana says to you, "How is your home?" What is your first thought? You know "how," you know "is," you know "your," you know vibrations, impulses. So, first is the word; it is vibration. But the mind is actually first. First is the All, the great Mind. The Word of the Father is vibration.

In Genesis what does it say? In the beginning was the Word. "In the beginning" means in the All, in God, the Father of all things. The first manifestation being the Word, the vibration, the continuous, perpetual vibration sustained and rung throughout all the ethers of the universe. The word is vibration.

You are all subject to vibration. You are all subject to words. If your neighbor says to you, "I have much hatred for you," are you not affected by this in your thoughts?

You most assuredly are. You feel ill at ease, you feel sorrow, you feel anguish, pity. You are affected. And if every day he says to you, "I have only hatred for you," you become more and more affected.

So the vibration is what affects you, not the word. How can the letters h-a-t-e affect you, the letters individually? They cannot, but the sum total of the vibration affects you. So it is the vibration which affects you.

If a man says to the one he is courting, "I have love for you," she is affected, is she not? If she has normal receptivity, she is affected. How can the word l-o-v-e affect her? It is only a word. Look at it in the written scroll, what is it? Only letters, hieroglyphics, wiggly lines, yes? Can this create emotion? No, but the vibration can.

***Student:* To what degree does emotion distort the relative absolute vibration of the word?**

Emotion distorts greatly. Emotion is of the mundane plane, the physical plane. However, there are varying degrees here. Emotion can be of a great spiritual nature as well, and can quicken the spiritual nature. Or it can quicken the mundane nature, all depending on which side of the road you are standing on.

Man is a most perfect receiver of vibration. He is a recipient. He is an antenna. He is a transmitter. Man is like a diamond, perfect in shape, form, structure and brilliance. He is like the perfect diamond in potential. It has taken eons and eons of time for the diamond to be formed. Its nature is hard, strong and solid, yes? And what does it emanate? Brilliance, perfection in natural law. That is the spiritual nature of man, symbolically.

***Student:* The diamond is also cold.**

It is not cold. It is a degree of vibration. What is hot and what is cold? They are the same potential but different in degree. Spiritual man is not hot. Hot is only a physical counterpart as a degree of manifestation.

Man cannot feel spirit as hot and cold. They are only degrees of vibration on your plane. You cannot have hot and cold in spiritual substance. They are only related to the physical plane.

***Student:* If someone is in resonance with say, Gershwin's work or Mozart's work, is it because his personal vibration or his nature is inclined in that general resonance?**

There is a harmony within him which is attuned to that frequency. Just as, for example, your keynote—Acumana has told you before of your keynote, that you each have a keynote—if this keynote is sustained for any length of time it would destroy you, disintegrate you. However, you may find your keynote and sustain it for short periods of time, but if it is drawn out at any great length, just as it will spiritualize you and rebuild you, it can, being overdone, destroy you. So it can build you or destroy you.

***Student:* Are we attracted to our keynote within the music, or harmonies, of the keynote?**

Yes. Each person has a keynote and some have the same keynote. When you strike that keynote it causes a rapid increase of the vibration in your body and your nature. Your whole being is revibrated. You may heal many afflictions with your keynote. You may change your whole mental attitude, if you are in a mental digression. Play your keynote and you may change your whole vibratory rate. But Acumana cautions you, do not sustain it for a great length of time or it will destroy you as well. The violin is of the greatest assistance for finding your keynote.

***Student:* You mean that by playing different tunes we could find out which note we respond to?**

Yes. The piano, also. Piano, harp or violin. Any of the stringed instruments have the full scale of the keynotes.

***Student:* Isn't there also a system of finding your keynote from the astrological sign, from your birthdate?**

Yes, if it is done properly.

***Student:* Then is it to our advantage to know our keynote?**

It most assuredly is to your advantage.

***Student:* When you say one can have too much of the keynote, what relatively should be the time by our standards?**

A great, intense pitch of your keynote would shatter you. Think of it in terms of pitch, volume, intensity, likened unto a tuning fork. If you strike one tuning fork, and another one, even though it perhaps be encased in glass, if it is of the same intensity it will respond. It is the same with people. If your keynote is known, you will respond to it. However, if the tuning fork is increased in its intensity it will shatter the glass around it. You have not the physical means to fully intensify your keynote for your own destruction. But if you play it at a great rate of vibration, constantly surround yourself with it, overdo it, as you can overdo anything, it will destroy you. You worry so about little things. You do not need to worry, just be assured when you know your keynote you cannot overdo it. Your own inner nature will tell you this. Be confident. Just know that the intensity of a note will destroy if it is sustained over and over.

You may have a symphony where your keynote is used many times and it has a great constructive effect upon you. What Acumana is saying is that the one note alone, if you persist to intensify its given rate of vibration, would affect you destructively.

Now, children of Light, blend your minds as one unit. Before you there is a blazing great, golden image of Christ consciousness. Accept the consciousness and the power of the Christ spirit. As this golden vision radiates its brilliance about you, there is warmth, a glow and a burning sensation within the center of your head where your spiritual eye lies dormant.

Now this center is radiating warmth throughout your whole body, and you are conscious of pinpoints of burning energy emanating from your eye. This is spiritual power, positive in direction. Your whole body now is centered in great, radiant power and energy. All conditions of a lower nature are being burned and disintegrated from your aura, by the power and radiance of cosmic energy, through the Christ Light.

Power, wisdom and love be yours throughout the days. Peace and love unto you, in the name of the Father, the Son and the Holy Spirit.

Know this, my children. You have the power behind your spoken word. For it is said, he who speaks commands the universe. Therefore, speak words of gentleness and tenderness, for words carry with them energy and power. Utilize that power for the betterment of humanity.

SLEEP'S MYSTERY

O God, my Father,
For the day that has passed, I give thee thanks.
O God, my Father,
For the blessing of repose before me,
I give thee thanks.
I ask that I may be united in the Presence
of Light and Purity.
I approach sleep's mystery
With the desire to serve Thee,
To serve the world.
With the blessings of light and wisdom,
May my body be renewed, revitalized,
And may I share
In the contemplation of reverie,
The beauty and the silence of the night.
May the mystery of the evening and the night
Enlighten my consciousness,
And upon awakening, O God, my Father,
If it is within Thy will,
May an awareness of the night's content
Remain indelibly engraved upon my outer mind,
That I may grow in wisdom and in strength
To understand sleep's mystery.
O God, my Father,
I give Thee thanks.

CHAPTER IV

Correlation

Thus far you have in reality had a summarization of numerous teachings which you have previously been given. Now they are put in a form for your edification whereby you may correlate all the facets, all the laws which Acumana has already given. You shall understand and see the philosophy of the All, Divine Mind, God, Supreme Infinite Intelligence, working through the universe and through all the various degrees of the universe, finally down to the degree of human consciousness known as humankind.

Now, let us speak of the primary principle which involves the mind of God, or the principle of power generating at a given period of time which has no beginning and no end, functioning throughout the endless cycles of time. Mind is the law whereby man, as a manifestation of mind, is housed in a portion of the Father's body. What, then, is mind? What do you conceive mind to be?

> ***Student:*** **Mind is the faculty through which the All expresses and through which we express.**

It is so, according to its various degrees and levels. Divine Infinite Mind, the All, is the mind of the Father. Operating through the mind of the Father there must be Supreme Spiritual Intelligence. Since mind reflects an external functioning within an internal system, which is your body, what operates the mind? Spirit operates the mind. Divine Intelligence operates the mind, and it in turn has a composite of numerous divisions.

So, within the mind of the All there are numerous divisions of Divine Infinite Mind which from the mind of the All, in turn, produces the phenomenon of the Endless Universe.

Man is a composite in a miniature form of this law of mental operation in the universe, this law of motion, this law of activity. The mind functions as a given law of activity. You cannot escape this. As you sit now, in this room, there is great movement going on within you. Your mind is climbing to great heights of spiritual awareness. Your mind is functioning on more than one level. It is working in rapport with Divine Mind and with mundane mind. Mundane mind being the faculty whereby you are able to reason and understand the causes and effects on your own plane of understanding, the physical plane.

Divine Mind is that asset, that quality, whereby the mundane mind is enabled to function. It is called Spirit. It is called God. It is the crown of all Omnipotence within every individual. That faculty is Divine Mind as reflected in the Father. You are only a personification of that Divine Mind, a degree.

How is your structure functioning? You all know that your physical bodies are made of substances of various degrees and various elements. This can be chemically analyzed by any laboratory. You have substances, minerals, chemicals, composites, in your body. It is composed of numerous cells. These cells, in turn, are composed of numerous atoms, each having a central sun or a nucleus and each, in turn, having a planetary system of its own.

The universe of your being is in continuous motion at all times, never ceasing. Therefore, you are in substantial reality, not dormant, not inactive, but dynamically in activity at this very moment.

What do you do physically to assist this spiritual dynamic motion in the universe? Do you feed yourself all the necessary foods? Not only physical foods, but the foods of spirit? Do you feed yourself foods of nourishment and health to assist in your rapidity of growth, or do you eat poisonous foods to destroy your nature? Poisonous foods being all forms of criticism, negation, judgment, doubt, fear, anxiety, and we may go on down an endless line on the polarity of negation.

You are all students in the annals of Cosmic Truth. And as students of Cosmic Truth you have a place, a plan, you have a cloud, if you wish, of pink white fluff in the universe which is yours and yours alone. That is, you have a given destiny, a fulfillment. The sooner each of you comes to recognize that fulfillment, the more rapid becomes your growth. It may take you eons of time to recognize it.

You may come back four or five lives before you finally arrive at the point where you say, "Why did I not see this before?" You have seen it numerous times, but remember, while in the physical state you are living in an illusionary condition. You are living in a reflection, not the reality. You are living in reflections, and reflections often blind the true reality. The true spiritual nature is not permitted to express its godhood because the illusions of the world present a different picture.

Acumana understands that there are places where there are rooms filled with many, many mirrors. These are called rooms of amusement, yes? Some of you have been in such rooms. Now, for a moment, conceive with Acumana, that you are standing in such a room, surrounded wherever you go by mirrors, but one which appears to be a mirror is not a mirror at all, but an arch. It is an arch, an opening, and beyond the arch is a mirror. You are in the center of a six-sided room. You look about you. Can you discern the opening? No, for the room is so conceived, so built in a pattern of geometric form and design, that you cannot, while standing in the center, discern which is the mirror and which is the arch. That is life, my children, that is embodiment. You see many things, but not the real.

How do you find the real? You have to grope for it. The first thing you must do is to move. If you remain dormant and do not move from the center of the room, then you must be content with your reflection and you cannot expect to progress. So first is the doing. The first effort you must take in the law of mind is to move.

So you move to any given point. Maybe you move straight forward, and right before you is the arch where you leave the room of mirrors, the illusion. You cannot tell. Only the soul growth, the soul that progresses over eons of time of esoteric training, inner plane instruction, and dedication to certain spiritual principles, can determine whether or not you must labor to find your way out. You must labor by groping. You may go to each mirror, touch it, feel it, move around. But if you become fearful and frantic, what happens? You bang yourself from one wall to the other, and you never leave the room.

So what do you do? You remain assured, confident, and positive that if you carefully, without fear and anxiety, systematically move about the room, you shall find the arch. And you most assuredly shall. That is life and progress.

Since that is your choice and that has been your choice throughout certain lives, then you must be content with the struggle to find the arch of Light and Freedom. If, however, according to your soul growth that is not the case at hand, then you shall find the arch with a little effort. But you must move. You must make the effort to progress forward mentally and spiritually. You always progress. Negativity is a progression as well. Perhaps on the morrow you will decide not to think good thoughts, only evil thoughts. You are still progressing. Only instead of going one way, you are going the other way.

When the illusion is gone, is past, and you come to the true realization of your purpose here in this, the six-sided room of illusion, you will soon learn that your growth, your destiny, is one thing and one thing only. In the endless life, the endless struggle, through all the turmoil, the sweat, the labor, the searching for the arch, one thing has been found to be the whole purpose for it all: *At-one-ment with Spirit.* That is the purpose and the reward.

Now, in the wheel there are many spokes, are there not? It is so. Each spoke goes to the center, the at-one-ment. Each one has his own *modus operandi.* Each one has his own means, his own given tasks. It is not for one to say, "Yours is wrong and mine is right." It is for each man to discern within himself whether or not his plan is the correct plan, according to the soul nature of his inner being. There are two avenues—the spiritual avenue and the material avenue. The material avenue will lead you nowhere. It is a circle, the rim of the wheel. It leads you nowhere but around and around and around. The spiritual is serpentine in its motion. It goes to the center, to the heart, for it is wisdom. Each individual must find whether or not his path is circular or serpentine.

You must come about it with gentleness and patience. You cannot suddenly decide on the morrow, "Oh, mine is the spiritual" because you are fearful if it not be the spiritual that something shall happen to you on the material. That is not the approach. It must be an inner conviction. It must be like a pilot light, igniting the entire unit. The pilot light being the divinity which is within you, the I-AM, the Christ, the crown of pure wisdom, recognized by you. You must see yourself spiritually before you can decide. Then your decision is of Truth. And then there is no limit to where and to how far you may go.

What Acumana is endeavoring to do is to impress upon the carbon images of your mind these laws of divine operation which are about you continuously at all times. You each individually have a major responsibility, and collectively you have a responsibility to the All. Your collective responsibility is to disseminate that which you have been given to help humanity, to serve humanity, to be informed, and to disseminate.

It is why over endless, endless cycles now—cycles relating to man's time—the teachings have been unfolded in various groups. Think not that yours is the only group. There are numerous groups on various levels. Some levels are lower than your level, and other levels are far higher than your level. But they all have one purpose, which is to do the will of the Father. To be about the Father's work, to assist mankind at this hour, this darkened hour of gloom, that he may see through the fog to the clear, pure blue sky of awareness.

This cannot be done in silence and prayer alone. You have to have action. You have to have the physical counterpart. Prayer is perfect in its realm, but without activity, without the physical counterpart to prayer, there is no avail, no purpose. How can you pray unless you begin? It takes the physical doing to pray, does it not? Then you pray. You cannot substitute prayer for action. You cannot pray and not do it physically, even if it is just putting the brain into action. So the two have to work together. You cannot have the spiritual without the physical, for then the spiritual would not exist. The physical is a reflection of the spiritual and the spiritual is a reflection of the physical. The two are closely allied, for each of you has within you a two-fold nature, a positive and a negative, as does all nature in the universe.

So the greater plan of the teachers is to give Truth and wisdom. More Truth has been revealed in these recent generations than there has been in the past five thousand years. They are all coming back—all the Truths, all the teachings, all the esoteric schools.

However, remember, there are many pseudo-esoteric schools, as there were in the ancient days. Throughout time, Truth may be tested for its own value. The way to test it is through your inner discernment. What value is Truth unless each of you can create within you a sympathetic atunement to your teachers and to the universal plan? If it is merely to satisfy a desire to know a little more for curiosity's sake, then Acumana bids you peace, love and happiness in your endeavor. But this information here is not for you—or any group—until you come to the full realization that there is a plan, there is a purpose, behind it all.

There is only one force which opposes Truth and that is negation. Negation has great power, depth and dimension, as does Truth. Throughout all the ages of man the one enemy of Truth has been negation. It has assumed the counterpart or the dimensions of various forms, shapes and creeds. That is your enemy, negation. It is for this reason that the quickening process of spiritual teachings has come to such heights. It is for that reason that the great Lords of Light from other constellations surround you and observe you. It is for that reason that many have been called to serve the Light, to disseminate the Truth, for their inner purity knows that negation is the enemy.

That is what you fight, and you must recognize it. The only way you recognize it is by knowing it and by serving the opposite, by giving forth the opposite to the greatest extreme of your endurance. Do not appease any opposite concept. Never appease it. Never tolerate it. Anyone who presents to you a concept which violates God and the true teachings, which is anti-God, or any principle not of Light, shake the dust. Your Lord tells you this. What did He say?

Student: **"If any man offend you, shake the dust from thy feet and go thy way..."**

It is so. In Antioch, did this not happen to the disciples? What happened to Sodom and Gomorrah?

***Student:* They fell because they didn't recognize the Light. They lived in a state of constant upheaval until the Light was no longer there.**

They did. So you must not oscilate with them. That is the key. Do not oscilate with them. Be strong and firm in your convictions.

In this course of study which we give to you, where you are concerned as an individual unit, it has been deemed essential that prescribed teaching material be read by you. There are three works most important for each of you to read. These are the works:

Life and Teachings of the Master Jesus
Life and Teachings of the Gautama Buddha
The Bhagavad Gita

These three books are most important. You will find a parallel so familiar in each that you will say, "Why have I not discerned this before?"

It would be good for each of you to become more familiar with the great Ascended Beings of Cosmic Light—what their purpose to the service of humanity and Light has been. However, it is your choice to read them or not to read them. Acumana will say this, never shall you find three more beautifully written and emotionally experienced books than these three. Never shall you find three more perfect esoteric teachings of Cosmic Light than these three books, particularly in the book which in your own day tells of the Christ.

***Student:* Is this the New Testament?**

Any volume which gives you the life and the teachings of the Christ, if it be the New Testament or if it be another volume.

***Student:* There are books written about the life of Jesus, containing actual research on His life as well. We have one. It is "The Life of Christ" by Reverend John A. O'Brien, Ph.D.**

Yes, therein is pure esoteric teaching. Reading such treatises brings a deepening of the spirit.

***Student:* Do I understand you correctly, Acumana, that you want us to read this particular book?**

Find your own. You do not have to read that particular book.

***Student:* What about the Aquarian Gospel?**

No, not the Aquarian Gospel. That is not the life in the times of the prophet. That is a concept. It is important for you to know the whole area, time, condition, political intrigue of the day, how the teachings were given and why they were given that particular way and why it is so hard for man today to understand. You will not find this in the Aquarian Gospel. The Aquarian Gospel is more of an esoteric treatise on the teachings rather than a practical approach to understand the power of the ray.

Forget religion as such. Though you are all of different faiths, it matters not. Those faiths have all gone down the stream of time. You have left them. You are beyond them. You are in true Truth, pure Light. You are universal in your approach; therefore, you are interested in all things, not one doctrine, but all doctrines. Wherever there is Truth, in whatever corner of the universe where there is Truth and Light, that is what you are interested in. So be not concerned with religion, with old conditionings.

You live in the new now. You have searched for the Light. You have knocked, and many doors have opened for you, and now that the doors are opened, enjoy the various rooms that you are in. Explore them. Find their hidden compartments and the treasures buried therein.

Individually, as Acumana has said, your purpose is dissemination of Truth, to reach a point where you may become a power center of Truth in your own capacity. Then when you are scattered like sheep upon the mountainside to graze you shall spread the Light of Truth wherever you go, not to remain like clinging vines to the side of an old, decaying building, but to become pure lilies of the valley. Before you can become lilies of the valley you must first, like the seed, be planted, cultivated, crossbred, pollinated. Then you shall be replanted—not in another life, but redirected in this life. It is why you have been drawn together for this assimilation process for a period of time—to serve.

Collectively, as a unit, you have a responsibility to one another and to your teacher. Just as you are responsible to one another, therefore it is reflected to the teacher, which means that you are bound to cease all criticism of each other. You are bound to cease judgment of one another's actions, words or deeds. For who among you is so perfect, so spiritual, that he cannot be made more perfect? Not a one. Otherwise you would have long since ceased to need a physical body for growth.

So these principles which Acumana has given you numerous times seem to be paramount once more. Cease trying to analyze and understand your fellow man, your neighbor, and his problems. Rather, direct positive Truth to whatever area is his problem. Each of you should become so loving, so kind, so noble, so benevolent to your neighbor next to you that his problem is your problem and your problem is his problem.

You each work for the betterment of the other through God and Truth. You do not sneak around corners and say, "Oh, isn't this terrible. So and so has a problem." "It is just as I thought" you say to yourself. That is not the way lambs of the Father behave toward their own. They share. The mountainside has much greenery. The grass grows throughout the world. There is room for you all to graze. Why graze in the same spot that your neighbor grazes in? You have your own perfections to work on. The best way to correct your own problems is to assist your neighbor. It is the only way. It is what Jesus taught the multitudes.

What did He say in the Beatitudes and in the Sermon on the Mount? He said to assist others as you would hope they would assist you. By assisting them you take your mind off your problems. For what are your problems? The more you consider your needs, your desires, your wishes, your growth, the less you are open to Light and assistance. Assistance can never come when the ego or the aura is clouded with self-indulgence. This fine, etheric substance can never penetrate such a hard shell. This fine etheric substance, which is abundance and peace and goodwill, in whatever dimension it happens to be, can never penetrate the hard, crusty shell of self-indulgence.

So as a unit you are bound in that capacity—to hear Truth, to serve Truth. Set aside desire. You must not even have desire for Truth. Do not say, "I must have more Truth!" That is desire. If on the morrow you never once again in your life had lessons in Truth, if you were cast into a darkened dungeon, thrown into the grossest material conditions, among material-minded people, and never had a word of Truth for forty years, you should have had enough by now that in your heart you would say, "My cup, indeed, runneth over."

Adopt an approach, an attitude, and an inner conviction, that you as a god-individual have a position in the universe to assist the multitudes, that is all, not yourself. When Jesus paired His disciples off two by two to go their way, He gave them total power to heal the sick, to raise the dead, to cast out demons. He said to them, "Go now. You have my sanction, my power, and my blessing. Disseminate the Word."

You are potential disciples. And He said to them, "Carry with you no provision. Take with you not an extra change of clothes, not a saddle, not a purse, not one thing but what ye have on your back. Let your faith be so strong, so powerful, my disciples, that wherever you go you will be fed, housed and clothed, because you are in the cause of your Father. You are in your Father's home. And he who knows that he is in his Father's home and doing his Father's work is never in want, never!"

That should be your conviction, only to do the bidding of your Father. If you cannot within all your soul's searching come to this conclusion—and some of you perhaps will not—then that which you do have should remain as a lasting ballast for your journey, that you shall not need more cargo. You have a fine cargo.

It is true an individual may separate himself externally from his esoteric purpose, but he can never separate himself esoterically. *Once you have stepped upon the path you can never turn back.* Externally you can go back into the room of illusion, the material world, search after treasures, the pot of gold, but that esoteric link is there and it shall haunt you throughout all your lives, until once again you return to the fold.

These are burdens, or what appear to be burdens, it is true. They are very hard burdens. They are what you would call, in a sense, crosses.

For when you are in service you have to sacrifice many things, and the greatest sacrifice you make is yourself to your Father.

How do you sacrifice yourself to your Father, God, which art in heaven and in all things? By doing His work only, by looking in His direction—straight ahead. It matters not to you that you have the worldly things, only Godly things. What did Jesus say when He taught His disciples what is called the Eucharist? What did He say to them of the bread and the blood?

> ***Student:* This is my body, take it in remembrance of me. This is my blood, take it in remembrance of me.**

It is so. He told them, eat of my flesh and drink of my blood. He said to the multitude and the disciples, eat of my flesh and drink of my blood, and you shall never thirst and you shall never be hungry. For he who eats of my flesh eats of the Spirit. What did He say at the well to the woman?

> ***Student:* Drink of this water (of the well) and ye shall thirst again. But drink of the water which I shall give you and you shall never thirst again, but the water that I shall give you shall be in you a well of water springing up into everlasting life.**

It is so. He does not say to you, rend my body and gnaw upon my flesh. No. He says, "In spirit, in service, in Truth, hold as your image the Christ principle"—not the Jesus principle, for remember, Jesus of Nazareth was the man, the physical form, the Christ was the Divinity operating through Him.

Your spirit is not operating through you yet. It is above you. Christ's spirit was in the man, Jesus of Nazareth, so what He was saying is, search after the Truths which have been given you through the Christ principle and you shall never hunger spiritually.

If you drink of the symbolic blood of the Christ, you shall never thirst. You are drinking of pure spiritual essence. It does not mean that you devour the vital blood substance in literal form. The body and the blood represent the full abundance of the entire universe. And He said, "Let he who has ears hear, and he who has eyes, let him see." The same laws apply today that have applied throughout all the centuries.

There is no easy way. Remember, you are in the room of illusion, and you have to make a little effort, but the doing is what brings the reward.

Digest these teachings, try to fathom some of the inner meaning. Try to find their relationship to your everyday world. Now, you may ask Acumana questions if you desire.

***Student:* Are we still on probation?**

You are on probation. It means that according to your everyday approach to Truth, whether or not you are motivated by fear, doubt, frustration, certain anxiety patterns which develop within your aura, until these can be cleared, you remain on probation.

When you become a disciple, then a vast door opens to you. But before you can become a disciple, many things have to be changed in the individual consciousness. These things reflect as certain lights in your aura. It is Acumana's endeavor and fervent wish and hope that you should all become disciples. However, if not, it suffices that even as a probationer you can do much to lend assistance and power. For there are many, many hundreds of probationers throughout your planet. And there are many, many hundreds of disciples.

There are various degrees of disciples. There are only two degrees of probationers. There is the probationer who is on the first or entry level. The second degree of probation is one who is so close to becoming a disciple that it is only a matter of his choice and how he handles certain inner problems.

***Student:* Acumana, you say that negation is our only enemy. If we could for twenty-four hours of this next week not admit negation to our world, our radiance would probably fill this room. But how do we go about this? All we can do is pray for constant awareness of the thousand small statements in any day which are shaded.**

It is better not to speak of that which is shaded. The first lesson given to the neophyte, in all the temples throughout all history of man in esoteric teachings, is silence. The neophyte is taught to be silent. Silence has great meaning. He hears with the inner ear. He does not speak words of power which can be negative. And above all he is disciplining the faculty of expulsion, of scattering his thought and energy.

Student: **But he still has his thoughts to contend with.**

Yes, but it is far easier to contend with the thought when you are not scattering it with words.

Student: **So we should truly bite our tongues?**

Truly bite your tongues.

Student: **Well, Acumana, it's physically possible for one to keep one's lips sealed twenty-four hours, but how does one keep one's thoughts sealed for twenty-four hours?**

Each time your enemy comes charging into your battlefield, face him and say, "Away with you! Get thee behind me, Satan."

Student: **Then he will get so discouraged that he won't even come into the battlefield, right?**

It is so.

Student: **I thought I'd say come back tomorrow, today I'm too busy for you!**

But he will come back on the morrow and he will bring reinforcements. Let him go on to the Elysian battlefields to meet defeat.

Student: **Acumana, you use the word enemy, but truly do any of us have enemies other than our own bad habits, which we have to overcome?**

Even the physical enemies you might have are reflections of your own mental habits. If you have a physical enemy, or one who is in animosity toward you, it is only a reflection of your own mental state.

***Student:* With a purified mental state you couldn't have an enemy?**

You could only attract goodness.

***Student:* But, Acumana, Jesus had enemies.**

Jesus had the opposition to Truth, the power and opposition to Truth combating it. That was not a reflection of His state. But Acumana sees what you mean. Jesus represented the dynamic energy of Truth in God, in conflict to negation. His enemies were the sum total of all negation. Remember, it was so written and fulfilled that it had to be.

Now, children of Light, be aware of this concept. You have all gathered so together in unity of thought, oneness of ideas, and a sincere desire for more Light. In your hours where Acumana cannot commune with you through the sense faculty that now is manifest, know this. There is a link, a thread, as it were, of communion at all times between you and your teachers. You are observed, you are watched, you are guided. Your needs for enlightenment are understood. Be patient and know that the mills of your Father turn exceedingly slow and fine.

If you will attune your ear now, in silence, you may hear the last strains of a symphony in the distance as Acumana leaves you with these words. In the silence attune yourselves to the heavenly realms, in the name of the Father, and of the Son and of the Holy Spirit.

ONE WITH THEE

For the day that is past, I thank Thee,
Oh God, my Father.
For the night that has come, I thank Thee,
As one with Thee and nature
I gratefully take the rest
Which Thou hast lovingly ordained.
Whether I sleep or wake, my body and soul
Are Thine.
Do with them as Thou wilt,
For Thy command is my joy
As I am one with Thee.

CHAPTER V

The Excluded Middle

To every student of Light upon the path appears a fellow student of Light, and soon they journey on into deeper avenues of understanding. Look about you and you will find that you are not alone. There are many followers of consciousness about the path. They are like the seeds of the dandelion.

In the spring the dandelion stands up tall with its angelic grace. Have you ever, as a youngster, held up a dandelion, blown it with the breath, whoosh, and scattered seeds into the air? Have you watched the hundreds and hundreds of dancing beings in the atmosphere? The wind picks them up and carries them all about. That is representative of those upon the path of Light and Truth. They scatter all about. Then each one plants its own seed and multiplies.

Now Acumana wishes to speak with you more on the laws of mind. This subject embraces many deep concepts. One basic pattern, or one basic universal hindrance which each of you, and many others in the avenues of Truth, are burdened down with is this: You say, how does one find self-recognition? How does one become self-less? How does one, if this be your choice, choose to transcend material density and soar into the great Empyrean heights of spiritual illumination?

My children, if this could be answered in one word, truly the secret of all the ages to the great universal system of evolution would be answered.

But each one of you must search, grow, learn and study this inward process in his own area. However, it is advisable while studying to give certain keys to the student.

As Acumana's teacher has often said to Acumana, "These are crutches. How may a lame man learn to walk with a crutch"? And Acumana used to say to his teacher, "It is true that a lame man may not learn to walk strong and straight if he always relies upon a crutch, but is it not possible, oh teacher, that the lame man will learn better to stand up first with the crutch? Then when he is standing erect he may cast aside his crutch and walk on his own."

And Acumana's teacher would smile at Acumana, for he knew the answer all along. But he waited for Acumana, when he was a student, to come to that conclusion. So, let Acumana give to you a crutch, enabling you to stand up. You will find, when you are able to stand up, that you need no longer rely on the crutch. For the crutch only gives you the ability to stand, not to walk.

Will, herein is the key. In our other esoteric studies, in our divisions of the universe what are the three aspects of God?

***Student:* Will, Wisdom and Activity.**

Right, and what are the three aspects of Supreme Infinite Intelligence?

***Student:* Power, Word and Motion.**

That is so. So Power and Will are synonymous. They are different in degree, but synonymous in actuality. Power and will, are they not alike? As we proceed you will see how they are interrelated with one another. Will, therefore, is essential. What kind of will? Does this mean you must have the will to proceed in Truth to better yourself mentally, physically and spiritually through willpower? No, not in the mundane sense. Not in your everyday awareness. It is a different kind of will.

There are two aspects of will. Bear this in mind, for it is most important. There is the mundane will which is clothed with desire. That is your will. Will and desire are what make a person. Now what of Infinite Will?

What of spiritual will? The inward will is the essence of spirit, the essence of your identity, your infinite being.

A man takes his measure and strips away bit by bit all of his personality factors. This is what you must do before we can find out who and what you are in the avenues of Truth.

Your personality is comparable to a suit of clothes. A fine radiant personality would be one who is well garbed in clothes, in color harmony. He is a well-groomed individual, they say. That is personality in symbolism. Take away his grooming, his fine pressed suit, neatly starched shirt, his immaculate tie and the rest of his garb and what do you have? You have a man, but you have taken away his personality. All that remains is individuality.

Then take away the individuality and what remains? The soul essence. Now we are drawing close to a definition of Supreme Will which each one has. Each of you, each essence in the whole universe, is endowed with this Supreme Dynamic Will. Let us call this will spiritual will, the essence and nature of your being. Consider this essence, this inner spiritual will. To do so you must first be calm, peaceful, and poised, and in this state of being in repose, take your measure. That is, consider your value, your characteristics, your good and your bad. For each one must unto himself be true.

Make a list. On the right hand side write all the positive values, on the left hand side list all your negative values. In your mind begin to strip away your personality. Remember, personality is desire. Outward will, manmade will, personality, are synonymous with desire. You have the will, for example, to become successful in business. You have the will to have material gain and abundance that you may not worry or be in need. However, this is desire. First is born the desire, the desire to do, and then it becomes a power. That power and the desire are outward manifestations of will. Do you see how it works? Desire does not motivate, does not activate. The activation or the motivation is brought about through the will. So the will catapults or propels you into action. Then you fulfill the desire. You must first eliminate desire in your endeavor to know who and what you are, how to master yourself and revibrate yourself, to attune yourself to great Infinite Cosmic Intelligence.

Eliminate desire from your meditation. Reach the point in your meditation where you cease to have desire. Become a void. Become, as it were, in a state of no-thing-ness. Moment by moment, drop away all your worldly desires in your meditative state. The desire for life, the desire for breath, the desire for food, for clothing, for shelter, for satisfaction in all the material senses, and for satisfaction in all the esoteric and spiritual senses. All that is desire and must be dropped away. And when you have stripped yourself of all the outward manifestations what remains? The true person. The I. The I AM. The Spirit. That is what remains.

Then you stand face to face with your true identity, your God-self, your Christ consciousness, your spirit, your soul. You stand face to face with divine will, which is your endowment. You will see, in this state of reverie, that this Divine Will is in reality the will which gave you birth. It is that will which built your personality, which builds your body, your egos, your mind, in every one of your incarnations.

That is the greater will behind the lesser. Now, what is this Divine Will? It is in reality the essence of your divine infinite being, Spirit. That, therefore, is the will of God. That is the Will and the Power. It is the Word set forth into action in the universe.

God said, "Let there be light." It took will to let there be light and that is spiritual will. Every day in your prayers begin to bring about this state of consciousness within your nature to strip away your personality, your characteristics. Stand, as it were, before yourself in your true essence. It will not happen in one flash. It takes time. It takes time for the rose to grow, time and patience. An ancient Chinese proverb says, "With time and patience the mulberry grows into a silk worm."

So be patient. The doing is what is important to find yourself. Suddenly you will find you know who you are. You have stood before your desire body, seeing what it is and how it works. Acumana will tell you a story, a story Acumana always uses at this point in the universal teachings, for it best illustrates a particular point. It is an ancient Hindu lesson that the teachers teach to their scholars. This is the story.

A long, long time past there was a great Hindu God, Indra. And Indra desired to incarnate, to take on a body. So he became incarnated in the body of a pig. And in the body of a pig he took unto him a mate. And they began to multiply and reproduce themselves. So the pig became the proud papa of many young sucklings. And it groveled in the mud and enjoyed its condition. And it soon began to say to itself, "I am a pig." Its friends, the other gods, the other deities, became concerned. For Indra had become too endowed in the personality of the pig.

They said to Indra, "You are not a pig, my brother. Know ye not that you are Indra, a god?"

And Indra, in the garb of a pig, said, "I am a pig, I am a pig."

So great concern spread throughout all the Hierarchy of all the gods. How could they impress upon the consciousness of Indra that Indra, in reality, was not a pig, but was a god? They could not impress it upon his consciousness, so the gods struck dead his mate and all of his young ones.

And the pig became violent, and in its wrath, in its rage, it condemned. It threw words of blasphemy to the gods, to the heavens, for doing this to him. Then finally, all other courses served no purpose, so they took the life of the pig that Indra had become.

And suddenly in glory stepped forth Indra, the true god in heaven. And Indra laughed and laughed and laughed at the folly of his belief. He had become so convinced that he was a pig that he lived only in that area of thought.

Now herein, in this story, is a perfect example of man. You see why the Hindus give this lesson? It is man. The pig, understand, is only symbolic. Each of you, through your desire, are so convinced that you are man or woman that you know not your potential. Each of you, through your desire and your desire-will, (now speaking of the two together, desire and will, for you have the will because of your desire), believes you are a man or a woman. You are material, so you live in a material sense. And you are so convinced of this that no matter how often the teachers deliver the Truth to you you still go about and say, "I am a pig," just as Indra said, "I am not a god."

But ever so slowly, some of the Truth reaches through. Do you see the parallel? Now part of what Acumana gives to you is an endeavor to illuminate your consciousness, that you may shake off the desire, that you may become aware of the true potential. This does not mean that you must eliminate desire from your daily activity. But then you will find in a truer sense, there is a greater desire, a greater activity, and a greater will. You have yet to tap it. But first you must become self-less. As Acumana has said many, many times, self-less.

It is impossible for those upon the path of Truth to have any aid or assistance as long as they continue to say, "But I suffer. But I have a need. But I long. But I...this." Not important. It is worldly desire that makes you say that, not divine will, only desire. You must be honest unto yourself and in Truth say, "It is desire that makes my body respond. My body responds to those thoughts, not divine will. It is divine will, the essence of my nature, that is desirous to express through me. Away with worldly desire and away with its activity. Now let me dwell within."

Then you begin to contemplate some of the greater inner depths. When this has been brought about in your consciousness there will be a greater activity, a greater motivation, within your whole spiritual, physical and mental natures.

It brings about a complete trinity of activity. Therefore, while in this state of trinity and activity you will find that every need, every sustenance, every effort, every contemplation of your own essence, is instantly cared for. There is never a want, if you only allow the law to begin to work.

Indra was so convinced in the personality of a pig, because it was able to grovel in the mud, eat the food before it, and nurture its young, that it believed it was a pig. So mesmerized was it that it was a pig that its own will, divine will, was lost until it was too late. Not in reality, in spirituality. Had Indra, in reality, recognized his true identity, suddenly there would have been a glorious reunion.

There is in all the esoteric teachings a phrase given. Now is the time for this phrase to be given to you. It is called THE EXCLUDED MIDDLE. The excluded middle. It is the missing link.

Let us now proceed on to the endless chain and find this missing link. Imagine an endless chain. Imagine it as having a beginning and an end, for our purpose of understanding. Yet how can we say which is the beginning and which is the end? Let us pinpoint it. Let us say one side is the beginning and the other side is the end of the chain. At this side of the chain is Will and at the other side of the chain is Will and in the middle of the chain is Will. Let us consider the beginning of the chain as Divine Will, the essence of your natures, spirit, true will and at the end is the same will, the essence of your nature. But in the middle is a different will. It is the negative will, or personality and desire. For desire and will are on the same pole and they are manifested as personality.

To exclude the middle means that you grow in the beginning of all things from Divine Will up to the middle. When you are aware of the detriment of the middle, the desire, you exclude that. And you go on to the completion, back to Divine Will. That is called The Excluded Middle. It is just to strip away the personality. Take your measure, cease to consider what you desire, rather consider Thy Will Be Done, not my will be done.

The Lord Jesus gave you this in a prayer. When He says, "Thy will be done, on Earth as it is in Heaven," it means the Earth being the desire of your nature, and heaven being the spirit of your nature, or will. Remember the principle, "As above, so below." Each of you, as a degree of manifestation, of spiritual essence, is a heaven, only you are a divided heaven. You are a heaven and earth.

Depending upon the density of your mental outlook, depends the degree of materialism or Earth that you are manifesting. The more earthy you are, the heavier your density, and the greater you are operating on the opposite extreme of the pole. If, however, you are more spiritually inclined, then you are living in heaven as the saints, the prophets, the sages, and the masters do. They live in heaven, but they may journey to Earth. That is, they may embody, they may walk in physical substance, at their own choosing.

So when the Lord Jesus Christ says to you, "Thy will be done, on earth as it is in heaven," He is saying to you in essence, as in true heaven or the spiritual nature of all things, when the will is functioning, Divine Will, there is perfection. As this exists in heaven, let it exist also on Earth. In other words, The Excluded Middle. Let the personality and the desire fade away so that Divine Will flows in one straight line. Then your desire shall not interfere with your spirituality.

Perhaps the best way for man to contemplate these thoughts or put them into practice is by this meditation, by this visualization: Sit in complete repose, alone in silence. Let no sound interfere in the vibrations of your thought waves. In this state that you bring about through your action, envision before you a great ocean, a great sea. Imagine this great ocean to be luminescent, vibrant—like when there is a phosphorous glow in the sea on a moonlit night. Imagine that you are in the center, in the direct center of this mighty ocean, this sea of luminescence. Imagine this vibrating, luminating sea to be spirit, pure spirit of power, Divine Will, and you are in the center of it. Be not fearful, but allow it to cover you.

Allow yourself to plunge into it, as you do into a pool when you swim.

Swim beneath the surface and open your eyes and you will see the same thing. Glowing power, spiritual power, permeating your very nature, your very depth, your every cell. Now imagine, and come to this conclusion—realize that you are a part of this. Say to yourself, as this image is before you, "I am a part of this. I am this." For is one drop of water from the ocean not the ocean? It is still the ocean, differing only in degree.

If you take a tumbler of pure water from the ocean and you drop soot into this tumbler of water, and it turns black and muddy, is it yet pure water? It is still pure water, essentially. Take away the soot and you again have pure water. What you have is a difference in degree. Therefore, as you declare your identity in this living pool of spiritual essence, say, "I AM this essence, I AM a living vital degree of this spiritual essence."

Above all have no thought of desire—give over freely. Give over so freely that it matters not to you whether you, according to your sense, live or die. You are so free, unrestrained, in this meditative state that it matters not to you. For you come to the realization that you are the embodiment of life and death, that there is no difference between life and death. Only in degree. And that you can transcend the degree when you come face to face with your true will when you have excluded the middle.

Every one upon the path must do this. When it is done is up to you, but it must be done. Let Acumana assure you of this—it is not an easy process. For some it has been described as an inward pain the likes of which birth knows no counterpart. This is symbolic. Great enlightened beings have embodied words comparable to the surrender of personality or excluded middle in a great book written by divine inspiration, through the Hierarchy, called *Imitation of Christ.* Another great book which has been written by an initiate, well upon the path, is called *Light on the Path.* It was given by divine inspiration by the Hierarchy. *Light on the Path* clearly sets forth this principle, the surrendering of personality.

You will find the sooner you set out to do this, the greater your growth, the greater your joy, and the greater your abundance in every sense, in every state, in every degree. Then, in Truth, you are attuned to Divine Consciousness. You become one mind. You become the embodiment of divine mind. Divine mind acting and motivating you in every degree of dimension. You then are what is called two parts of the three-part trinity,

You are Will and Action. The Will being divine mind and Action being that you are in action upon this plane. What is the third step? Wisdom. That you gain by the use of the other two. You gain Wisdom, for truly when the Will is recognized, then the Action becomes greater.

Are you not wiser? If you are not wiser, then you did not practice it correctly. You are then wiser and are in a degree the Trinity. You are in degree Will, Wisdom and Activity, the three aspects of God on the seventh Cosmic plane.

When you choose to do this is up to you. You may start today or you may start tomorrow, or the next day. But it must be done, in this life, or the next, or the next. Perhaps it would be far greater and far simpler for you to approach it now and wait not for the morrow.

For on the morrow you will find there will be other things to deter you from this practice. You will say, at the conclusion of the morrow, we were unable to approach it, we will do it tomorrow. And on the following morrow there will be other things to keep you from your goal. And you will say, in the evening of that day, again I was unable to approach it. I vow on the morrow it shall be done. And on the following morrow again you are deterred. It is an endless chain. Your worldly desire, your physical motivation, does not desire this to come about. It is the negation of your nature. It does not desire for you to have illumination. It does not desire for you to start to practice, to learn who and what you are in this great universe. So it will keep you from it in every possible way. But you will then learn to have the will to will.

This very evening, before you doze off into sleep, begin to observe yourself, but do not analyze and say, "Oh thus and so and this and that," and harbor and dwell upon it. That is not the correct way. Simply state the conditions you aspire to have. Imagine the old condition you have falling away, and the spiritual condition you desire in its place. Perhaps this would be a good way.

Once, a long, long time past Acumana, when contemplating the inner nature and the parallel of these teachings, observed in a small hamlet, a young boy plucking a goose for the roast. Acumana sat upon a log and observed the young boy as he plucked the goose, and he found that the boy uttered a mantram for each feather. He held the goose first by the neck, and then by the feet, and each feather that he plucked the boy uttered a mantrum. And he said, translated, "Oh, my Father, though this goose is lifeless in form it is endowed with spirit, and as I, my Father, pluck the quills from this shell, let my body perceive the pain of growth that this goose would feel." That was all he said.

And each time he plucked a feather the boy would go "ow." He would squeal. And Acumana said to the boy, "My son, why dost thou torture yourself"? Acumana knew why, see?

The boy said, "Oh, teacher, my father has commanded me thus, to pluck the goose for supper. And it grieves my heart that we should partake of the sole manifestation of this goose into our belly. So I am asking my God's forgiveness for stripping away this goose."

Acumana said to the young boy, "It is a fine, noble thought, my son. Thou shall grow up to be a teacher, but remember this: Let not your soul be grieved over the goose. For the goose has long since gone to search for greater fields of endeavor. Rather you should say as you pluck the quill from the goose, my son, these words, 'Thank you, Father, for the manifestation of every degree of life. And as I pluck the quills from the goose, Father, may my wisdom and Your wisdom put to good use these quills. And may I have a soft downy bed to prove the wisdom of Your use.'"

The boy smiled and he gave his thanks.

Now, can you see a parallel here? From the point of view of plucking away your personality, thank God for every desire and every trace of your nature. It is there for a purpose. Thank the Father for that purpose, that you have grown, learned, and profited by that purpose. For remember, as Acumana has said to you, your own will, not desire, your own essence of will placed those very desires and that personality around you for your betterment, so that you could come to the point where The Excluded Middle would be recognized and that you would transcend it. Do not, above all, criticize yourself or condemn yourself, but remain objective.

By all means, drink the full glass of elixir. Leave not one drop even to cling to the rim. Otherwise, that shall dissolve and shall blend to the rain clouds above and rain down upon you again and fill your glass. Let not the rain of time fill your cup, drain it. This must be done sometime or another.

Acumana has chosen to give you this lesson now, at this time, in order that you may better understand how you may open the great door of your own chamber to allow wisdom, untold wealth of wisdom, to flood your valley with vitalizing waters, that the crops and the deeds of your soul will bear fruit and the harvest shall be great and plentiful. And the multitudes shall feed upon your harvest. That is joy, untold joy.

There is not a one of you that is incapable of taking your measure and beginning to go toward your inner contemplation and stand face to face with Divine Will, your soul. Each day the more you do it the greater you become in shedding the shackles, the bonds, the noose around your neck. Your desires, indeed, choke and suffocate you. There is a greater desire awaiting you, if you will only open your eyes and look.

Think not that you shall leave the world. Be not concerned that you shall not have the things that you thought your heart wanted. But, rather, realize that there are things greater for you, and only your own inward destiny knows. Be not concerned from one day to the next where they will come from, the benefits, fruits of your labor. Only know that they shall come. The mills of your Father grind slowly, it is true, but do they not grind exceedingly fine? They do, indeed. So it must be. Be patient with yourself, that the silk of your nature will be recognized and the fine granules being ground in your mill shall produce abundant loaves of bread to feed the multitudes.

Now, you may ask Acumana questions if you desire.

***Student:* It's quite obvious, isn't it, that when this is applied in meditation it then becomes part of the subconscious, which, in turn, translates it into conscious action in everyday living?**

You will find, most assuredly, when you meditate and bring about this state of consciousness your whole physical motivation is radically changed for the better. Unawakened, you are only half, not even half, alive. You are only, perhaps, one-quarter alive. That is all! Would you not like to be four-quarters alive? The first thing is to become half alive, and that is to begin to meditate, to pray.

Let Acumana no longer hear, "Where do I go, where do I begin? I have need of this." These are words belonging to the dead past. They belong six feet beneath the ground, buried. You have no needs, you have no desire. You must become aware that you are not Indra the pig, but Indra the god. So do not say, "How do I meditate? What do I do?"

Rather you should say, "How soon may I do this?" Then you may answer your own question for as soon as you do it you will have the will to will. That is, you will have the Divine Will, which is the hidden essence of all your nature, to redirect, remotivate your desire into greater channels. It will change your entire physical life.

There are numerous approaches to meditation. Each one will choose his own approach, according to his own nature. What you must all do is eliminate your desire, face it squarely, recognize it, battle with it, be honest. You know your inner nature. No other knows it, only you. Stand before yourself, without personality, without ego, without human will or desire, and you will stand as you are intended to stand, in Divine Will, in the essence of spirit. Then there will be a greater desire and a greater physical manifestation of will, than you have ever yet realized. This is the whole system behind evolvement. That man will come to recognize what is meant by The Excluded Middle and what is meant to surrender personality.

It is better now to surrender your ego, your personality, and your desire, than many lives from now. Why not lessen the burden now and become in greater control or mastery over yourself? Step up your whole evolutionary process. Or would you rather wait lazily around until the showers of time drown you once more? You need not die if you only recognized the Truth. It is true that anyone is capable of ascension, providing he has reached a point of understanding.

Do not be fooled that only the masters may ascend. Are you not Indra? Are you not as Paul said, gods? It is not beyond your capacity, according to your own area of development, your own area of consciousness, to become ascended in great spiritual consciousness. It awaits you. Let life, therefore, shower upon you its true purpose, your true purpose and goal.

Waste not a moment, waste not a second. Let yourself be filled, your very thought be filled with the expectation that each breath you take is bringing you closer and closer to a greater consciousness of the universe and God, so that you look forward to the next breath with the expectation that it contains the secret of God. That will within you motivates you to move forward to take that breath. And that movement brings you into greater activity whereby your every movement, your every thought, your every action becomes so filled, so powerful with the realization that you are endowed with living spirit, that it is impossible, impossible, for you to conceive of anything contrary. And each movement, each action brings about greater stimulation of your whole spiritual nature.

Perhaps it sounds simpler than it is in practice. Is not life filled with the same value? Things are said easier than they are done. That is part of the goal. You all choose to learn in this school, in this corner of the universe. Therefore, be not content but be expectant, be radiant, be active. Too many people are content today. Go beyond contentment and become restless and active to move on.

Contentment is the beginning of indolence. And indolence is the beginning of decay, and decay is the beginning of retrogression, and retrogression is the beginning of devolution—going back to the beginning.

Your desire will not propel you to produce. You are not propelled from desire to achieve. Instead, by living in a state of at-one-ment with divine law, things will come about automatically. Let Acumana ask you a question. How hard must you concentrate to take your next breath? Of course, it's automatic without concentration. There you have the whole key. Everything will be automatic.

How hard must you concentrate in order to become materially successful? Let Acumana say this. Under material conditions a man must concentrate with great effort to produce material abundance. He must drive himself until he has a heart condition, and ultimately the condition of many pounds of dirt upon him. All this is unnecessary. Why is he driving himself? To what purpose? Desire.

You may have the same things without the drive and the force, when you recognize the divine supplyhouse through your own nature and you attune yourself to this divine substance, this divine energy, through the greater will. You know, therefore, that since you are a part of this spiritual essence, in this great sea of spirit, that all things that exist above exist below. And since you are the personification of all things, then you may, indeed, share all things.

Remember this axiom, this proverb: All things are worthy of your sharing. However, nothing is worthy of being possessed by you.

Let that be a key, a guide, for you. All things are worthy of your possession, but all things are not worthy of being possessed by you.

***Student:* I was reading something very similar to that, the third Chapter of John, where John the Baptist was explaining and his disciples said, "Here is Jesus who is doing the same thing that you are," and he said, "That which is given to a man comes from heaven, comes from above..."**

But that which a man takes comes from the Earth. That is the difference. What is given to man truly is from heaven, as you say, or above, but what a man takes he takes from the Earth, and when he takes he must pay back. So there is no need to take when you know that all that you require will be given unto you.

Carry this thought in the inner chamber of your heart. The great depth of your true nature is white, pure, sweet and glowing. You are likened unto the bridegroom. You must win love, affection and devotion. You do not take it or steal it, you earn it by proving your worth. Then the fruits of your love are manifested in multiplicity.

God's blessing to you, my children. Be productive spiritually. Be not desirous. Rather be endowed with the will to will, the will to will away The Excluded Middle.

RELEASE

Oh Father, I thank You for the lesson.
I see its value.
Yet if there is more to see,
I pray Thee to reveal it unto me,
That I may gladly and in joy
Accept the value
And release the condition.
I have worked with it patiently.
Now I wash my hands of it
And release it unto Thee.
Guide me in my patience, that it may pass.
Guide me in joyous acceptance
Of the new that awaits me.
Assist me in rising above all outer circumstances,
That I may be
In perfect Oneness with Thee.

CHAPTER VI

Blood on the Moon

There is in the world today a great spiritual esoteric activity. You can discerningly observe among mankind his various centers of Light growth. The reason for this activity is well known to all students upon the path. However, it is on this reason that Acumana desires to speak for a while.

The great Book of Revelation in man's Bible speaks of twelve tribes of Israel. It speaks of the seven churches of man. In relationship to these churches within man, there is a relationship between man and his esoteric centers and the root races, the seven days of God's week, the seven churches in the Book of Revelation. Each one may orient his own seven-fold spiritual nature to prepare himself for the great days ahead.

The Hierarchy, the Great Illumined Ones of Light, who guide and assist humanity in its hours of need, have prepared, as it were a banquet, a feast. It is a spiritual feast. Many ages past when God's tribes, the original tribes of Israel, were scattered and sent about the world to produce their own kind, to multiply, to bring forth the harvest of God's abundance, there was endowed within certain individuals spiritual leadership ability. These leaders, high initiated ones, brought to each race great progress. Chaldeans, Babylonians, Egyptians, Mayans, North American Indians and numerous others, which we need not go into now. History will reveal them to you.

When, in the course of man's evolvement, these high initiate ones bring about a degree of spiritual consciousness within the people they then leave them to decide which avenue they must choose in Truth, be it spiritual or be it material.

Then what is called free choice, free will, begins to operate within each individual within each race, so that he may learn the full value of his Father's abundance.

Now, when the masters have taken their physical presence from the Earth, they then guide and direct, from their mind of spiritual power, from other centers or areas. They must not, nor can they, interfere in the free will of the races. What they do is stimulate a one-directed activity within each race to bring it to its fullest perfection, to bring, as it were, a symphony before the Father. Each race represents a part of a great celestial symphony. When, as the Father has declared, in the seventh day of His creation, Vulcan, the day of rest and assimilation, God's great symphony must play.

What of all these races? Where is the enlightenment? Where is the balance? It is when each individual, consistently, from incarnation to incarnation, has set aside personal ambition, personality (therein is the key—personality). And when he has set aside these aspects and held only to the inner concept of God-awareness, stimulated and helped to bring about rebirth in his own nature, then he becomes a soloist in the great heavenly symphony.

Now, in the seven churches of your Father's kingdom there are many degrees. These degrees are the sealed tribes of your Father. And it says, when the day of great scourging, Armageddon, the day of tribulation and trial comes about, when there must be blood on the moon, all will be known.

Acumana will give this to you. Blood on the moon represents, symbolically, this concept: When the first physical creature, that is, manifested as man, is able to set foot upon the surface of Earth's satellite moon, there, in truth, will be blood on the moon, will there not? Not flowing blood, not spilled blood, but nevertheless blood upon the moon.

In this day of great tribulation many will go and others will proceed to the Light. The determined number of each is not known. However, in each person there are two avenues. There are two chapters in the Book of Life, the left-hand chapter and the right-hand chapter. The outcome is not known, for free will and collective will for race and nation cannot be interfered with.

When these races within man have continued to cling to the one Christ concept of Light, the true and only God-self, they unite themselves in positivity and prayer. They do not interfere in the will or the thought pattern of their negative brothers. What they do, however, is bring a change of their own inner consciousness. They stabilize negative influence. That is important work.

And now the time is here to stabilize negative thought in the great magnetic field surrounding your Earth which for ages and ages has been known by all teachers and seers, and which science has given the name of Van Allen Belt.

This magnetic field of energy is the primary source or storehouse of universal energy, cosmic energy, which is being radiated and directed from each group, from each unit. In this force field about the Earth there is scattered great positive cosmic energy. That energy, in turn, by the direction of the Hierarchy, is scattered and directed to areas of mankind.

Man receives his spiritual inspiration and energy from the sun through his feet up through his entire body. He redirects his nature by the power of his mind through concentration, meditation and contemplation. Then he, in turn, surrenders his personality, directs that universal power within him, lends it and blends it with the greater universal power, where it becomes one power, one great dynamic source of energy. This great dynamic source of energy, through the Hierarchy, the great Brotherhood of Light, is utilized as a force field of action to stabilize and harmonize negative conditions.

All of you who are students of the deeper philosophy know that under the law of polarity there are opposites. These opposites are different only in degree. You know the law of Light. The opposite of Light is darkness. The opposite of God is Satan. The opposite of love is hate. They are on the same line, only different in degree.

Darkness and negation manifests in physical form as surely as does positivity. Each of you is a physical manifestation of the positivity of Christ-conscious Light, of God-wisdom, or universal Light. However, there are equally manifested the darker shadows of Light, all negative forms. They have manifestation. For remember, there are two sides within the nature of man, his spiritual nature and his material nature, and in order for him to overcome his material nature he must first surrender his personality and become one with Universal Mind.

This negative force is stabilized by the union of combined prayer and study brought about through the collective consciousness of the unit. As a unit you represent one mind and one body. Your unit or group is one mind, one concept, in the greater concept. The individual thought, the individual desire, is not of paramount importance. What is of paramount importance is the one mind, the one unit, the one power, which is brought about through the unselfish action of each individual to blend his intelligence, psyche, his spiritual nature and his material nature into one.

Individually you are personality, collectively you are one mind under the direction and influence of a great ascended master of Light. That ascended master of Light has under his direction many teachers of high initiation, many other masters. He has many above him in a greater degree of Light. It is an endless chain, on and on, ad infinitum.

Your one Light as a unit or your one mind, at this very moment of time—since you are limited by time—gives off a frequency of radiation at a great rate of vibration. At this very moment there is emanating from each of you, individually and collectively, spiritual power of enough magnitude to heal the most severe physical condition. There is enough power emanating from you now to quiet the thoughts of negation within the mind of the most evil individual you could comprehend, that is, your power could quiet it for a time.

These things must be sustained. Therefore, in the greater ashram of the Father there must be many power centers, many units collectively working for the betterment of civilization, that this century may have in its last chapter peace inscribed, that it may have its last word, *love.* This is brought about in the greater ashram. There are many ashrams within the greater ashram. Each ashram has its units or sub-units. They, in turn, add to the one essence, or the one power of the overall ashram. Then it lends to the greater ashram. The greater ashram, in turn, in its power, dimension and energy, lends to the greater degree of power to feed the world, to stand balanced, to sustain equipoise about the world.

Personality must cease to interfere in any class work or any individual work. How does one cease to become cognizant of personality? You are aware now of what is called in ancient philosophy, The Excluded Middle. Let us examine this further for a moment, that we may all have a clearer understanding of this concept.

There are two degrees of will within man. First there is the greater will. This greater spiritual will which is God-conscious, which is spirituality in creation going through all phases of physical manifestation, that spark of Light within each individual which endows him with the attribute to breathe, to think, to see, to hear, to utilize all his physical senses, is Divine Will.

Divine Will never was not, and never shall not be. It always is. Therefore, Divine Will is, in a sense, a degree of the will of Supreme Infinite Intelligence, or it is a degree of the will of God. For we have God in our visible universe, and then we have the Infinite beyond God.

In the seven spiritual planes of man you ascend up through the seven into God concept, and from God you ascend up into the greater cosmic seven degrees where the number of hierarchies, the degree and number of dimension, is beyond comprehension. At the apex is the All, which is beyond comprehension. Let us call this Supreme Infinite Intelligence, the great ever-expanding 0. On and on It grows.

Each of you is a degree of this Divine Will of God. When this Divine Will must densify itself, take on substance, when it must become cloaked in the garb of physical density called flesh, blood, substance, the greater will, or Divine Will, is dormant. It becomes completely dormant in the lower echelon of man's evolvement. Then man must evolve up through and to the state of consciousness whereby that dormant state of God Will, God Action, begins to ascend within him, as in Christ it ascended. When it was crucified it ascended. The crucifixion must come about in each individual, symbolically. That is the surrendering of will, the setting aside human will, which is naught but desire.

You must grow and expand in consciousness. Your younger brothers on the path cannot, in this life, surrender their will, their personality. They have not reached the point in the scale of evolution where they are capable of understanding, nor of operating, this degree of power. However, they will learn to follow the will of a greater being, of a greater concept, if they are shown and given that concept. It is freedom in a greater capacity.

Desire deters you from your spiritual growth. Desire deters you from recognizing and utilizing the greater will. And when you take your measure, that is, when you follow the axiom, "To thine own self be true," and make a list of those assets, those virtues within you which are cultivated through desire, you will find that when you strip yourself of all your encumbrances, there seems to be naught left within you. And yet you become aware, when you have the desire for food, the desire for shelter, the desire for love, the desire for protection, the desire for gratification, the desire of all physical senses, the desire of all mental senses, then, above all, even the desire for spiritual growth, that all is given unto you even though you are desireless.

You must reach the point in your consciousness where desire does not motivate you, but Will, great Divine Will, motivates you. And when that will motivates you, you become one with the flowing substance and you are then the perfect reflection. You are then the great microcosm within the macrocosm in consciousness. Then you will the will to motivate.

That is the missing link—The Excluded Middle—the unconsciousness of divine will in evolution, growing toward recognition along the great scale of life, where in your chain of evolvement you reach the point called perfection of personality. You will the will to exclude that nature. You jump the gap. You say, "Not my will but Thy will be done."

When you exclude the middle, personal will, you then bring about an inner quickening of your spiritual nature, and Divine Will begins to motivate and function within you. Each of you have had this consciousness. In your endeavors and in your studies, each of you, at one time or another, has recognized, while in a state of peace, repose and meditation, that you have transcended the mundane area of mind and have ascended into an abstract state of reverie. And while in this abstract state of reverie you have become aware of a greater purpose, of a greater being. You have, in truth, esoterically glimpsed your own spiritual nature, only a fleeting glimpse. Each of you have had this experience. Some of you consciously are able to recall this. Others of you are not able to consciously recall it.

You will reach a point in your studies where you will surrender desire and personality. And you will work, as you are growing now and being prepared, and as others are growing and being prepared, daily to say, "Thy will be done." *"Thy will be done."* And then Divine Will shall take hold of you and motivate you, and a greater purpose in your spiritual life will unfold before you like a great lotus as it blossoms its beauty to the world. Then the nature of your being is revealed, and when you gaze upon the cosmic flower of life—your own beauty, your own purity—you are gazing into the heart of your Father. And when you gaze into the heart of your Father, you become the beat and the flow of the blood of your Father. And to become within the beat and the flow of the blood of your Father is, in reality, to become one with universality throughout all time.

This is your goal. This is your direction. Daily you grow toward this. Daily the world as a whole must grow toward this. Remember, you are a universe and you live on a world. Your body represents a great universe. Contained within that universe, contained within the nature of your being, every cell, organ and essence of your body vibrates, emanates and evolves. There are millions and millions of degrees of evolution going on within you. You are, as it were, in the great philosophy, "As above, so below."

The Father is above and you are below. Then you, in turn, represent the Father, and below you, your physical nature, is the below. And within this concept, there is going on within you your mineral structure, your animal structure, and your esoteric structure, evolution, growth, progress, in order that you may ascend into greater Light.

Your Lord, Christ, could never have ascended in His full nature unless He had reached the point of complete self-mastery and perfection in His whole being, which He had long since done. That means that every mineral essence in His body was so pure, so high in vibration and in frequency, that its degree of evolution was comparable to that of the highest degree of maturity and consciousness of man. Within each of you there is consciousness. You are living on a planet of consciousness, and contained within that planet is its own consciousness. It makes one realize that the universe, this small world that you live on, your temporary abode, your school, represents in life universality, a great dimension of growth. There are millions upon millions of lights of evolvement, each one assisting the other.

And wherever that assistance is going on it is harmonizing the opposites. For there are opposites in all things. The opposite of your spiritual nature is desire. The opposite of the spiritual nature of God is negation, and there are many degrees of negation. Therefore, through these laws, these great concepts of spirituality, man shall and will, through collective work, bring about, in the dawn of a coming day, a state of cosmic consciousness. That is, those beings who shall incarnate in the new age, depending upon the work as it progresses in this age, shall be incarnated in a greater degree of consciousness. The masses, the multitude, your younger brothers and sisters, will cease to incarnate as they do now. They shall incarnate in another area more to their liking.

Each of you endeavors to perfect your seven-fold nature, but before you may become one with God, your planet must become one with God. It must melt, as it were, back into the Sun.

Mercury, the closest planet to the Sun, having the greatest degree of evolution upon it, is growing closer and closer to the physical manifestation of God, the Sun. This Earth must, in its course of evolution, in its serpentine motion, its circular motion, draw closer and closer to the Sun. You cannot measure this, except in an age, which takes millions of years to evolve. So as you perfect your spiritual nature, the Earth must perfect its spiritual nature. The only way this is possible is by free-thinking man in his spiritual nature uniting to bring about a quickening of the inner vibration of the Earth and all of its degrees of evolution, that it may equally in balance with man, reach cosmic consciousness and therefore, be ready for the great banquet that the Father has prepared.

This banquet is naught but the day of fruition, the day of great Light, the day when man will walk among the angels and the angels shall walk among men.

That is, man's consciousness will have expanded to such a degree of evolution spiritually that his eyes will be opened and he shall see, and his ears shall hear, his physical nature shall change, and in truth he will once more inhabit the Garden of Eden—the Garden of Eden being the most perfect state of condition of spirituality, which is united in perfection with materiality or the lower substance of vibration.

The greater obligation to Truth, and to the Brotherhood of each ashram, of each student, is to bring about this quickening process, to bring about this stabilizing process within the world. That the world may move into its spiritual enfoldment in balance with man and in balance with the plan of the Hierarchy. If the world goes into positivity in the next seven cycles, it is all predetermined what shall happen. If, however, it does not, it is equally predetermined what shall happen. That is why teachers say there are two sides in the Book of Life—the dark and the light. Both are predetermined, both are known. But it is not known in which direction they will proceed. If it is in the left direction, it is known. If it is in the right direction, it is known. But in which direction, that is not known.

This, therefore, is the purpose, the plan, that it may become stabilized by those upon the path of Light, by those who are of the White Brotherhood. Each of you have pledged your spiritual allegiance to the Brotherhood, that you will serve as a physical manifestation of the Brotherhood, that you may be receptacles or channels for the greater abundance of man. This is your goal. This is your direction.

As the Sun rises in the east on a new age, a new unfoldment of wisdom, cosmic consciousness shall be brought about to the world. Great universal secrets shall be revealed. The past one hundred years have marked the greatest transitory period of evolution and progress for man. There has been in the past one hundred years more progress, more growth, than in the whole recorded history of mankind. Daily you are preparing for tomorrow, and tomorrow is indeed close at hand. These past years have brought about a complete change in orthodoxy, a complete change in politics, a complete change in esoteric knowledge, to reveal to man the teachings which have gone down in time. All that has been concealed shall be revealed. All that has been hidden shall be found.

Today these teachings are once more being brought to man that he may benefit by them. Once more God in His great compassion gives every creature upon the Earth an opportunity for spirituality. Regardless of how devious, how treacherous, his deeds may be, he is, nevertheless a child of God, and God's compassion and mercy are so great, so vast, that each one is given opportunity after opportunity.

Blended with your power, your love, and your assistance, these things are brought about. If a man falls to such low extremes on the ladder of life that he must suffer the second death, that he must return in some other age at the very bottom of the scale of evolution, it is still a blessing of the

Father. He is not forgotten, he is given an opportunity to begin anew. But within his consciousness there is always the memory, the idea, that somewhere along the line he had taken the wrong step.

Man is truly the fallen angel of his Father. Each of you, fallen angels, are standing erect in purity, Light and service. Your teachers, your individual teachers and your master teacher, give you daily direction. You are attuned continuously to their frequency. The only way you may remain attuned to that level is by the purity of your own Light.

A channel of Truth is protected, but that protection is only as strong as his own personality and mentality can make it. If you continuously surround yourself in the radiance of Christ Light, the great ring-pass-not, but you harbor thoughts contrary to that nature, then you are vulnerable and that ring of protection is dropped. So your protection and atunement is only as strong and sustained as you make it. These are some more lessons on the path man must consciously adhere to daily to strengthen his tie with the world, to give forth in prayer, and daily to strive to imitate the consciousness of Christ. Imagine, with a great expectation of feeling, not desire, but feeling, that at any moment one of the great, glorious ascended masters, Christ, Kuthumi, Morya, Venutian Kahuna, the Tibetan—imagine that one of these great dynamic powers of Light were to step forward and become your guest for one day. How would you receive them? Would you receive them in your home if you were angry? Would you receive them in your home if you had argued, if you had judged another, if you had had any thought contrary to all those teachings you were given? You would instantly feel humiliation of a greater sense.

And yet you are told, "Chastise not thyself," for to chastise thyself is to deny and criticize your own God-potential. But rather you should hold the concept that perhaps today, at any moment, my great beloved teacher shall bless me with his presence. How shall I receive Him? He is all knowing, all wise, all loving. He will know my every thought. He will know my thought of yesterday. He will know my deed of yesterday, my deed of today. Are these things worthy of His presence? Ask yourself this question. If with this code of conduct you motivate day to day, Acumana will guarantee you that by living in this state of expectation, that is, the expectation of God-consciousness motivating continuously through you, it will be impossible to harbor any thoughts on a mundane realm.

There shall be periods of trial. There shall be periods of failure. But when you slip, you know you have slipped. Those in Truth have this great advantage, that they know they know. And when they know they know, they are able, as a rider who is thrown from a horse, to stand up once more and proceed. Each day your Father gives you a new day. And each morning you should arise with this thought, this prayer:

> *"God, my Father, I thank Thee once more for the light of this day. God, my Father, I thank Thee for this opportunity to learn once more the beauty of Your lessons of life. May the sun, the warmth of Your countenance, as it shines upon me, may it shine upon the entire universe. And may each other have the same understanding, the same joys, the same thrills, the same expectations, that I have."*

And at high noon, let this be your thought:

> *"God, my Father, at this time of day let my being be filled with the contemplation and the beauty of Your manifested works. For the light of the day is brilliant upon the world, and with my eyes I am able to see, and with mine ears I am able to hear. And may the world share in this joy. And may they see and may they hear the glory and beauty of Your world."*

And in the evening, let this be your thought, your prayer:

> *"Oh, God, my Father, the radiance of Your smile sinks behind the clouds in the west, and as the blanket of night soon shall enfold Your countenance, may that warmth, that peace, that radiance which is within my being and may music of your sunset fill my evening ahead with the memory of the beauty of the day you have painted before me."*

And at night, let this be your thought:

> *"Oh, God, my Father, for the day that has past, I give my thanks. God, my Father, for the blessing of repose before me, I ask that I*

may be united in the presence of Light and purity. May I serve the world in my hours of repose and, with the blessings of Light and wisdom, may my body be renewed, revitalized, and may I share in the contemplation of reverie, the beauty and the silence of night. And may the mystery of the evening and the night enlighten my consciousness. And upon awakening, oh God, my Father, if it is within Thy will, may the consciousness of the night remain indelibly engraved upon my outer mind, that I may grow in wisdom and in the strength to understand, a little of Your nature once more."

Let that be your thought to carry you into the hours of repose. May every moment, every second of your day be filled with prayer. Better still, Acumana says to you, *May every beat of your heart remind you of prayer. May every breath you take be the inhalation of wisdom, and as you exhale, may you exhale the power, prayer and love.* Then you shall surrender your personality, your ego, your desire, and unite in the loving arms of your Father. And let the Mother of the world nurse you with the sweetness of Her breath. And let the angels, the great masters, the illumined ones, work through you in purity, clarity and sharpness.

Your bodies have been prepared for eons of time. It is not only for this life that you have prepared your tabernacles. You have built this and prepared this many lives before. Now have the faith and confidence, the intuitive awareness to know, as you know your breath, that you may turn the knob, as it were, toward wisdom. But above all, believe in what you believe. Hold to what you believe. Let no man deter you from your goal, and expect, above all, that at any moment your teacher may step forward in your presence to give to you a greater blessing, a greater lesson, and to prepare you for something else. You know not how, when, or where it may come about. But you will know that by contemplation of those thoughts your mind is held in a state of elation, and the vibration thereof that you emanate is of great service.

DECLARATION

I am a disciple of Truth,
In the name of the Father, and
Of the Son, and
Of the Holy Spirit.
I am a servant of God.
I am surrounded by perpetual illumination
Through the grace of God,
Creator of all things.
I am oneness with the Great One.

CHAPTER VII

Shamballa

Truth may be given as a tangible or abstract Truth, the tangible being that you are able, according to your finite minds, to analyze and understand. It has tangibility according to your reasoning capacity. It has abstraction in its dimension or its depth. The Truth or parable has a two-fold meaning. It means the reality of the parable as well as the esoteric value yet unrevealed.

Many of the Truths which Acumana and other teachers have endeavored to pass on to you throughout the ages of your time have been substantial Truths. However many other Truths have not been fully revealed. They yet remain to be revealed. Some will yet remain concealed, in order that you, who are spiritually upon the path, may progress mentally and physically through meditation to uncover that which is intended to be revealed. One of these facts Acumana now desires to reveal.

Through the successive course of your incarnations, through the successive cycles of birth and rebirth, cause and effect and the Law of Karma, you have been trained and prepared. The banquet has been prepared and the invitations engraved and sent out to the guests to come to the great feast. What is this feast? It is the feast that you all strive for. It is the enlightened day when the great prophet, the Christ, descends in its blazing glory to humanity. This takes preparation of action, spiritually, mentally and physically. Some of these secrets that you have now shared throughout the ages with others are being more and more uncovered.

In the ancient day of Lemuria, approximately, according to your time between sixteen to twenty million years past, the great Lords of Light, the angels and hosts with all their cosmic glory, descended upon Earth to help evolving humanity. This then was man walking among the angels. The Lord of the Flame, the great Godhood of your universe, who is called Sanat Kumara, embodied, that is, took on etheric form of great dimension, and he brought with him the Hosts of Light, the Angels of Light, the administrative, executive branch of the Logoi, to organize and to administrate unto man, order, evolution and progress. Man shared then in mind and spirit, with the great Logi.

Man was then in the process of building the vital body, the vital body being that etheric substance of reality, the soul. Your vital bodies existed in what is called semi-gaseous or etheric form. You had dimension, depth, but you had transparency. That was your vital body. You were drawing unto yourself substance. You lived in two areas. You lived in pure spirit and you lived in the mundane or the Adam body.

All who were ensouled with the conscious ego of evolution were then in existence in Lemuria. You had evolved in that cycle of time from the lower kingdom and were building your vital bodies, building the reality of existence. You dwelt in pure etheric form. You were able to live spiritually and materially in completion.

At that time in man's progress for illumination, Sanat Kumara and the lords of destiny, the world teachers, the great enlightened ones, held in their council important concerns. It was deemed essential at that time to allow humanity to enter consciousness through evolution up until the Atlantean day.

Prior to the Atlantean epic the spirit of man entered evolution through the lower form of evolution, primarily the animal kingdom, it being the next step down from human. The door then was closed, meaning that from the Atlantean time until the next epic of evolution comes about no soul shall have transition into consciousness. This means in a literal sense the entire animal kingdom shall not have consciousness until the seventh root race is complete and a new chain of root races begins. This means that younger souls have not evolved from animal hood as recently as you may have thought. There are seven cycles of evolution.

Why was the door of evolution closed? What was the purpose? Humanity must grow as a unit. As one unit the world representing humanity must progress. The continuous action of newer souls leaving the various lower kingdoms, coming into physical existence with a lack of intelligence, a lack of understanding of their level, would continuously hold back and deter the progress achieved from that day on toward the seventh root race. There are many younger souls who come from other universes, other constellations, other solar systems, to journey and experience lessons upon the physical plane. The animal kingdom remains as it is through successive cycles.

During a cycle of evolution, the angelic hosts, the Hierarchy, achieved illumination. In literal terms they embodied and lived in a depth and dimension comparable to yours. The great exalted masters of Light learned all the lessons you are learning. Then they went on into higher levels of expression.

Your elder brothers existed as you do. Perhaps they sat in a room similar to yours and listened to their elder brothers and they, too, learned. Perhaps you were their household pets, if you like, or you were the beasts of prey in the jungle. Then the cycle moved forward, they graduated, they progressed. And those who taught them, their elder brothers, also progressed on up the chain of the cosmic ladder and you became embodied. You became ensouled in consciousness. It is a continuous cycle on and on, ad infinitum.

This, therefore, means that those of the animal kingdom of your world are in truth your brothers, as are the birds in the sky, as are the plants around and about you. They are your brothers in consciousness. Their time shall come. Humanity existed in gaseous, mineral form for eons of time. It existed in the vegetable form for eons of time. And then the cycle moved. When the full chain of all those kingdoms are completed, life moves into the human, the next is the angelic, and on and on. Therefore, express kindness to the animals. They are your brothers growing. They must exchange and reexchange life after life in a successive cycle, throughout eons of time, in order to become acclimated in that dimension of consciousness. Then they will step forward in the vital body in a new day and a new age.

This then is one of the mysteries revealed to you, that the door of evolution is closed. You may say, "What of the wild savages? What of the men of wild natures, the Africans?" True, they are younger souls, but remember, many of the races have become crystallized in their patterns of evolution. When a race refuses to progress as a race it becomes crystallized. Consequently something must be done to uplift that race, that unit.

Many of the natives in Africa have become crystallized. They refuse to progress. They are, therefore, slowly dying off. You have heard of the Pygmies? They are becoming an extinct race. They are so set in their ways, in their habits, they have become crystallized so they are becoming extinct. Their term of evolution is over. Their will has not allowed their race to progress. They have become laggards. They must be redistributed throughout the universe to become stepped up in evolution. So it happens with many other tribes, many other races.

The Jewish race of today is becoming a crystallized race. They refuse to progress. Orthodoxy holds them down, the letter of the law, the Mosaic law. Many are becoming crystallized in their thoughts. They refuse to read behind the context. They read only the letter, the punctuation. The period is the end. There is no more. They read not between the lines. They do not realize the esoteric value. Some do, and they begin to promote the Truth that they do know. The evolved ones, the enlightened ones, have broken away from the old concepts, the traditions, and have become universalists.

The German race went through a similar pattern. The Russian race is going through a similar pattern, according to their group karma.

In the great hierarchical chain of Universal Brotherhood exists the Infinite, the God, Sanat Kumara; Sanat Kumara representing Wisdom and Activity. Working with Sanat Kumara are called the Buddhas, the three great Buddhas of Wisdom. They are the Lords of Flame. The three Buddhas are a trinity. The three Buddhas representing Sanat Kumara are the embodiment of Will, Wisdom and Activity throughout this universe. Each of these beings of great dimension and Light were in body at one time. They were not created from legend and myth. They grew and evolved to that state of consciousness in which they now exist.

There are also subdivisions of each of the Buddhas into seven. There are three divisions in each group and there are seven groups. One group is primarily concerned with Earth and its evolution.

You also have what is called the Manu. Working with the Manu are great ascended archangels of power. The next principle is the Christ, the great exhalted Christ, and working with the Christ principle is love. The Manu represents wisdom. Christ represents the love. There are great exalted masters who work under the Christ concept. Down the successive chain in this group you find all of the disciples and initiates. It is Acumana's great privilege and distinction to have Kuthumi as a teacher.

Each of the great exalted beings connected with man's evolution have their archetype concepts, their workers in successive chain. The embodiment of this great council is in Shamballa. You have no concept of what Shamballa is. In the ancient day when your teachers and the great Lords reached their point of illumination, Shamballa in its geographical location, which is comparable to your Gobi Desert, was the peak of civilization. It became a great power center of spirituality. So the great Council of Lords decided to help struggling humanity, in its next cycle of evolution for the seven root races, to establish an esoteric center upon the Earth and to pick geographically the Gobi. Since the Gobi had at one time past, millions of years gone by, been the center of great spiritual evolution, the vortex of power and energy emanating from Shamballa would be the esoteric center. Where is Shamballa in the Gobi? This is only given as an individual secret. It must be sought after and found. Each of you may find it in your journeys, physically and astrally.

The size of Shamballa is immense. It is etheric in substance, for its rate of vibration is extreme in its power. Shamballa is a relay station for the great Lords that they may dwell in their own supreme power in close proximity to the world and its evolution. They have in their hands the reins of the destiny of the world and this universe. To bring about race evolvement and the completion of the seven root races of man to one state of consciousness requires infinite understanding and spirituality. Many will achieve it before the multitudes do. Those who do not achieve it will, as has been said, be set aside for another cycle.

Shamballa is the place of the council chamber. Like the capital of the United States, Washington, D.C. represents your capital of the fifty states of your union, Shamballa is also a capital. Council meetings are held there by the Lords, the great Archangels, to decide new approaches, when to bring into the world teachings, how to infiltrate into the consciousness of man the true depth of understanding. These plans were made thousands of years ago. No plan of action is decided upon instantaneously by the Lords. Man works that way, not the gods.

The gods decided millions of years ago what would happen tomorrow, and they prepared the way. They must work with and through the free will consciousness of humanity to see to it that all nations, the national karma, the racial karma, and the individual karma, are all coordinated. In Shamballa there are the great Archangels working under one of the great Lords. The Archangels who are in charge of all akashic records of the universe must maintain, manipulate and sustain world karma, national karma, racial unit karma, and individual karma.

Try to coordinate those, if you can, so that you come out with a score of A on the card when you are dealing with free will consciousness.

The tabulation, the coordination of all this information, takes indeed the power of a god. In their power and dimension they are practically gods. These Archangels are part of the Hierarchy, or the Executive Board. They have working with them thousands of Archangels and helpers who daily, moment by moment, keep up every record, every progress, pro and con, positive and negative. They must maintain the karmic record of the political state of every nation as well as the individual state.

Your United States has a karma as a unit. Each of you are part of it. Therefore, you are part of the United States karma. You are part of a unit karma and each of you have an individual karma. These things must be coordinated, maintained, so that all the teachers, the Masters and the Lords who work to bring about complete brotherhood and fulfillment know how to work every second. Their plans are well laid out. The progress is there, man only determines the time factor. They assist man with every beat of his heart in this progress. They know that his free will is his greatest hindrance. They will never go above his free will, or subjugate his free will, but they will work around it.

All of this is done in Shamballa. The teachings are disseminated from Shamballa. The teachers of Light from around the world all teach from one focal point.

Sometimes teachers build a body and return to Earth. Not through birth, that is unnecessary for the Masters. They do not come through the womb, through pain and suffering. Man is born in pain and suffering being born of the womb. Masters simply know how to build a body.

Far beyond Shamballa is a great sacred valley in the Himalayas where nothing can penetrate. The vibratory rate is so powerful that if one were to wander into the valley unprepared he would be instantly disintegrated by the radiation. And in this great secret place exists the Master Jesus, the Master Kuthumi, the Master Morya, the Master Saint Germain, and other masters. Very often Sanat Kumara journeys down to spread its rays of Light.

***Student:* Acumana, is that the Wesak?**

The Wesak is one of the adjoining valleys.

***Student:* Is it Shintomani?**

Yes, indeed it is. It is in this valley that power emanating toward the world is directed. The Christ concept working through all the Masters is directed from Shamballa. Often the Masters and teachers are called from Shintomani for council in Shamballa. They must journey there as your representatives in Congress must do. So the teachers must do. There they meet with the great exalted Lords of Light to day by day observe the progress of man.

Visualize high mountains, jagged, reaching toward the sky, their height beyond measure. There is a mist in the valley, a warm mist which keeps the foliage semi-tropical. It blooms in abundance, and there are plateaus, ledges, in this valley. On these ledges some of the Masters have their homes or their chambers. There is a huge lake, crystal in its purity. There is a mist upon the lake, and the mist rises and feeds. The birds sing, the power is great.

As you walk down one of the mountain paths, through the growth, you feel the balmy air. The temperature is seventy-one degrees Fahrenheit all the time, although the mountains around are covered with snow and glaciers.

You may enter that valley when you have sufficiently purified your minds, your bodies and your consciousness. The abode of every Master in the valley is open for deep teachings. You need not journey across the seven seas. The Masters see you and observe you. At this very moment the great exalted Light, Kuthumi, has this unit under observation.

Each of the Masters in this valley continues his work. Silence is profound in the valley. Only nature speaks its celestial music of peace. If you could wander through the valley you would find simplicity beyond understanding. Your first concept would be this: Why should these great exalted Lords and Masters live in such simplicity when they could build within their mind-consciousness a universe of their own?

You will then learn that *simplicity in all things is self-mastery,* simplicity of living, simplicity of thought, simplicity of expression. For remember, they have surrendered self to the universe. They are the universe in embodiment. All they need is a place to meet and to teach. The simpler, the more profound.

Your day-by-day progress determines the path toward this valley. Self control, mental control, and spiritual control, these are the determining factors. To be patient with yourself and others, day by day. Your every experience of impatience holds you back that much longer. You must express love and kindness with every beat of your heart. It matters not what you think or feel. You are only finite, and you are often in error.

It matters more that you think, feel and be in compassion and love. Who are you that you may think you have desires, that you may think you have feelings and that you think those feelings may be offended? Oh ye of ignorance, how long must you journey in this death that you are in to learn that those are only illusions? You are not hurt, you are not offended, you are not in pain, you are living in a mighty universe of cosmic love, wisdom and understanding.

When will you cease to be children and grow up to be men? The sooner you decide, in your own selves, to forget self, to forget feelings, and express love and wisdom in your heart, the sooner will every one of your individual problems be answered. If you continue to have problems, you shall continue to struggle and suffer accordingly. It has been deemed a law unto you. You shall struggle, slave, and want day by day, until each of you in your own consciousness can rise above the limitation of your thoughts. Do not chastise yourselves, do not condemn yourselves, but recognize that you must become one with the universe.

Realize that you cannot be hurt, that you cannot be in want, that you cannot be offended, that your feelings must become cosmic in their dimensions, not personal. Your personal things will be taken care of accordingly. All who have stepped upon the path will continue to suffer until they rise above it. It is the law of that path. And that law shall be transcended by your own progress. It is this way because it is the only way.

Suffering shall fall away from you like a dead flower upon a bush when its purpose has been fulfilled. All want, all desire, shall fall away and you shall become radiant beacon lights. You are each brought into incarnation at this time for a purpose. You are to prepare the way for the great advent of our leader, the World Teacher. And it is important that you start now. Much must be done in preparation.

If you must, beseech in your prayers. Perhaps it might be of benefit to you. It has been proven, consistently throughout certain orthodox faiths, that to beseech the elder brothers is indeed to reach them in sincerity. Then beseech them if you must. Lie prone and beg and beseech, call the names of the glorious Lords of Light. Confess the desires of your heart and soul and body. Tell them that your soul desires more Light, more Light. Whatever is necessary in your prayer, do it for the release. Each faith has certain concrete proofs, proven consistently throughout the ages, for its value.

In the Catholic faith the value of confession is beyond measure in its power. For when you confess the mundane desires of your body and your mind, you free yourself from the bondage and limitation of those very conditions. Express them verbally, audibly, or however you may desire.

Discipline that Satan within you, your body, your mind, your desires. You must let the Christ within you reach out victorious. Stand upon the mountain peak basking in the glorious sun of God Almighty. This is possible by acknowledging the two faces of existence within you. For you are composed of the duality of God, the right and the wrong, the positive and the negative. Surrender that negative and make it neutral day by day. This is your progress, this is your growth. So confess, if you must, and enter the valley, my children, enter the valley.

This is not harsh, it is discipline. Acumana is not hard on you, Acumana is kind to you. The world is harsh and cruel, the teachers desire only your peace, your love and your devotion. You must affirm where you desire to be in the universe. On whose side of the army shall you fight? If you are for right and Truth, then you must uphold that and live by it every second of the day. If the world of glamour, the world of illusion, the false world, calls you, then choose it. You cannot live in the two and hope to be victorious in both. It must be one or the other.

You live in the world of illusion and strive for reality. That is the Truth. It is untruth to say that the illusion will bring you closer to reality, that is false. Millions upon millions of people live in the illusion only. They are aware of Truth, they know of its existence, but they are more concerned with the senses and the illusion than this substantial reality. To them it is reversed, reality is an illusion and the illusion is the real. But to you upon the path, your discerning eye says the illusion is true and reality is true. You live in the world, but rise above it.

***Student:* Acumana, is there such a thing as time in Shamballa?**

No. Shamballa is above the Earth. It is a rate of vibration in the etheric. It would be comparable to a cloud. Is a cloud physical? Does a cloud have enough substance for you to stand on it? This is Shamballa, it is suspended above the Gobi.

You will also find great power and spirituality in the Grand Tetons. In most great mountain chains, in the great Colorado Rockies there is great power. There are Masters upon each of these mountains. There are small centers scattered about, Shamballa being the direct power center.

Do you know why you have such chains of mountains around the whole world? They were placed there by the Lords during the cataclysmic ages so that they could be transmitting stations for the Ascended Ones to look after their younger children.

There is much, my children, awaiting for you around the corner of your destiny. The great heavens have opened up their infinite knowledge, love and patience to mankind. Stop for a moment and realize that you move and have your being in one of the greatest eras of man's whole evolution. You who have chosen to return at this time, in this cycle, live in a time of great inner contemplation. You live on the cusp of one age to another.

You will live to see great mental, physical and spiritual changes wrought upon your home, the planet Earth. You live in an era and a time when the advances in science will yet come forth to astound the world. This is a time when religious convictions will go through the greatest upheaval the world has yet to see. Man will stand forth and proclaim the Truth and acknowledge the Truth as it has been prophesied.

Move forward in the wisdom, in the awareness that is before you, with assurance, and clear-sightedness. Blessings of the Father, the Son, and the Holy Spirit. Blessings of Ahura Mazda.

I AM A UNIVERSE

I am a universe.
I am a power,
A light, a force,
Capable of great achievement.
I am the great AUM,
One with the Father,
One with the son,
One with the Holy Spirit.

CHAPTER VIII

Redemption

Acumana wishes to speak with you on matters which ultimately all students upon the path, at one time or another, must come to. This is the point often referred to by initiates as "the crossroads." Or as one student would say, "the jumping off place." Teachers always come around to this point.

It is avoided by many upon the path who feel they cannot cope with such disciplines. They find material excuses. They find reasons for not disciplining the carnal man, the satanic principle. They find it much more convenient and desirable to give vent to the Satan principle, or the fallen man, as referred to by Christianity, rather than to redeem that man which the Lord Jesus promised would have redemption.

Redemption occurs when the spiritual, mental and physical man are reunited in one dynamic entity. That is, when the spiritual, mental and physical bodies in man have recognized the identity of their own nature, each in its own place, and the spiritual man has been given full reign. The mental man now is in control of the physical man, the fallen man.

When desires of the senses have fallen off and your one goal is more Truth, more Light, more spiritual food, that is redemption. Before you can possibly enter the deeper mysteries you must go through disciplinarian periods for your own growth. There is a world of abundance waiting at your feet. At your fingertips awaits the promised fulfillment of all your dreams, all the desires of the soul. They cannot be fulfilled until you have been consciously brought into the Light of discipline.

The ascension is the ladder which is referred to by many as Jacob's Ladder. All things ascending must be on a firm foundation. Truth is on a firm foundation. It would be of no value to you to proceed any further in Truth, up the ladder of knowledge, unless the ladder of your faith and discipline were set on a solid concrete foundation of discipline.

You all know, when climbing a ladder in the physical sense, that it is a foolish man who sets up his ladder and tries to climb it when it is balanced against no object. It is a foolish man who places his ladder in the middle of the ground and starts to climb. He knows it will topple. But with a ladder well balanced, a man may climb in safety. Place your ladder not against an object, but against God. Place your ladder against a foundation of solid cosmic matter in the universe which is based on faith in the *I AM Presence,* then you may climb the ladder in safety.

Before we go into the disciplines, it is paramount we discuss certain matters. The primary concern is your three natures, the mental, the physical and the spiritual. You have been dealing with spiritual matter or the spiritual man for some time. It is this spiritual man which we have been feeding, which you have been recognizing, or striving to recognize. But remember, this is an intangible substance. Spirit is a dimension, a vibration. It is based primarily on faith. And yet faith alone does not sustain spirit. Spirit is sustained by growth and wisdom. Spirit is fed and sustained by discipline. Without spirit you would be a non-functioning, non-thinking, non-evolving entity in a void universe of non-existence.

You would not even be a speck of cosmic dust without spirit. So spirit is all-pervading. It is the incarnating principle. Spirit is incarnated within physical man, the fallen man. In your esoteric studies you read of Adam and the fall from Paradise. You have been given many teachings in regard to this. They are not in error, but there are more depths to the teachings yet to be revealed. Some of these Acumana shall give to you now, in relationship to the fallen man, the carnal man, the desire man.

Long past in another cycle of creativity when your elder brothers were as you, and you were the younger ones, the newer souls, you were warned and told by your elder brothers not to abide in a certain race of man. Not to take unto you the Adam principle, not to take unto you the sins, the burdens of the world. You were given in that day, that age, a being to assist you. There was an animal kingdom similar in size, structure and nature to the present day man. This was the laborer. This was the server, the servant, the help-mate unto the angelic man.

Some who were free souls who had been endowed, as all have been endowed, with freedom of will and consciousness, crossed the seed with this animal concept. In other words, they united and bred offspring, thus rooting themselves to another kingdom, a denser kingdom. A man today who would commit such an act of fornication with one of another kingdom would change his whole cycle of evolution. This is the most heinous of all sacrilegious things to commit. Perhaps that other kingdom cannot bear an offspring but the purity even of your own seed flowing in that of another kingdom is indeed inviolate of all God's laws. Only great, great harm can come to the individual. That individual begins to decay day by day. He little by little turns into a most gross creature.

Herein is the answer to the Abominable Snowman. Those beings who have, out of physical desire, shed their seed into an animal have digressed, lost the immortality of their soul, for eons and eons of time. And they must wander in herds and packs. There are many such creatures in the world. Many of them go down into the deep abyss of the Earth and crawl and grovel.

Man fell from the Garden of Eden when he crossed the seed. The door was closed. He no longer walked among the angels. The elder brothers had reached the peak of their evolution and they soared upward. Adam was abolished from the Garden of Eden. The Garden of Eden symbolizes the perfect state of spirituality wherein the physical and the spiritual abide together like husband and wife and become one. So Adam and Eve represented, symbolically, the husband and wife who crossed the seed and were abolished from the Mother-God principle of consciousness. That was the fall of man esoterically.

A whole new root race must come about so that man may be redeemed. In other words, the offspring who are part carnal and part angelic must be made one. The animal nature, the mundane nature must become spirit through the evolution of the seven root races, through redemption.

Each of you has the same strands flowing through your being that flowed through the first colonization, the Adam race. You are the Adam race in evolution. All of your humanity today is that race of man in evolvement. Those of you who have stepped upon the path have chosen to eliminate from your psyche, from your karma, the animalistic nature within you. It is the nature which desires eating of the flesh, eating of your brothers. It is that within you that desires the gratification of the senses. Your younger brothers, the animals, are imprisoned by their instinct, you are not.

Man has the concept of liberty. It is given to man that he does not have to be imprisoned by instinct. But if he chooses to, then he must suffer the burdens of all those who become crystallized in this pattern. For those of you who are upon the path it becomes essential, in your ascending, that you begin to shed the tendencies which are dormant within you. This is not to say the body does not respond biologically, organically, to certain things.

Spiritually you know that through the laws of transmutation all things may be surmounted. Earlier in your teachings upon the path you were taught certain concepts for that stage of your growth. Now you have grown. Now other doors have been opened unto you, greater wisdom and Light awaits you. There is not a one who is not capable of handling the tasks before you, not a one. The only thing which can hinder your growth is your mental approach. If the physical man, the carnal man within you, is allowed to be undisciplined and run rampant in your universe, then you must spiritually suffer the consequences. And the consequences indeed are great.

Now before you can relinquish any condition which is physically and mentally negative you must convince the subconscious mind. You must win it through love, not force it. You never win your woman in love by beating upon her and forcing her. You win your lover by kindness, gentleness, persuasion and love. Then great is your reward. Never do you win a friend by beating upon his door. You only make an enemy of your friend.

So with your disciplines, never chastise yourself, never force yourself, never beat upon yourself. Never perform tortures to the physical body. It is not necessary. Persuade gently. Imagine you are with your lover, your secret desire, God awareness, and you desire this God awareness to spark the flame of your soul into recognition. How would you set out to accomplish this most difficult task? By gentleness, not by impatience with yourself. Not by impatience with others. You would talk to yourself. You would reaffirm the subconscious mind and allow the subconscious mind to open up to the superconscious, the spiritual.

If you have a problem or a difficulty with a condition, talk to the problem, say to yourself in essence, "My friend, we must live together our lifetime, the three of us." There are three of you living together—the spirit, the mind and the body. Three, the trinity. Never forget this. The spirit operates the mind, and the mind and the spirit operate the body. Yet the body has predominance if you give it predominance.

Allow the body to be won over by the spirit. Not the spirit and the mind to be won over by the body. Let the spirit say through the mind—for the mind will do as the spirit says—"My friend, we must share the same bed together, the same clothes, the same fork. Could we not, therefore, become better friends? Let us meet on neutral ground. Let the mind be our mediary. You, my friend, are the material man, the desire man. I am the spiritual man, the I AM. The mind shall be our neutrality. Through our neutrality let us eliminate all weaknesses within our basic nature."

Ah! but your new-found friend will say to you, "Bunk!" Yes, he will say, "Bunk! It is not valuable. I do not desire this ally. I am happy and peaceful as I am." And it shall go out and try to appease its base desires. Say to it, "But, my friend, what you do I must do. And what I do you must do. You are tortured and you suffer when I strive for spirituality. And I am tortured and suffer when you strive and crave for materiality. Can we not meet?" Reason, divine reason will make the material man within you say of its own wisdom, "It is so. We both suffer." And he will begin to come around to your way of thinking. It is a slow process.

Recognize that you are three individuals. The mind will work for you. The mind is the strength over the body. Day by day discipline it. Talk to it. This does not mean you must begin the most severe disciplines. It does not mean you must stop all things instantly. What is paramount now is that you become conscious of the nature within you, the three faces, the three bodies within you, the spiritual, the mental and the physical.

Win the physical man that he may be ascended. You do not have to be a master. You do not have to be the Christ to bring your body with you, but you must become redeemed. You must become enwrapped with the cosmic glory and the mystic beauty and the celestial harmony within your own being through the disciplines. You are now sufficiently aware of the teachings to demonstrate and begin to put them into practice.

If you fail, it matters not. It is the doing which is important, not the grade, not the success. The application is what you are measured on.

Acumana suggests that for a short period of time now you conserve the cosmic power within you, this reproductive power, by redirecting it spiritually and mentally. The mystics, the sages, all come to this point. They must abstain periodically. This does not mean that for the rest of your life you become a celibate. You may have happy, contented, joyous lives, those of you who are in wedlock. And those of you who are not shall have happy, joyous and contented lives.

But certain periods of the year you must set aside the self. It is an act of humility. It is an act of giving up the self, the material man, and giving over to the spiritual. It is for this reason that monks, yogis, all who are dedicated in this life to the one concept, must abstain. They are spiritually attuning themselves to the mystic Light before them, and they know the mystic Light of awareness can never light their path unless they redirect the physical energy within them. So for three months, abstain. However, you are not forced or compelled to do anything that you do not desire to do.

You say, biologically, physically, how does this affect me? You are thinking of the self first of all or you could not conceive of what it would do to you. The "you" saying this is the carnal man, the spiritual man cares not. The mental man cares not, for it is not mental, it is not spiritual, it is the physical man who speaks, the desire man. You know the laws of transmutation enough now that if your mental concept is that you must have satisfaction in the material sense, the very process which brought about this mental concept may be redirected by the process of transmutation. It is simply a thought.

The thought which produces the physical act is a desire. It is an emotion brought about by thought. Think upon it. The physical man shall not suffer, the spiritual man shall not suffer and the mental man shall not suffer, if you work your laws. Win yourself over, as Acumana has said, by being friendly with your opponent. Say to it, "Look, my friend, we together have had good times. We have shared, we have laughed, and we have had the joys. What harm shall it do either of us for the time being if we set aside those trivial things?" Reason alone will say to the material man, "It is so. It cannot harm us for the time being." Win it over. Transmute the thought.

If you have a thought of desire for satisfaction, redirect that thought. Think of that desire and that satisfaction as a spiritual concept. Hold that same thought and desire for a moment, and then say, "If I could only enter meditation with that same desire. If I could only enter prayer with that same desire." Then instantly enter prayer and imagine this great golden fluid of awareness, this golden Light of creativity and productivity within you, up to the golden Light of awareness. It is a mental world you live in, and a physical world. Now bring about the spiritual world, in awareness.

Of food you are well versed. Change your eating habits. It is desirable that you cease forever to eat of your younger brother. It is the carnal man in you that desires eating of the flesh. Acumana has said before that it is the material man, for it desires to stay rooted to the ground and the only way it can stay rooted is by partaking of the gross dense matter of its origin, flesh. Eating of flesh is symbolic of cohabitation with the other dimension. You do not need it. God produced abundance for you in other areas. He gives you the fruit on the trees, the berries on the bush and the herbs in the ground. And He gives you nature's abundance in by-products. They are given to you unselfishly.

Do not take from the animals their very lives. Cease all toxic poisons. Keep the temple pure. Cease to eat and partake of those things of carbonated nature, those things of unnatural sweetened nature. Honey is the greatest elixir you can partake of in a sweetness. Keep your system pure.

In the process of eating there are three primary things to remember. The taking in, the chewing and the swallowing. Your eating should be reverent. Do not overeat. It is better to eat less, but to eat in more fullness. Eating should be done as a prayer. The worst thing you can do is to sit down, gobble down food and then jump up and run off. It is sacrilege. Think of the universe for a moment when you eat. You are redirecting positive energy to bring about more productivity, more creativity within your universe, and thereby bring about a greater state of evolution in your own nature, through eating.

As you chew the food, think for a moment what you are doing when you chew. The chewing is important. It is a meditation. In all cloistered orders, students are taught three functions of eating. The taking in, the chewing and the swallowing. It is a meditation. It has a rhythm and it has a cadence, taking in, chewing, swallowing.

Eating is a dedication. Take only enough to sustain the body, no more, no less. Eat less, eat only essential things and enjoy it more. Bless the food. Recognize and realize what it is doing for you and your being. Man pays so little attention to his habits, his functionings. Think for a moment as you eat, where the food goes, what it does, how it sustains you.

In the morning eat fruit. In the afternoon you may have nuts, vegetables, grains, in moderate proportions. And in the evenings, have only the light foods. Never over-indulge in eating. Fasting is equally important, in that you not become over-burdened with food.

For your children, they may eat three times a day nourishing things for their growing bodies. You parents must not poison your children. You are responsible for their material growth. If you give them things which are unnatural you poison them. Would you willfully sit down and pour cyanide down your children's throat? No. Then you must cease to permit your children to partake of things which will poison them. Condition them and win them over by love and communion to the new concept. Never force them to eat. Be gentle. All things are won by love, kindness and gentleness. It is better that they do not eat at all than to force them. They will eat when they are hungry. And if you have only things for them to eat that are good and eliminate all other things from the home which are not good, they have no choice but to eat the good things. It is a discipline. It may be hard, but growth is not easy.

As your nature begins to change you may find yourself becoming impatient with yourself and with others. You may lose your temper and raise your voice. You will become irritable, grumpy and disagreeable. You will be like a hungry animal in the jungle, and your aura will be the same. That is the material man. But he is being won over and if you continue to love him, pray with him, bring him to your side, in a short time the resistance will be over and a new life awaits you. You will enter greater awareness than you can possibly imagine!

When you have become purified, fully united to the spiritual life, then you will see what is meant by the balance of the spiritual and the material. You think you balance it now. You do not. You live out of balance. Let us show you what true balance is. Then you will begin to know and understand how to master other laws of matter. Then you will become an alchemist in the true occult sense. You will learn, when you become pure by conserving the vital force, purifying the body and the mind, that you have within you the capacity to, at will, go through walls.

You could not possibly now perform any of those mystic arts that so fascinate students upon the path. They are everyday practices by devotees. A devotee who has been fully prepared may arise from where he is, walk through the wall and go wherever he desires. He may also say, "There is my abundance," and produce it. Only that which he needs. No excess. You cannot do this when you are rooted to the Earth. How can you expect spiritual power to be yours when you fight to hold onto material power? When you win material power over, then you are a cosmic being.

Now unto sleep. Acumana desires for you now to recondition the consciousness to less hours of sleep. You all spend far too much time sleeping away your life. The body only needs four hours of rejuvenation. You should have certain hours where you do only spiritual work, prayer, healing, treating, enlightenment, and then certain hours for your material work.

This does not mean for you to right away go and sleep only four hours, for you will awaken exhausted. It is a slow process. If you have been doing extreme physical work, then you require more hours of sleep. You must also learn how to sleep. There is not one of you who has learned how to sleep.

There is a mystical way to sleep wherein you are instantly released from your body, instantly released from the mind and the physical dimension. Then the soul soars out to the great heights of the cosmic universe. Then the great angels will come and heal the body, using the cosmic currents of universal healing. The vibrations will penetrate the body and rejuvenate it by natural law. Then the soul re-enters the temple and once more you are ready for your material and spiritual work.

Acumana would like for you to awaken at five in the morning. Five in the morning, not eight, not nine, but five. That is the beginning of your new day. Now, at that time spend one hour in full prayer and preparation for the day. Give thanks for the night, thank God for the new day.

You will not be tired if you do this. Your day should be planned and organized. Do this in your prayer. Then from six until seven do very light work, light mental work. You may treat, you may heal, you may write, you may do whatever you desire, if it is light mental work. And then begin your work-a-day day.

Now, unto going to bed, it is up to you. If you desire to go to bed at four in the morning, fine. You can only sleep one hour. If you desire to go to bed at eight or nine, you will have more sleep. First we want you to discipline yourself to be up at five in the morning, and to take a good breath of fresh air before you begin your meditations. See the sun and the silence of the world in the morning.

Plan your day in prayer. Treat the day before you. You are treating all those you will come in contact with although you may not know who they are. And you will bring about transmutation of your day. You will bring to you only positive results during the day, if you will treat the day beforehand. You are facing the day before it begins and it will have to meet your approval. System and order is the law of the universe.

***Student:* Acumana, I have a couple of questions. I had never thought about this ascending without being a master. I have always tied the two together. Without being a master have we the possibility of taking our bodies with us?**

You have the possibility of taking the esoteric body with you, the atomic body, not the physical body. The atomic, etheric structure is what you take with you, not the substance, not the weighty body.

***Student:* Is there an advantage to that?**

Yes, there is an advantage. It means that you have eliminated all karma. You may come and go in the universe as you desire. You have taken on mastery over self. Also, it is like having only one valise to take instead of seven.

***Student:* You can be ascended without being a master, and you can be a master without being ascended?**

It is so.

***Student:* The purity of food will greatly aid us, Acumana, won't it, in the months ahead?**

You will find your whole life altering, your whole health pattern changing, your mental pattern changing.

***Student:* Is it possible for us to become conditioned so that we do not need to depend on the clock?**

It depends on the nature of man and the set condition established. Each of you is an individual temperament unto himself. You do not all approach these disciplines in the same way, but according to your own capacity. What may heal you may not heal your neighbor. Each individual is a perfect reflection of Divine Law. You must begin to study yourself and know yourself. Find out how you may treat one condition from another. You may not be able to use the same mental concept with every condition within you. It is an experimentation with yourself, with knowing yourself. Most students when undertaking disciplines take anywhere from six to eight months to come to the point where they will decide they intend to do the discipline.

You now have arrived at the point of understanding in your finite minds that you know that spirit is divine, and you know that the mind, the mental body, can be your enemy. You are functioning in three separate bodies, as are all people. The multitudes function in the mental and physical body. The spirit is silent. It waits patiently. It does the great soul work of the universe within. But it does it in silence, without one sound, without one syllable. Not one whisper is uttered in the soul. The spirit is the motivating force within you which brings about the continuous states of evolution and involution.

The mind works in rationalization, in reason. It is a conditioned mind. It is fearful and does not work in accord with the spirit. The flesh is that which must be disciplined. It is the animal within you, the Eve within you. It is that aspect which day by day crucifies you, which day by day waves the apple of temptation before you, like unto Adam. The flesh eats of the apple, for the desires are gratifying. The desire world is the world you function in. The desire body, your flesh, desires of all forms of sense sensation, all forms of physical gratification in all capacities. It desires food. It desires pleasure. You may go the whole scale in the physical realm, and you will find that your desire body is indeed your greatest enemy.

These three separate entities are working within one divine body, the kingdom of heaven. For the Lord Christ said, "The kingdom of heaven is within." And it is so. He deceives you not but affirms positively to you that the kingdom of heaven is within you, as it is within all mankind, all celestial beings, all cosmic beings, all Supercosmic Beings. It exists within man.

How do you therefore, tap the resources of cosmic understanding? How may you take one step forward upon the altar to glimpse the heart of the cosmos flower? How may you move forward one inch upon the road of destiny so that you may open the door unto the mountain of wisdom? By one way only—discipline and silence!

You must unify your three aspects. It is for this purpose that the disciplines have been set forth, not as a means of punishment, by no means. Not as an avenue to deny you, but for one purpose, that you may become true spirit, true power, the master of your own senses. That you, like the blinking eye do not blink involuntarily, but blink consciously. That you may motivate consciously, that you may become aware of who and what you are in this great universe of your Father. Only through discipline is this brought about.

Do not command and attack the body to win it over. Do not persecute the mind to win it over to spirit. You persuade the body and the mind through positive affirmations of love from the heart, that you shall unite with the flesh and the body to the one purpose of spirit. You should make into a marriage the mind and the body. Unite them as husband and wife, under the roof of your Father, the spirit. Then as one body, as one entity, body and mind flowing through spiritual awareness, you become united. You become the Trinity, you become Father, Son and Holy Spirit in recognition.

Discipline does this for you spiritually. It identifies your spirit with the purpose and nature of its existence. For spirit desires only one thing, reunion with the kingdom of the Father. That is all the spirit desires. Reunion with the Father.

In order to have a perfect reunion with the Father, the mind and the flesh must suffer the stings of all forms of bitterness, frustration, growths and evolvements, until finally the spirit speaks forth within the evolved man and says to the mind, "Now, my friend, let us unite as one principle that we may reunite with the Father." This, therefore, is the purpose of discipline. It quiets the mind, quiets the body, and permits the spirit to shine forth.

Your spirit is dormant within you. The only time your spirit glows as an ember of awareness is when you sit in meditation, in your silence. And then it only glows faintly. It must become a blazing light of awareness. The beacon unto your own soul awareness must light and illuminate your path, through the disciplines this is brought about.

Now the next step of discipline is before you. This involves correlation of the teachings and the discussion and explanation of yoga.

We shall now endeavor to teach you the basic steps in proper breathing. As you breathe you reflect your soul awareness. To breathe properly, in rhythm, is to breathe by the spirit. It requires only a few moments a day, once or twice a day, morning or evening, whichever is suitable, to practice a few basic steps in breathing.

Postures in breathing will help do this for you. This then is the next step forward. We assume that you have adopted the attitude of cleansing the body. We say only assumed, for time tells within each one the progress of his discipline according to the nature of his response to discipline. Assuming now that your bodies are cleansed and as you progress they shall become more cleansed, we shall proceed.

Your breath is your spirit. Your breath is your vital force. Your breath is the energy which brings into your lungs and heart life giving vitality, and which feeds your microcosmic universe with cosmic food and elixir. So your breath is vital.

Now, therefore, how do you breathe? There are two ways to breathe. There is a way for the woman and a way for the man. The constitutions of the two types of bodies are different. The constitution, the sensitivities, the intuitional awarenesses, the nervous systems are different. Therefore, there are two approaches to breath.

For a woman breathing must begin at the top and she must breathe down. She must breathe from her shoulders, down to her diaphragm.

The first thing for the woman to do in this practice is to recline or sit in a comfortable position, either early in the morning or late in the evening. You will need fresh air. Open the window, be surrounded by fresh air. Have a mat. Acumana suggests each of you have a prayer mat, a grass prayer mat. This is very important, for it symbolizes simplicity and dedication. All students of esoteric yoga have a prayer mat. It becomes a place from which to go within. You shall learn as you progress that you need not go in the temples, into the buildings, to find God. You shall truly find that the kingdom of God, the kingdom of heaven, is within, just as the Christ prophesied and proved.

The woman must have nothing binding about her waist. She should wear loose fitting garments. It is most important to be free, to allow your abdomen to be free. Then exhume the air from your lungs, from your shoulders by allowing your shoulders to sink down. Exhume the air from the shoulders down through the rib cage, through the thorax, finally down through to the diaphragm, until all the air has been expelled. Envision that the shoulders working down are pushing the air out. Keep your mouth partially open as you exhale. This is so that the air leaves you through a thin opening in the mouth. Do not have the mouth wide open.

When your lungs are completely empty fill them again, starting once more from the shoulders, by expanding the shoulders. As you breathe in deep, expand the shoulders, expand the thorax, expand the rib cage and expand the diaphragm. The whole importance here is to expand your chest area. This takes practice. It is not an easy process. You shall have to force yourself to learn to envision this process taking place. You must proceed gradually in the studies of esoteric yoga. Also, the visual is what is important in the esoteric.

Gymnastics are unimportant. Avoid gymnastics, for they can be injurious to the body. Some schools today which teach the yoga practice teach the gymnastics, not the mental and spiritual attitude of mind. It is for this purpose that many are advised not to study or take up the course of yoga breathing, yoga postures, because they go in for gymnastics and not the mental and spiritual. The mental and the spiritual work together to discipline and control the physical, which is your whole purpose. To control the physical body, to reunite it with the mind body so that spirit may soar forth into Brahma. That is your goal. To have true prayer. To have true meditation. This you can do if you proceed slowly. Follow the instructions carefully and be patient.

So for the woman, you understand, breathe from the shoulders down, contracting and expanding. Try to expand the chest and the bust area and the shoulders. For now just be aware of the breathing. Learn to breathe properly. Then it will become an automatic function later. All singers know this function. They have been trained to breathe this way and they breathe this way instinctively now. That is the first thing for you to learn in breathing. Every day practice it, five minutes at a time, in the morning and evening. Perhaps you may feel a little woozy at first. It is normal, for your lungs are receiving purer air and they are utilizing their full capacity.

Now, the man must breathe the conventional way from the diaphragm up. The man does it in reverse. Have the stomach not binding, be free. It is best for the man to be naked from the waist up. Have a very loose fitting garment. Have the crotch free. Have the whole abdominal region free. Yogis have a very scant loin cloth, just to protect the genital region. Anything on the body which is distracting to the mind deters the growth. It is why so often you see the contemplative figures of the yogi as they were born. For the garment distracts the body. The less garment the better.

The man breathes up from the diaphragm. He pushes the air out from the diaphragm all the way up, through the rib cage, in the chest, until all the air is exhumed. Then he draws in air the same way by sucking it in from the diaphragm, filling the lungs, the chest. As an athlete would breathe. Those are the first steps for you now in a study of breathing.

***Student:* Acumana, inhale through the nostrils and exhale through the mouth?**

Inhale through the nostrils and exhale through the mouth, yes, keeping the mouth partially open, leaving just a small sliver.

Now let us concern ourselves with the physical body. Do not correlate the breath that Acumana has just given you with the body positions coming next. That is something different. We must learn one thing at a time. Practice the whole thing but do not practice them together yet. We will give them to you together later.

Now, for body control, in the morning or evening, on your mat, stand erect, straight. Have the body free, unencumbered by burdens. Stand erect, arms straight down in normal position. Head high. Remain still. Also have a still mind. These disciplines will produce a more stilled effect in the mind and body as you proceed. Stand erect, shoulders square, in what is called a conventional army position. Shoulders square, stomach in, chest out. Then raise both hands up in the air, palms facing forward. For both men and women, palms facing forward. Keeping feet flat on the ground, reach as high as you can, stretching the whole body. Do not lift your heels from the floor. Stretch and stretch. Stretch the whole body. Stretch those internal organs that have become so set in their natures for so long. Stretch them, utilize the vital energy flowing through them. When you have done this for a moment, relax slightly. Do not strain. Keeping the hands above you, now very slowly bend forward from the waist. Do not bend the knees. Do not lift the heels from the floor.

Then bend slowly, keeping arms straight down, your palms flat, until you have the palms of your hands flat on the floor—approximately four or five inches from the palms to the tip of the toe, or a little closer. Do not bend the knees or lift the heels. Stretch, stretch. Then palms flat on the surface, the goal is to touch your forehead to your knees. You will be surprised that when you begin to learn these processes, time and practice, like any skill or art, you will be able to do feats of control over your body you have not done before. You are then the master of your body. You must become aware of the blood flowing through your veins. You must control and be aware of the beat of your heart, that you may stop it at will if you desire. Then you are fully aware of your own universe. That is your goal now on the path, and you must not avoid it, for it must be done. Be patient with yourself. You cannot expect to do this in one morning's try. It will take you perhaps two or three months, depending on your application and agility.

Now, with your palms flat on the ground, assuming you have reached that goal, move them very slowly, slide them, until the end of your palm touches the tip of your toe. Then touch your forehead to your knees. The next step is to stand erect immediately, arms straight up. Then drop the arms to your side once more.

When you have resumed your standing position you will feel like collapsing. You may have the sensation of great dizziness, wooziness, spinning perhaps, nausea perhaps. But remember, you are stretching, utilizing internal muscles, internal system functionings which have remained dormant for years. You must redistribute the energy in your body. These disciplines can never harm you. They can only benefit you if you follow instructions carefully.

Do not approach gymnastics. Do not do knee bends as are taught by the gymnastics and health culturists. Up and down, up and down. This is injurious to your heart. It is not advisable. It starts the blood circulating too fast in the body, raises the body temperature and can cause a severe internal condition, ultimately. Calisthenics of that nature are dangerous. That which we give you now is esoteric yoga and will never harm you. It will give you greater health, greater mental freedom, greater control over your mind, your body, and allow your soul to achieve its true value. Above all it will give you a constant state of peace of mind, no matter where you are, what the condition may be.

That is the goal we desire for you. Peace of mind, perfected and radiant, that you may control and begin to use the universal laws. What value is it if we give you these teachings so that they may be filed away in your three-ringed notebooks to be read at leisure? That is of no benefit. A blank page would be just as important. You are being given these teachings to use. But you cannot possibly use these occult laws until you have disciplined your mind, your body, and let the soul come forth.

There are divisions to this exercise. The first step is stretching, raising the arms forward. Phase two, stretch the arms as high as you can. Stretch the fingers, imagine them growing in size. Phase three, bend slowly forward keeping knees straight, heels on the floor until ultimately your palms are flat on the surface. Phase four, move the palms to touch the tip of the toes and at the same time touch your forehead to your knees. Phase five, stand up erect immediately. Phase six, lower the hands to the side. Then start the cycle all over again. Do this with a beat and a rhythm.

There is a variation or an alternate to this if you desire. The alternate perhaps would be easier for your lazy bodies. Stay with the same process, standing erect, hands in the air. However instead of bending forward and placing your palms flat on the surface of the floor, bring your palms down and grasp your ankles, keeping your forearm so that it runs parallel with your leg. Your forearm rests against the side of your leg. Grasp the legs from the outside. Then touch your forehead to your knees. That is the only difference. Then stand erect. Even this, at first, is not easy. Be very slow and very cautious so that you will become aware of the body movements. Ultimately we shall restretch the condition to perfection.

Be not upset with yourselves, my students. It is not easy. This is difficult, but be patient. That is the first physical discipline to learn. You have the faculty of breath, to learn how to breathe. Practice this every day. If you are doing menial work stop for a moment, become aware of how you are breathing, and try to breathe correctly, until it becomes a process as automatic as blinking your eye. Then you are drawing in greater cosmic energy, greater vital force.

What is the purpose for this? Acumana shall reiterate once more for your edification. We give you this so that your spirit may have the liberty it desires to reunite with the Father. This is only possible by the control and the oneness of the mind and the body. The spirit must control the mind and the body, not the latter the former. The desire now is that you may become aware of true meditation, that you may have a state of bliss, a state of oneness, that your lives may be altered, physically, mentally and spiritually.

You have work to do. You have laws to put into effect, and discipline is the only way this is brought about. The teachers desire not to torture you. You are not living in the Dark Ages when you would be placed upon the rack. You place yourself upon the rack. You are the executioner, you are the beheader. So discipline.

It is advisable, if you desire, that before you approach meditation, to practice the first breath as you were told. Then practice, for five to ten minutes, the physical exercise. Then do your meditation, and you will find that you are in a more relaxed state of mind, a more receptive state of mind, for the spirit will become a little more aware of its identity. It is unloosened from the bondage of the flesh.

The flesh holds the spirit back. That is why you have the conflicts, the annoyances, the emotions. It is the flesh. It does not want the spirit to have liberty. And it will fight, and fight, and it will use the mind as its weapon. Then the spirit becomes dormant. It is said man may lose the flesh, may become corruptible and he may lose the mind, but he can never lose his spirit. And it is also said, "Woe upon the man, pity unto the man, who loses the mind, the flesh, and the spirit." That is what is happening in your world today. Human beings are literally losing their spirit. Their spirit becomes more and more dormant. It is like a light which becomes less and less in its glow and its intensity, until finally it is extinguished to a point where it is not even discernible. This must be altered within you.

***Student:* Once we have these disciplines to the point where they are automatic, is this within our soul in following lives, or do we have to go through it all again?**

You never lose the growth you have gained. All teachings, all esoteric experiences, all knowledge on the physical plane, is retained within the superconscious mind of the soul. But the soul is silent. The soul cannot possibly proclaim that wisdom until it is brought forward. So you do not lose anything, you only gain. When you have gained much spiritually, in your succeeding lives you are given more awareness quickly. Awareness comes to you at an earlier age and you begin to utilize that awareness earlier. Consider what is called the prodigy, the child prodigy. They are the ones who have had the most experience on certain facts. Musical prodigies, for example, have become so fully oriented in music and its uses, it is so much a part of their nature, that it cannot become dormant. It buds forward continuously from life to life. It is the same with all other things. The more fully oriented you become in this pattern the greater it becomes in its external use.

***Student:* Would these exercises help in losing weight?**

You may be assured of this: If you follow through this whole course set down by the teachers, and follow the disciplines, you will find yourself shedding many pounds. It is the natural way.

***Student:* Would this, then be good for children to do?**

No, this is not for children. In India children learn yoga. They are taught at an early age. Your children may be taught portions of this for the discipline but not the full esoteric value yet. You may teach them the first body position, if you so desire. Remember that the mental attitude is what is so important in these exercises, the maintenance of the mental attitude. When you have started your first position with your arms lifted upward, and you are bending down, exhale your air. Let all your air out slowly as you bend so that it is in rhythm. For a woman let it out the way you are taught, for a man the way you are taught, so that by the time your arms have reached the floor, your air is gone. Then as you rise, breathe in.

Your prayer mat must be large enough to accommodate your body lying down or standing. Ultimately, when the body has become stretched and supple, you will be able to assume the lotus position without any difficulty. It is called the position of the hero, the Buddha position. The hero position, or the lotus position, is the position wherein your seven chakras are perfectly aligned, perfectly flowing. It is the ideal state in the universe. It is the full trinity, the triad, the triangle. No other position offers the esoteric release that the lotus position offers. All bodily energies and currents are redistributed with the crossing of the legs. When the head stands erect in that position, back straight, you may assume that attitude for hours or days without moving, and the body is in a perfect state of being.

***Student:* Could we also do this breathing exercise lying down?**

No, standing or sitting. While you begin this breathing exercise, if you desire to sit while you do this, sit in a chair, back straight, head straight, with hands on your knees, palms upward on your lap.

***Student:* How long did you say that the breathing should continue?**

Spend five minutes on the breathing, and five minutes on the body position. That is sufficient. At first you will not be able to take more than five minutes. Include this in the overall time now of your meditation. If you have an hour for meditation, ten minutes of that hour are devoted to these two exercises.

Have discernment in your worldly life, in your mental and physical life. We are now concerned with your spiritual life. Discernment and spirit do not go together. Discernment and mind, discernment and the body, but not discernment and spirit. For spirit is all-encompassing. Spirit is all things. That is the course of action you are upon, the liberating of the spirit.

Apply diligence now to your endeavors. Remember, this is the way in your journey to liberty of the spirit, to peace of mind and inner satisfaction. You shall be opposed by many things. Two primary opponents shall be the mind and the body. You are warned of this. Be alert. Let the reasoning mind of goodness work with the spirit to guard the body. For the body will decide to fight. It will not want to be disciplined. But be diligent, have faith and know that all things are fulfilled when one endeavors to fulfill them faithfully.

Move forward now in the coming days before you with surety, knowing that the ladder of your evolvement rests against the shoulders of God, and that as you climb God watches and assists. The faith of your nature is based upon the foundation of your being. And the foundation of your being is built upon the solidity of God. So all is one and one is all. Be patient with yourselves above all, and be patient with each other.

Kindness wins many battles. Violence causes war. Love brings about peace. Harshness brings about bristles. Gentleness brings about beauty.

THE PATH

In Truth and in Light,
The path is never long,
But is always strong
And always pleasant,
If we but view it
With the eyes of Truth and Light.
We walk upon this great path
In search of perfection and Godhood.
I seek perfection and light.
All men seek perfection and light,
Even while struggling in darkness.
May I always understand this truth.
May I never condemn another.
Giving forth Truth and Light
That others may see and believe
That in Truth and in Light
The path is never long.

CHAPTER IX

Personality and Individuality

The development of personality is a very important study which fits into the panorama of the whole view of the studies of esoteric wisdom.

A great Lord of the universe said, "There is the microcosm and the macrocosm. As above, so below." The universe, in its endless depth, is filled with order, symmetry and balance. However, the individuality of the universe is often filled with chaos, just as each man is filled with chaos in his own personal individual life. For example, man has a mental body filled with mental thoughts. He is filled with desires and emotions. He is filled with goals and ambitions. His mental, physical and spiritual natures are composed of millions of various identities of individuality.

Take into consideration the entire structure of man's physical body. Each cell, each atom, in its nature is an individual expression of perfect law and order. Each is a universe. Each cell and each atom, therefore. represents an identity, an individuality of its own. It has a goal, it has a drive, it has an ambition. Therefore, man is pitted against thousands upon thousands of various and sundry desires and goals, all fighting for survival within him. His body, representing the microcosm, is a teeming mass of chaos and confusion. He is born as an individuality or an individual spark of reality from the whole, the whole of the universe being the perfected state of law and order, the opposite of chaos and imbalance.

The individuality is never lost, but is indelibly engraved upon the consciousness of the universe throughout all time. This individuality is like the snowflake in that no two individuals are ever alike. A comparison can never be made between one person and another. Each is distinct in his own being. That distinct nature is the composite of millions upon millions of various desires or identities, and these identities are just as real, just as alive, just as growing, as you as a whole are alive and growing. You have heard Acumana say to you before, your entire being is made up of thousands upon thousands of entities evolving within you, constituting your earth. These evolved beings—they may be thought forms, they may be emotions, physical desires, senses, moods, whatever they may be make up the nucleus of the whole, of the individuality.

Now, from mental darkness begins the trek forward toward personality, for personality is the balancing factor in the evolvement of the individuality. That is, the personality arrived at a state whereby that individuality is made whole, mentally, physically and spiritually, within itself. The chaos has now become balance and order. This balance and order is arrived at in the personality stage, and when it is completed is likened unto the Master.

The Master is a personality and is the sum total of balance and order. Through endless struggle the chaos of individuality within him has been reoriented and balanced. So there are the two extremes of the pole, the individual in mental darkness and the perfected personality in transcendent spiritual depth, wherein you find the Masters.

The journey begins now, not tomorrow.

With each step the individuality of the personage who is the composite of many individualities, is learning various lessons and is progressing toward the perfected state of personality. As it arrives closer to the balanced state of personality, the chaos within becomes less and less. The emotions become balanced. The desires become balanced. The higher and higher on the scale of perfection one climbs, the more the outer chaos falls away and the inner confusion and chaos take on order and symmetry. The soul consciousness, or the identity, that which you call individuality, which is never lost, then turns inward on its journey. And as it turns inward, it is reflecting the soul life. The soul light is showing through the personality, just as the individuality is the outer expression of the soul life.

The soul light of those who are in mental darkness does not shine forth. They are the reflection of their soul light as an individuality, and as they progress physically, mentally and spiritually they also progress psychologically and physiologically. They become more balanced within. Then their individuality becomes more dormant and goes within. The soul life begins to become more and more aware. The candle grows brighter. Then the true soul essence shines through the personality. The personality becomes oriented and balanced. It learns mastery and control over the mind and the body, then over the forces of nature and ultimately over the universe.

When it arrives at the point of perfected personality, it is still reflecting the individuality, for though personality is eventually lost, individuality is never lost. It is indelibly engraved upon the consciousness of the Father. If you had two personages of equal power, you would remember each for his individuality. You may call it personality, but mark you, it is not personality. It is the individual impression, the individual radiance, the individual countenance, which is indelibly engraved upon your conscious and subconscious memory.

Therefore, individuality is never lost, but personality eventually is set aside.

The exact opposite exists in the beginning stages of growth. In the beginning, there is the individuality but the personality is dormant. Then as the soul transcends higher and higher toward perfection, the individuality becomes internal and gradually gains soul growth and expression. When it arrives at its highest stage of development it is then the full expression of soul radiance and power, which is called personality.

Personality being a word or a term for the concept of a balanced state of the mental, physical and spiritual nature within a being. Personality is that balanced state of the mental, physical and spiritual natures within man, wherein all three divisions have become oriented and are aligned in perfection. Then you become in Truth the microcosm. You must become the microcosm before you can grasp the concept of the macrocosm.

The teachers, the masters, are all individualities who have expressed through personality. It was like the clothing they wore, such as a suit of armor or a coat. And as they dropped the shell or outer garments, what is left is the radiance of their individuality, their individual mark of distinction as a perfect balanced state of mental, physical and spiritual consciousness. They are, therefore, the essence of the microcosm. This is the stage of consciousness which each of you are striving toward.

Now, what comes beyond personality? Ah! Therein are the things of the spirit. Therein are things long since forgotten by the ages of man. Things of the spirit can only be gauged and measured by spiritual depth and spiritual depth is only perceived by those who are upon the path of spirituality. Not all members of mankind are upon the path toward spirituality, but those of spiritual discernment may, with discernment, measure personality. You may go behind the garb of the reflection of personality and you will find one essence always—individuality.

For example, two tables are made by a carpenter. One is made of walnut and one is made of maple, but they are made identical in size, shape and form. Why does one person choose the maple and another choose the walnut? It is the individuality of the table, its distinctiveness. It is that difference which is called individuality or in the progressed state of spiritual consciousness, it is called personality. Personality is the outer manifestation of the inner motivating individuality.

Now, for a moment we go back to things of the spirit. When you are born into mental darkness as an individual, you are filled with myriads of individualities. These are disciplined throughout the endless cycles of life until you arrive at the balanced state. When the balanced state is reached, then things of the universe must be blended. Then that personality, which no longer exists as a personality but as a distinct, radiant individuality, different than any other spark in the universe, becomes a light in the universe. It becomes like a star in its brightness in the heavens. Then it must learn the endless slow process which is the cycle toward spiritual perfection on the inner planes.

This has been called the Christ-conscious state. It has been called by some the Elvina. It has been called the god-state, the lord-state. It is the ascension toward the Logos. Call it whatever you will, nevertheless, all roads lead in the same direction and all must traverse the same road with the same burdens and the same cares. Each in his own distinct way will walk differently than his brother preceding him and the one following him.

When you have mastered the entire physical dimension, when you have mastered the mind, the body and the spirit within, you have won half the battle. It has perhaps taken you millions of years to accomplish this. Now half the road is won. You have another half to proceed upon, and that is the angelic kingdom, the God kingdom, where you must at some distant time arrive at the pinnacle of the Logos. This takes equally as long, sometimes longer, for you then must travel and journey throughout endless space in the universe.

You must become a Master, you must become a Lord, you must become a Planetary Ruler. You must become a planet, wherein are housed over cycles of time millions of beings of evolvement, and you must do well by them. You must not, like Lucifer, allow your planet to blow itself up and be destroyed. You must master it from the God-concept, a power and a depth and a dimension beyond your present understanding. What would it mean to you? Acumana cannot even convey in words what it could mean to you in terms of power and depth in the universe. There are no words for it. There are figures for it, there are equations for it, but it cannot be defined by semantics. It cannot be placed in the limited capacity of man's finite mind.

The personality grows toward perfection through endless avenues of self-mastery. Each individual is a reflection or a potential personality, but the personality does not begin to radiate and manifest until the individuality has fully gone within at the halfway mark of the cycles of physical evolution. Much depends upon whether or not the person is upon the path.

Herein is a key of great importance. Acumana said earlier, not all of mankind are upon the spiritual path, for a purpose. There are thousands upon thousands of individuals who have not consciously or unconsciously chosen a spiritual life. They have not consciously or unconsciously chosen liberation from bondage, and therefore they shall be held in bondage, likened unto the children in Egypt who were held in bondage. They have chosen the bonds and the only way they may be free is by clinging unto Moses and the law. Moses represents law, spiritual law, law and order in the universe.

When a person turns toward that spiritual law consciously and says, "What does this life afford me?" he takes his measure, and he measures himself on these standards. He figures that his life affords him food, clothing and shelter, the three basic needs taught to all elementary school children. Then these basic needs may be expanded. It may be food to an abundance, clothing to surplus and shelter in grandeur. He may conceive of any of these three basic needs in any dimension of consciousness that he chooses, but those basic needs which he chooses to satisfy are the instincts of the physical senses. In taking his measure, he has found those three things essential to his physical being, but that is all.

Then he says, "What is missing? I have provided all the food that I need for myself and my people. I have provided all the clothing for my nakedness, for my body, and I have provided shelter and protection from the elements of life for me and mine. What have I not provided for?" One thing—he has forgotten his welfare. When one forgets the origin of his nature and is only concerned with providing for his food, clothing and shelter, he has left out providing for his spiritual growth.

Instinctive man, primitive man, does not consciously say, "I must assist my spiritual growth." No. He has another approach. He perhaps makes an image or an effigy, a deity, something to cleave to, something to gaze into the heavens and desire, something to set in his heart and his spirit, though he knows not what they are, wondering. This is the nature of his spiritual needs. Even the cave man, the primitive man, who gazes above him into the universe, is filled with a sense of awe, and he begins to worship some image and pray to it. He, in his own finite way, is providing for his spiritual needs.

The progressed man provides for his spiritual needs in various and different ways, according to his level of consciousness. When he takes his measure and finds he has forgotten his spiritual needs, he is filled with a void and an emptiness, a gnawing and a sickness within. He says, "I have no faith. I have no heart. I have only been concerned with the physical senses and desires. God has meant naught to me. Worship, spirituality, are only hollow, empty words to me. How can hollowness and emptiness be satisfying?"

He must first of all approach it this way. He must say, "I have neglected my spiritual needs. Therefore, I appeal to whatever it is within me, within the universe, that affords spiritual depth to guide my feet in that direction." Faith is what he is saying. Faith and the spiritual need are the two allies. You may not have one without the other. One cannot find spiritual satisfaction without faith and faith does not exist without the spiritual, for what is faith but the full measure and reflection of things unseen? In order to believe in things unseen, you must have faith. The two are inseparable.

When this has come about he then steps upon the path, but if he does not take his measure because he is still too concerned with the food, the clothing and the shelter in all of its ramifications, he is lost. Lost not in the eternal sense, but lost in the sense of the age or the time. We have said to you so often, time is unimportant and yet time is important in its infinite sense. The goal of the universe is measured not in an hour, not in a half-hour or a quarter of an hour or a minute, but within a fraction of a second. It is measured even to a portion of a fraction of a second.

When one is lost to the age or to the time, he has lost the potential personality. Then he slips, as it were, down into an abyss of nothingness. Since his life has been filled with nothingness he has, therefore, built his world of nothingness, for as a man thinks in his heart, so it shall be. So his world has been filled with materiality and materiality does not exist in the true reality. It is only a reflection, and when that reflection is shattered, when the garb of the personality is set aside, only then is reality seen. Since he has clung to materiality and it does not exist in reality he is lost. For he has not built for himself a mansion in reality by clinging to spirituality from the material side.

You are now living in your senses. The world calls this reality. You know from the mystic point of view it is not so. You know that reality is beyond your vision, therefore, what are you living within? You are living in only one dimension of reality, the dimension called materiality. It is only a state of consciousness called materiality. Since you are living in this materiality you must, therefore, provide the three basic needs, or the three trinities of that materiality (food, clothing, shelter) but you must not neglect the spirituality.

Building your spiritual mansion is like having a savings account or tithing unto yourselves. If you do not plan to provide for your future because you say, "Tomorrow it will not be needed," tomorrow comes all too fast. What does tomorrow mean to you? What does ten years mean? Ten years to you now means so many days, so many hours. You say, "It is a long time away," but look how fast a moment goes, look how fast a year goes. So if you do not plan today for tomorrow, when tomorrow arrives you have no food, clothing or shelter. However, if you have faith, spiritual depth, and you have balanced that faith in the material sense, and provided accordingly, then when tomorrow comes you face it as perfectly as you faced the moment. Thus you will enter tomorrow with equal armor and equal strength. Then the morrow means only a transition of time.

If today you do not plan your spiritual tomorrow, when you arrive at the reality of tomorrow where will you live? What will you have? Nothing. So the one who lives a material life, though he knows better, and does not prepare for his spiritual growth, when he arrives in the true reality, when he is deceased (that is the reality), he has no home. It matters not how highly-evolved he is, he still knows better because of his individuality. If he has not prepared his way, defeat leads him down to the pit wherein he must learn the hard way because he has clung to the things of illusion.

That is what is meant by being upon the path. That is the plan, preparing your spiritual banquet toward reality. It is only the truly enlightened ones upon the path who have been able to grasp this concept, that there is no importance in what the physical world has to offer.

It matters not to you if on the morrow you must lose all your physical possessions. It is a foolish man who thinks he is upon the path, and says he is interested in spiritual things, yet clings to the world of materiality. If anything happens to shatter that world he is shattered. He has built his foundation on sand and a wave has come and washed it away. But the man who says, "It matters not. It is easy to obtain material things as long as I am in the material world," is a man of vision and he is a man of monumental faith, for he knows that wherever he is in the physical world he will be able to provide for his food, his clothing and his shelter. He must surrender all and move on and not look back as Lot's wife did. Lot's wife, remember, upon looking back, turned to salt. She pretended or feigned building her spiritual mansion and yet desired the pleasures of the physical.

It is not wrong to desire but it is wrong to cling. And when they said, "Go from Sodom and Gomorrah and look ye not behind you," she said, "Yes." But her heart still remained in Sodom and Gomorrah, and when she cast an eye over her shoulder she turned to salt. She was lost.

Salt is the most highly absorbent mineral on the Earth. It is of great mystic significance. Your body is composed of various salts, which are of different chemical origins. Salt represents spiritual absorption, and that means you must go back to the origin of all things if you cling to materiality.

The man who is a true pillar of faith is one who knows it matters not what he builds. He may build a great mosque, or he may build a humble grass hut, whatever is his vision. For his vision will be different than his neighbor's. That is his individuality. He may express it in any way he desires. Solomon built a great temple. Another man may build a mud hovel. Which is the greater? Both are of equal importance. Both are perfect. Solomon built according to his level of understanding and another built according to his needs and his understanding. The man who built the mud hut was no worse or better than Solomon and Solomon was no worse or better than the man who built the mud hut. Each utilized his capacity to his level.

Moses came to offer man liberation and to deliver him from bondage, from Pharaoh. Pharaoh represents material law, material senses and desires. The Pharaoh within you is holding you down to the sense sensations and you are in bondage. Moses represents spiritual ideas. He represents the highest concept on Zion receiving the voice of God, does he not? The Zion within you is the highest spiritual consciousness you can reach, receiving divine inspiration, divine guidance, through the ten basic commandments. Through Zion you are delivered from bondage.

Jesus represents the same thing. Each age brings a different concept. This is what the path means. So you see in the world about you today numerous personalities and numerous individualities which are not all upon the path. It is the eye of discernment, the voice within, which is able to recognize those upon the path, the clue being the eyes.

The eyes are the window to the soul. Regardless of how highly evolved or lowly evolved a person is look into his eyes and you will know whether or not he is highly evolved, whether he is upon the path.

In the Book of Revelation you are told, "On the great day those who have the mark of the beast on their forehead are lost. Those separately marked shall be spared." It means that those who have chosen the path, who are marked with the esoteric signature of spirituality, are the only ones spared. Mankind will suffer great purgings, great devastations, but your signature will mark you, and that signature is perceived spiritually through the eyes. This is why the mystics and priests in Egypt, in

Chaldea, used the eyes for their contact.

What do you know of the eyes other than the axiom, "The eyes are the windows of the soul"? They convey radiant energy. They reflect the depth of your understanding, and, above all else, they are the mystic windows toward esoteric wisdom for good or for evil, for they are transparent and elusive. The priests used to mesmerize from the eyes, as they do sometimes today. And it is your eyes that give you knowledge. It is your eyes that give you sensations. When you see something, you desire it, not when you feel it. If you see a beautiful structure, you desire it. If you see a garment of silk in bright glorious colors, you desire it, not through the touching, but through the seeing. So, indeed, your eyes are your most cherished possession.

Let us say you meet a man and you say to yourself, "I wonder if this man is upon the path. How may I reach him?" Look into his eyes. You will be able to tell. All who are upon the path have a similar light, a sparkle, that is recognized throughout the whole universe. Those who do not have the light are not upon the path. Their eyes are deep, hollow and cold.

The personality is the key, and when that personality is fully surrendered then things of the spirit shall be embraced. It is the individuality which will long be remembered. Each is a distinct individual in an endless universe, peopled by stars of countless ages. The heavens proclaim the glory of God's work of individuality. Every star in the galaxy, every sun in the universe, every meteor in the atmosphere, is a reflection of the individual nature of your Father. In God's home are many mansions, and to grow toward those mansions you must become the microcosm in the greater macrocosm. As above, so below. You may now ask questions of this if you wish.

***Student:* I wanted to ask whether each time we come back we have the same personality or a new one.**

You have a basic individuality. Depending upon how you have progressed in the previous life, how you have motivated or learned the various lessons, how you have consciously mentally, physically and spiritually grown, determines the change in your basic nature. The basic individuality remains the same but it is progressed a little more. The individuality then functions through a progressed personality.

> ***Student:*** **Then your new personality would develop with the new incarnation into which you came?**

It is so, exactly. If in a previous life you were a Frenchman or a Frenchwoman, your personality expression would be different than it is now. The individuality is always there, but it progresses, reflecting in the personality, until it becomes a radiant personality.

> ***Student:*** **If a person accidentally dies or meets with an accident before he has finished a particular incarnation, does the development of his individuality stop right there? Where does he take up in the next incarnation?**

He takes up at the point where he finished. There is no such thing in the universe as accident. There is nothing in the whole vast universe, in the many universes of God, that may be termed an accident. Therefore, according to his life cycle, as it existed at that time, there was a completion and events were brought to a conclusion which were essential for his growth at that time. When there is a completion then there is a drawing in. A drawing in, or gathering together in the harvest, is termed by man transition or death.

> **Student: Aside from the possible karmic origin, what is the esoteric significance of a blind person?**

There are two. Blindness may have two significances—karmic or voluntary. For example, you have had in your generation a great, highly evolved individual, Helen Keller. Helen Keller volunteered to embody under the most extreme hardships possible to assist all those who are burdened with those physical maladies to reach the same state of consciousness that was hers. If it is voluntary, then it is manifested in deeds similar to those of Helen Keller in another capacity, depending upon the need. When voluntary, it is to elevate others to assist humanity in knowledge.

In some very rare cases people have lost sight of their eyes so that they may have an inner revelation, that they may not see the ugliness of the world but see only the spiritual beauty. That is very rare. Usually blindness is karmic. Perhaps ninety-six percent is karmic. The other four percent exists for various other purposes. For those who have karmically attracted that condition unto themselves, the great extended hand of mercy of your Father gives even to them one more assistance. He says symbolically, "Come all of you who have earned such a deed, let us help you out of your malady." So He sends one such as Helen Keller to assist the suffering.

Student: **Why does the old Hebraic Bible contain this reference on two or three occasions—and eye for an eye and a tooth for a tooth? That doesn't sound very Godlike.**

Remember, according to the age of man (speaking now of the progress of the race), the individuality is born into mental darkness. You know the transition it must take to reach perfection as an individual. This works collectively as well. There is a race consciousness, and that race is made up of individual people making the whole. The law is determined according to the time in history, the cycle of time in the race.

It was a law at that time. It was the only law man understood. How would man who was nomad, who wandered the plains fighting and killing, be able to comprehend any other law? Imagine your prehistoric ancestors who had to struggle for survival against nature, confronting creatures that roamed the Earth ten times their size. Imagine saying to him who must fight for survival, "Love your neighbor." It was beyond his understanding. All he could understand was, "An eye for an eye and a tooth for a tooth." He was more like an animal than like a man. When that race had perfected itself through numerous growths, a new law came.

Student: **That would explain then why Christ in the New Testament says, "If a man smites you on the right cheek, let him smite you on the left cheek."**

Yes, the exact opposite of an eye for an eye and a tooth for a tooth. The race had reached the point of evolvement as a whole to accept the new law. Each individual had evolved to the point as a whole whereby his consciousness could grasp and understand, "Turn ye the other cheek."

***Student:* That's why, then, people who sometimes quote that old Hebraic saying as authoritative are archaic in their thinking?**

They are indeed archaic, and how unfortunate for them, for if they try to live by that old concept, verbatim, then they are not giving themselves the new food of sustenance. They shall have, indeed, a sharp awakening, for the new law has been in effect for many years, and a man who has not in that amount of time learned the new law had better quickly get upon a horse and find out what has delayed him. Unfortunately in your world there are numerous diehards who refuse to conform to progress as a whole. If the laggards persist in holding back the minds of other people, then they must suffer the consequence.

***Student:* It is stated that though sometimes the great ones are beneficent forces bringing peace and contentment with them, more often they have come as agents of destruction, breaking up old forms of religion and government in order that the life within might be set free and build for itself a new and better vehicle. Then are such dictators as we have known in our time, such as Hitler, possibly ranked among the forces that were sent for the purpose of breaking up old conditions?**

Herein there is such a difference between right and wrong that unless it is so stated in an exact precise way you may misunderstand. Yes, it is true, they oftentimes have been classified as masters of destruction to break up crystallized conditions that have existed. Now, where the avenue of wrong-doing is concerned is when the personages which are given this responsibility lose the purpose and suddenly conceive of themselves as being the All within the All. Things of the spirit are undefinable. They must learn lessons you cannot even conceive of yet. Think of the responsibilities they must handle. It is far easier to fall at that point than it is from your point. It is why there are so few Masters, why so few ascend in comparison to the all.

> *Student:* **So actually to fulfill their true purpose they would have to break up the crystallization without becoming dictatorial or without predominating with their own personality?**

If the will of the Father be, according to the great Council of the Lords, "Break up this condition, for this condition is leading to the corruption and the downfall of mankind," then it must be done, and the power and the force to maneuver and manipulate the condition is entrusted to a highly evolved being. Sometimes power is entrusted to highly evolved individuals in the physical body. Whether or not they correctly wield this power is not the Master or the Lord of the Ray's concern, as long as it is done.

When you find a highly evolved individual who forgets the God concept and begins to manifest within himself the concept that he is God, he actually believes this. You may say, "What can those who do this possibly think they will gain?" They lose intuitive stability. They lose intuitive balance. All who have joined the darker side believe that they are going to be the rulers and the sages. Each individual believes that he is helping mankind and the race of mankind and that somewhere in that great struggle he will be a pinnacle of Light. Just as you believe that you are a good student of Truth and that you believe in the teachings, they believe in the opposite. Many of them are so bathed in their own ego, their self-centeredness, that they believe themselves to be the guardians of the world, the keepers of the flame.

They have lost one aspect. They have lost the identity of their soul awareness. They did not take care of the spiritual. They were too concerned with the material. Yet that is their choice. You are free in the world to think as you please. That is the only way you are free, to think as you choose, spiritually or materially.

Remember, the Lord was tempted, and what did He say under temptation? "Get thee behind me, Satan." There is the key! Everyone is tempted. Those who are highly evolved are tempted by even greater forces than those that tempt you. And sometimes they are not able to overcome those temptations. It takes the strongest power possible in universal development to overcome temptation. They are offered everything in the world. You might say, "If they are Masters, what more could they want?" They are offered everything from a physical sense, and when they are in the physical body, the senses are distorted. When your Lord Jesus was tempted He was in the physical body. When you are in the physical body your spiritual senses are distorted. You are alone, you are cut off, and you may fall. That is why so many fall and so few volunteer.

The darker forces wait for much time until you are at a vulnerable point toward perfection. They wait until you lose your will. Do you know when you will lose the will? At mastership. And when you have lost will and gone fully into creativity, then they will come and tempt you.

It is likened unto this. You know that there is night and there is day. Now, imagine that you are at the apex in the world where light meets darkness, and see there an imaginary line. Here is light and there is darkness, and they come together. Day and night come together and you are at the apex. Who will win? You have no way of knowing, except this. If you know that it happens to be the time that the sun is to come up, then you are on the side of the sun and you are bound to win.

Student: **Acumana, would you please explain, once more, what individuality is?**

Individuality is like the stars, like the grains of sand on all the beaches and all the deserts in the world. It is like every snowflake throughout all time. Each one is different. Not one is duplicated. So the individual is the expressive magnitude of every creation, never duplicating itself. You have never been duplicated. You are unique. Not another snowflake, grain of sand, star, drop of water, ever was or ever will be, the same. That shows the magnificence of God. That is individuality. Its purpose is to sustain its uniqueness, not to be a copy of another, in an idea, in action, in ability or talent, but to remain pristine in its individuality. That is God expressing through individuality, and that is you.

Personality is a suit of armor, the coat, the way an individuality expresses. Your personality is what you have gained over many lives, which is what you dress your individuality in. Personality is your way of doing things, your unique way of expressing individuality.

The main thing is to be individual. Don't be a collector. Don't be like the mob. Be a step above mediocrity, always, and you will shine throughout the whole world. For if you go to the level of mediocrity it will consume you and you will be lost. This is where man stays, because he cannot step one step above mediocrity. When individuality is conscious, then personality is used like a coat or cloak, and you can change it. You can put on a red one or a green one or a black one, because it is infinite.

As long as the individuality is expressing through you, your personality changes as each experience in life brings you new encounters. Your personality grows. It takes unto itself, like adding another garment. Keep it free and flowing and individuality will then express.

So individuality is what you are. It is the spirit of you, incarnate. You are God spirit incarnate, individually, with the clothing of personality, which is the way you do things. And that is also individual. Each of you is different, so each is individuality also. But you are all one. You all come from one whole, the Absolute, divided up into many different pieces.

Acumana will tell you a story now. Once upon a time, before there was time, where there was only pure spirit, nothing else, nothing created, only Being, Being was in an absolute complete state of ecstasy. And Being said to Itself, "I am God. I am Being. I am God of everything. But what am I God of? I have nothing to be God of. I am God, but I don't know what I'm God of. I think I will make me God of something. I think I will make Me." So number one, in order to become something, It had to divide Itself, yes? You cannot have two from one, can you, unless you divide one into two. So God, Infinite Being, decided that it was very dull being God with nothing to be God of, so It divided Itself into two, here and there. Now It had made for Itself time and space. The division of one into two created time and space.

Now there were two. Now with two you can multiply, yes? So now the two multiplied. First Being divided from one to two, and then those two multiplied, which is again a division. So It divided more. It made for Itself a universe of vast space, because the moment It divided Itself, time and space were there.

The first creation was in the word, "I AM GOD." That was the word. Then came the next creation. Being divided Itself again. And It filled the space, which is the solar system, with bright lights, stars, planets, infinite suns, moons, star dust. And Being said, "How lovely. I'm God of all of this. How pretty. A ball here and a ball there and a ball there. A moon, a Mercury and a Venus."

"But let us have them do something," It said to Itself. "We'll put them in an orbit and we'll have things happening between them. Energies. And We'll see what this does. We'll let this be." So it says in Genesis, and God then let it all come about, letting it do what it wanted to do.

And then finally It made Itself. Being said, "Now I'm God of all of these things, I think I'll make Me. Personality, yes, that's what I think I will do. I'm all of this but I will make this more interesting for Me, this life, this Eternal Being's life. I think what I will do to Me is I will make part of Me forget what I am doing, and the other part of Me know what I am doing, so it will talk to Itself."

"Part of Me will say to Me, what are you doing? And the other part will say, I don't know what I am doing. And it will have fun with Itself." So It made part of Itself know and part of Itself not know. The part that doesn't know is the beast. It is asleep. And Being said, "I will make Me in My own image." So Being called, "Poof!" and made Itself a body. And Being said, "Oh, I've made for Me a world. Very lovely. This is My planet."

So Being walked about upon Earth and said, "I am this. I am the soil of the Earth, and I am the air, and I am the apple tree there, and I am that lovely flower, and I am that lady and I am that gentleman. And I Am Me. I Am who I Am. I Am what I Am. I Am that I Am, that I Am."

And the being was divided, from one to many. Is one better? Is the piece less than the whole being? Or is it all one? So you are one. *Thou art one.* You are the reflection, the perfect, creative reflection, of Infinite Being, God. You are not God, but God is you, and there is a big difference. The beast in you will say, "Oh, I am God." No, God is you. You are not God. Contemplate upon this.

Peace be unto you now. Always be good to one another, kindly to one another, because the world is not kindly now. We are trying to generate kindness, because, you see, the part that forgot about itself forgot that the other part of it is kind. So we are going to wake up the kind part and let the other part go to sleep.

TRUTH STANDS BEFORE ME

Truth stands before me
As a stalwart tree
Arms raised in victory.
The solid trunk,
Far-reaching,
Holds forth the limbs
Which bear the fruit of life,
Ready for the picking.
If I pick not
The fruit of life,
I am in the shadows
Of the truth
Which stands before me.
Let me stand erect, Oh God,
In the light of the sun
Reaching upward,
To pluck the truth
Which stands before me
As a stalwart tree.

CHAPTER X

Balance

The more you serve and adhere to the path of Christ-awareness, the more you receive. You know the symbolism of your Lord, the Christ, who carries the cross. You all bear the cross.

You all have the potential of Christ-awareness. Christ-awareness is a state of consciousness that the man, Jesus of Nazareth, achieved. That is why He was given the title, Jesus, the Christed One. The man, the body of Jesus of Nazareth, bore the cross. The cross symbolized the burdens of the whole world upon His physique. Think of the weight. Think of the pain. Because He bore the cross, He was Christed. The law is, if you adhere to the Truth regardless, you are given rewards. His reward was to be relieved half the way. A man named Simon relieved Him of the burden of the cross, did he not? This man Simon was not the disciple Simon. This was a different Simon, and his sole purpose was to carry the cross.

Jesus volunteered to stand before Pilate, before the world. Pontius Pilate symbolically represents the judging world of man, the material, judging world. The man, Jesus, stood before that judging world, taking mockery and criticism, and He was stripped before them. Soldiers came and stripped Him of all His garb. He was naked before the world. He was chastised. The King was stripped before the populace. "Since He is a King," they said, "let Him wear a crown," so a crown of thorns was placed upon His brow. This was extreme mockery. He suffered three extremes—judgment by the world through Pilate, nakedness before the populace, humiliation, and the crown of thorns to symbolize the king who stood naked in the bleeding Truth. He was proven by the populace to be a fraud and a deceiver, for they said, "If you are a King, surmount this." He could not, nor would He surmount it, for He knew this must happen. He allowed this to happen. He knew their suffering and He bore the cross, with great physical pain.

Who of you could lift the world? That is the symbolism of Atlas in ancient mythology. It is the forthcoming or the prophecy of the coming of a Christed man, bearing the cross of the world.

Jesus was relieved halfway up the hill of the cross. And because Simon volunteered to carry it, it was his reward. Do you see the symbolism? Because he volunteered he was given the power to carry it. He had the strength to carry the cross. He came for that purpose. He did not have the physical suffering that Jesus had, for when the crown of thorns, the judgment and the defacing had been completed, the Lord was stripped of prana. Since He was stripped of prana the cross was extremely heavy for Him, and yet it was not heavy for the other man.

When each of you bear the cross, serve Truth in all its honesty and only serve Truth, you are given many things. Much of the cross you bear is removed. Many blockages, many stones in the path, are disintegrated and blown aside.

Now if students have any questions of a various nature you may now ask.

> *Student:* **Something has come to me that is kind of disturbing because I don't know if the relation to me has to do with the crucifixion. Should I not be trying to discover what this is at this time, or can I know?**

It is this. Your own soul is aware of the deeper significance of the crucifixion in relationship to the physical act. All deep concepts have a counterpart in the physical. All Truths are manifest in the physical. Crucifixion is a concept, an ancient concept. Acumana's physical teacher, Zoroaster, at the time of his physical existence, taught of man's daily crucifixion upon the path of life, that man, to be born again, must be daily crucified. All the celestial beings, the cosmic teachers of Light, teach of the plane of crucifixion and suffering as being the Earth plane, where each of you, daily must suffer and die upon the cross of your physical being. Your body is your cross. Your bodies are the densities of your existence, and you must suffer them and be reborn again every moment. Each moment of each day you must guide your thoughts toward positiveness, toward God, toward Christ Light. That is to be reborn.

When the body, that cross of yours, sends pain through you and says, hate, envy, lust, desire, selfishness, greed, all the opposites to the pole of life that you desire, then you are being crucified by your earthly condition. You must counteract this with positiveness. You must be reborn. The counterpart to this Truth of daily crucifixion is the physical act of the crucifixion of the Master Jesus.

What Jesus personified in that age was the development to the highest state of consciousness that the physical man can obtain. When Acumana says physical man, understand, it is only because when you are in the density it is called physical, it is that rate of vibration. His body, His soul, His mind, His consciousness, is at a rate of vibration so high and so rapid that it is the highest. He symbolizes the concept of the law, daily crucifixion, for all the positiveness. For what did He teach? Love, forgiveness, gentleness, healing, goodness, honesty, the attributes of God, the true, pure Light.

And what happened? He was murdered for this, for teaching goodness. He daily taught goodness, and rather than being crucified daily, it all culminated in one act, which symbolized man. So the physical crucifixion represents symbolically man's daily suffering in his goals and in his desires upon the path of life, in his desire to obtain more Light.

Now, your soul begins to recognize this concept, and when it begins to recognize a concept it goes into that concept more deeply, and it is felt fully. Does that answer your question?

***Student:* Yes. Then that is part of what Jesus meant when He said, all men shall do what I do?**

Only partly. What He meant is that all the greatness that exists in God's world which He has obtained, you may obtain. One day you may have the consciousness that He has. You, one day, may heal the sick and move mountains. What He is saying to you is that one day you may evolve to this point of understanding, as He has evolved.

***Student:* I'd like to know how we can be more creative.**

First of all, remember those words of Jesus when He said, "All that I have done, ye also may do. It is not I. It is the Father within me which doeth the works." What does He mean? He means that unto yourselves, unto that carcass which you are wearing as a robe to move you about, you are capable of achieving nothing. You as an individual are capable of achieving nothing because you are made of mineral substance, of dense gases and vibrations of the physical plane, and these vibrations are incapable of coordinating creativity. You say. "But how is this possible? I can do this, I can do that." It is not you, it is the Father.

There is in the universe, all pervading, the great substance, the divine flow. It is called the All, the all-embracing God, the great ever-expanding 0. God is all things. These things we need not reiterate over and over. You know this. God is science, wisdom, intelligence, love, all things. And there is at all times vibrating throughout the universe a balance and a consistency in all areas.

Each of the seven rays of service are in constant vibration, and like your television or your radio, you are attuned to them. You are only a box, that is all. You are plugged into the divine source, the divine essence. Your body is equipped with various mechanisms to receive and transmit vibrations from the divine source. It attunes itself, according to your ray, according to your area of understanding, to this constant flow of divine energy and ideas coming from the mind of your Father.

However, if you do not do something with them, someone else will. An idea or an inspiration coming from God flows through the mechanism of your mind and you digest it. You contemplate it because you are attuned to it. It is given to you to use. If you do not use it, it still goes on. Someone else will pick it up and they will use it. It is not lost.

You may be anything in the universe you desire to be, anything you contemplate upon being. You may be the greatest in any area of any field, ultimately. As long as you have life within you and as long as your heart beats you are magnetically attuned and psychically attuned to universal thought. It shall always be carried on from age to age. If you do something with what you have, then you are increasing God's supply house. And it is important to increase and multiply the great storehouse so that the younger children may equally share in the wisdom, just as you have shared.

Attune to the universal source of ideas, for the universal source contains all wisdom, all things, and you will be fed the thing most appropriate for your need. Universal source also knows what you are looking for.

> ***Student:*** **Suppose you receive an idea and you formulate the idea in the material sense and then you are ready to motivate the idea, but you meet blockage here and blockage there. Are you permitted to call upon help for motivating the idea?**

You may call for help, yes. But you must discipline yourselves to overcome those obstacles. This must be done by the individual ego, the entity, through self-mastery. Remember, the body does not desire to respond to spiritual vibrations. It desires the low vibration of the physical sense and all of its desires. It desires inertia. It will fight you all the way. This is what the Masters have all taught. It is the most difficult of all things. And in all ranges, in all areas of understanding, there are different degrees of the eternal struggle. Only through discipline of the mind can this be controlled, until you have reached mastery. Then you have coordinated the three aspects of your nature. They are not aligned within any of you yet. Only highly evolved Masters and those who are in self-mastery are able to function from that level.

A Master is one who has learned control of himself, as well as control of universal force. One who is in self-mastery may control himself but has not as yet learned universal control.

When you have these blockages, these obstacles, you must first decide what they are. Are they phantoms created in your own subconscious mind or are they conditions of the world which have been projected upon you? Or are they your own lack of self-confidence, self-inflicted, self-imposed? They could be any number of things. You are the only one who has the key to unlock the secret.

What does it profit a man if he must always have assistance from the other planes? Then he does not learn the greater lessons himself which he must one day learn. Those who do not progress are always asking for a crutch, always asking for aid and assistance. They do not desire to lift one corpuscle in their own nature to assist themselves. They would have the spirit world do it for them.

Acumana will tell you something of the spirit world, since it must be your home for some time between lives. There is a great misunderstanding of the world of spirit. The true spirit world is progress and wisdom. The true spirit world would in no way interfere in your growth, nor would they assist you in your day to day progress. They have enough to do in their own world. They will not lift one finger (though they have not a finger), to do your work for you. They must equalize other conditions of greater importance.

Student: **Why is it the Spiritualists don't accept reincarnation? With all these messages they get, all these disembodied souls they profess to talk with, supposedly highly-evolved souls, nobody ever comes through and tells us about reincarnation. Yet we know it to be a fact.**

Many Spiritualists are in different ranges of awareness. They cannot nor would they understand or accept reincarnation, the law of consequence, of rebirth, as it is called. However, they accept life after death, and they attract to them, by the law, water seeking its own level, only those of their own understanding. For if you are a man given to stealing and lying continuously, would not your friends also be of the same nature? If you lived in a world of filth and vulgarity, would not your associates live equally so? They would indeed. But if you live in a world of milk and honey, then your friends also partake of milk and honey. You always seek your own level of awareness, even in the spiritual world. It is a natural magnetic law of the universe.

Student: **It works on the inner as well as the outer planes?**

Most assuredly.

***Student:* So a person on the outer plane who didn't believe in reincarnation would only attract the spirit world that didn't believe in reincarnation?**

Absolutely. The only reason they do not believe in rebirth on the inner plane is they have not taken the time to investigate.

***Student:* May I ask a question regarding my meditation and the problems that I'm having with it?**

It is a difficult lesson to learn. To learn to give in to the benefits of meditation is essential, but you must be persistent. Be patient and be consistent. Daily take time to become quiet and listen over and over consistently to maintain one thought and nothing else. One way is to do the Lord's Prayer over and over until you become a part of that prayer. Then you can have a state of semi-meditation, a state of reverie, and, gradually, the more you persist, the closer you are to going deep within, where there is the silence. If you feel yourself dozing into sleep, wake up and start again.

Each evening when you retire ask your Father in your prayers that you may consciously remember those gifts awarded to you in your hours of night travel. Protect your body, bless it with radiant Light, and ask, if it is in divine grace, in divine order, and if it is the wish of the Father, that you may remember those things of the night.

***Student:* If I concentrate and ask will I be able to hear my teacher speak to me?**

Perhaps when certain things are initiated by you your teacher will speak to you. Begin to move and motivate, cease to wait. Become active. Begin to move.

***Student:* In which direction, Acumana?**

It is up to you, my son, it is up to you. For you cannot say, "Where is the moon? Where is the sun? And when, why and how can I get there?" You must first say to yourself, "I know the moon is there, I know the sun is there, and I know I shall find the way by doing. I must first build a boat to conquer the sea and then I must build myself a great ship of space to conquer the air. Then when I have come upon the moon I will gaze at that which I have done and say, 'It has been a goodly day I have led.' And then I will set about to explore the moon by doing, and when I have explored the moon I will build myself a greater ship, of greater speed and greater height, to ascend to the sun. And when I climb the stairs to the sun I must then become aware that it has been a goodly day that I have won. And as I merge into the sun I will look back upon the things that I have done and say unto myself, 'These are goodly things, it is a goodly day I have won, and I thank my Father for the doing! There is your riddle, my son."

What Acumana means is you must *do,* cease to wait.

***Student:* But I could go in the wrong direction.**

Any direction you go in is not a wrong direction if it is a productive, working, motivating direction. The day will come when you must cease to ask where and how, but simply do. There is no way in the universe for the great golden key to fall into any man's lap magically to lift him and elevate him to a height whereby without effort he can surmount all things. In many ways, you are looking for just such a golden key. To find such a key you must create it.

***Student:* In our going toward the path of perfection, what place does what we term personal love have? There seems to be a great need for that with many of us. Does that have to fall away ultimately, or is it possible to pursue the path of perfection with happy personal love?**

You must understand the definition of personal love. That which is called personal love never falls away, for when you love an individual you are in a sense loving the God presence in another. Therefore, there is perfection. Possession is entirely different. What often happens in personal love is that the individual mistakes possession for personal love and cannot give up that possessiveness.

***Student:* I have a question I've been wanting to ask. I have heard of cosmic fire. What is it exactly?**

Ah! God is cosmic fire. Cosmic fire is that central core of the universe from which issues all else. Think of the great flame of your own sun. What is the sun but a molten body of fire? Thus it is with the great central spiritual sun. It is a great cosmic fire. God is the cosmic fire, and there is no separating yourself from the cosmic fire. For there is no separating your self from God. For if for one second or for one one-hundredth of a second or one one-thousandth of a second the sun ceased to emit its rays, what would you have? The cessation of life in the whole universe. So God is the cosmic fire.

***Student:* Now I am confused, Do you mean that the sun . . .**

Acumana will make a correction for you, my son. Never use the name of God preceding "confused." What is the name of God? I AM. So you uttered to Acumana, "I AM confused." Cancel that totally. Never use the name of God before any negative word, for you then make it a reality.

Look in your Scripture where Moses goes unto the Mount and he receives from God the Ten Commandments. He has, below, down in the plains, all of his people living in mass confusion, living in blasphemy unto the name of God. And after he had taken down the Ten Commandments, he said unto God, "Thank you, my Father. How beautiful that you have given unto me the salvation of my people. But what will I say unto them about where I obtained the commandments? They will not believe that I, a humble shepherd, could have such wisdom. Who shall I say has sent me?" And God's reply was this, "Say *I Am* has sent you. I AM that I AM. Let that be My name for all generations." So *I AM* is the name of God. So it is most important for students upon the path to be very aware of how they use the name of God. For if you declare in the name of God that you are confused, the name of God will willingly display for you more and more confusion. Say instead, "I am interested in more revelation upon this subject."

***Student:* I'd like to know more about my master teacher.**

A master teacher is one who has tutored with you throughout many successive lives. This teacher has worked with you in the body and out of the body, as it were, to bring you to a point of self-recognition, self-mastery. When self-mastery has been realized and recognized, the duty and obligation of the master teacher is complete. Then you, in turn, become one of the many to serve others.

Not all have a master teacher. This is only given to those who have chosen a path of service, who have chosen to become members of the great Army of Light that serves humanity. They are given, by their own degree of evolution, their own background of esoteric training, their particular teacher, who gravitates to them according to their own degree of magnetic energy. This teacher may, in a meditative state, be called upon at any time, for he is with you at all times in mind, body and spirit, in telepathic rapport. You are in constant communion with him, for he has an archetype image of your entire nature within his presence at all times, and reflected upon that image is every thought, word, deed and action of your being. The teacher has an identical carbon copy of you at all times in his presence, so that he may know how to administer, how to coach, according to your own attitude, or auric impression, at the time.

***Student:* Acumana, is there a certain time when one gets a universal name? Would I have one?**

Yes. Each life earns for you a portion of your eternal name and at the completion, when you have learned the lessons, all the many lessons of physical density, when you have paid back all your thievery to the world, and you no longer need to incarnate, you may then wear an eternal name, a soul name, throughout all existence.

***Student:* Acumana, would you explain the distinction between what the spirit is and the soul is?**

God breathed upon man as man was being born. God's breath is the "Holy Ghost." That breath of God is the Holy Ghost. The Holy Ghost is incorporated into the individualized consciousness, and that then is the spirit of the man. The spirit, nebulous in form, then incorporates into form as the soul of man. The soul then is the container of the spirit and the Holy Ghost, which is the breath of God.

So you have the Holy Ghost, which is the breath of God, the spirit which is the individualized breath of God, and you have the soul, the container of the spirit. Then the soul becomes incorporated into the physical human third-dimensional self at birth, and you have what is called the personality.

***Student:* Why do they call it "ghost"?**

It is just a word, perhaps a wrong translation, for it is really the Holy Spirit, the breath of God.

God's breath creates your breath, which is the spirit. The spirit of God creates you through breath, through speaking the word of creation through the breath. For how can the word be spoken without breath? The soul is the container, like the cup which contains the water, and is thus individualized. You go into your cupboard and reach upon your shelf and take out cups and place them in a row and say, these are the souls. Then you fill the cups with water from the faucet, the water then is the spirit for each individual soul. From whence did the water come? It came from the Source. The faucet is representative of the channel from the Source. The Source is that unknown indefinable place.

Can you tell Acumana specifically where each cup of water came from? You perhaps could if you would go and search, but in reality you know not that total source of water which comes from the faucet. It may come from the mountain stream, it may come from underground streams. You know not, but you know there is a source. The source springs forth with that water into that vessel called the cup. It is the same with man.

***Student:* I would like to know a little more about transmutation. I have been working with it and thought I could do it better.**

Let us simply say this: If, for example, you have a condition of anxiety and you wish to mentally transmute that condition, what is the opposite of anxiety? You know you are anxious, so say to yourself, "What is the opposite of what I feel?" You say, "This is what I shall concentrate upon." And you set out consciously to concentrate upon the opposite of that negative emotion which you are feeling. You transmute it by consciously directing yourself to the opposite, to being peaceful. It will never work if you keep going back and forth and saying, "I cannot be peaceful when I am anxious." You must, first of all, imagine that anxiety is here, and peace is there. And you see yourself like a thermometer rising upward to peace. Imagine it happening. Then assume all the things which peace will bring. Assume the attitude. Assume that thing you are anxious about is now peaceful and that, therefore, all its aura is peaceful. Feel the peaceful effect that it has upon you, that all is well and good. Visualize it and imagine it as being that way to such an extent that you actually believe it so. Mesmerize yourself. Transmute the condition out of existence. Redirect your whole nature, your whole being, to the opposite of that which you are working on.

To transmute thought, first you must find the opposite. For instance, the opposite of envy would be charity. So every time you have a thought of envy, transmute that thought, through mental discipline, to charity. Daily, moment by moment, substitute that thought of envy with a thought of charity. Change each negative thought as it comes. You know your thoughts. Only you are the guardian, only you know your being. If you have a feeling of anxiety or fear, hatred, greed, lust, whatever feeling on the bottom of the scale, substitute it immediately for its opposite.

Each thought that you project has a reaction on something in the universe. Some degree of matter is affected by your thought, whatever it may be. If it is on the opposite end of the pole or the negative, then that negative thought will have a negative effect on matter. You will learn that the matter that it affects is you! It is your universe that it affects, not the outer universe. So each thought that you project affects your universe because your spirit has projected it. Your will willed it. Therefore, it is important to transmute thoughts through mental discipline to rise above these conditions.

Student: **I have been dealing with an inner conflict and I would like clarity on where these inner conflicts come from, whether they are self-created out of another life. In this particular case it**

happens to be an extreme case of fear, unfounded fear of something that I can't even identify.

Now, the first thing to remember is this. Whenever there is restlessness there are many ramifications externalized which all are offshoots of internal restlessness. Your spirit, your higher self, desires creativity, expression, expansion, and progress. However, the world you are presently living and motivating in is limiting and confining in more ways than are apparent. Your restlessness begins to build up like a great volcano within and it must have an avenue of escape. All the seeming avenues of escape are frustrated, for they are never completed. You attack one area and are met with defeat because of conflict. You approach another avenue of expression, and it is defeated temporarily, because of conflict.

Now, understand, conflict meaning because of conditions. When this conflict and frustration begin to build internally within the subconscious mind, it needs a means of expression, and oftentimes it takes many directions. In this particular case, one direction is fear. Fear is an avenue of escape, for it re-directs the creative energy, only in the opposite direction, into non-creative, non-productive energies. In this way it becomes fatiguing to you. You are overwhelmed with constant fatigue because of the worry of fear, the worry of anxiety, the worry of things which are non-existent. It is the re-directing of the creative spirit within, not negative, but a different direction of non-productivity. Also, you are not fully centered within yourself. You are not fully centered within your inner light. You have allowed it to become dull by workaday frustration. It all has a chain reaction.

When frustration sets in, non-productivity, the inner light becomes dull, the guard goes down, the wall is dropped, and the mundane forces of the world around you penetrate the aura more easily. Like a wave band on a shortwave radio, you pick up many frequencies, and they are transmuted mentally, subconsciously, into all forms of fear and non-productivity.

You must realign yourself, reaffirm yourself. You must become so positive, so strong, in your inward conviction, that nothing will deter you from the creative urge. This creative urge must be handled with peace, poise and confidence, not with force and brutality, but with quiet determination. Patiently, patiently, handling every situation and detail with a total lack of emotional attachment to whatever the condition is. One major lesson that you are learning is the balance of emotion.

This can be handled with patience. Patience, remember, represents the fine needlepoint that holds the world in balance. Imagine that on the point of the needle rests the mighty world. What holds the world in balance on the point of the needle? Two things, law and balance. These two things are synonymous, and are in harmony with patience, quiet faith and determination.

Each time impatience builds up the Earth sinks a little heavier on the needle, and it pierces the surface and cuts. If it is not handled adequately, eventually the Earth will settle down entirely upon the needle and it shall be very deep within the flesh to hurt and wound later.

The moment the guard is down, then the mind—the mind of the Earth being the conditioned mind—relates itself to all forms of material thoughts. Fear is the primary thought which attaches itself to the mundane plane, fear of loss in any dimension. However, spirit can never be destroyed, and all those things to which your spirit belongs are protected by that great impenetrable light of protection, providing the guard is kept at all times envisioned.

> ***Student:* Well, that is the thing that concerns me, because I know that by permitting that state to exist that I let the guard down.**

You allow it to happen by thinking and dwelling upon it. You must re-channel your mind, redirect your mind.

> ***Student:* I've tried to do this but I've found that it approaches at unexpected times and usually in the depths of the night when I'm not in the position or I don't put myself in the position . . .**

You are not resting, you are not relaxed. You have not released the self. You are in the astral area, therefore, you awaken unrested, just as fatigued as when you retired. This is up to you to handle. No teacher can help you to handle that situation. Each one, in his own way, must master his mind and handle it the best way he can.

***Student:* How does one stay centered?**

Only one way—by turning to the Father, turning to God. Prayer centers. Enter into the temple of your own heart and say a prayer to your heavenly Father for guidance, for Light. Learn to pray. Learn to meditate. It is not possible to take from one who is centered, for when you are centered you are one with the All.

The only way this centering of your being can come about is from your own effort. It means that you of the human sense and you of your soul are at one, at peace. That is centered. All of the chakras are spinning in balance, and the rod of Light is going from your whole being up to your soul being. How can anyone give that to another person? He cannot. He can only give it unto himself through the practice of prayer, meditation and understanding.

Be not concerned with worries of the day. Become selfless. For those in Light must cease to think of themselves as individuals but as spokes within the wheel to help the strength of the wheel as it turns. If each spoke were aware that he is a spoke working together with the others and would say, "Well, I desire my own wheel," and he would leave, the whole wheel would be weakened, yes? Cease to think of others as orthodox or that they are creating a hindrance, for there is good in all things.

Even out of darkness comes good. It is only a matter of clarity of understanding. Those in the realms of freedom—your teachers, the Masters, and the Lords—understand the law of polarity. They recognize that all things are in balance. They live and dwell in the center of the law of polarity. You must come to understand the relationship of these poles.

Help others through your prayer, that they unite. Help each person to reunite himself with his faith, his belief. As to those who have no faith or belief, try to bring them to a point of understanding the laws and principles. If they cannot understand God or do not believe in God, they can at least believe in nature. Then have them believe in nature, for nature is God as well.

Now, students of Light, go about your daily work gently. Do not attack it like an army. Conquer it through love, patience and understanding. Do not attack and chastise yourselves, for the moment you criticize your own nature you criticize your Father and your Father is perfect in you as He is perfect in every man. Perhaps the faults you see in others are weaknesses within yourself that are made visual to you, which you have not seen because of your own lack of discernment. By correcting yourself, you correct your neighbor.

PRAYER

Prayer is a whisper.
Prayer is a thought.
To suddenly stop in the busy day and say,
"Oh yes, my Father and I are one.
How wonderful! How delightful!
I had forgotten!"
That is prayer.
And when you go into your profound prayer,
In humility you say,
"Yes, yes! My Father and I are one."
You look into the eyes of one who loves you,
And know God.
You look into the heart of a rose,
And know God.
This is prayer.

CHAPTER XI

The Law of Consequence and Rebirth

Now let us speak for a moment of the law of consequence and rebirth. The Lord Jesus taught His disciples rebirth. This is in your own Scripture, even though in early times Scripture was changed to hide the law. This is also called the Law of Karma.

In the time of the Lord, when He was working and traveling about the land with His disciples, He often referred to the reality of the many lives, or the one life being expressed in the many lives, the many incarnations. For the word *incarnation* simply means a repetition of the life of the same soul in many expressions. He often referred to this and said unto His disciples, "It is this or it is that which this man has done in the past which has caused him to have this condition." And then the Lord would heal the condition, thus bringing the person into freedom, forgiving him of his karmic obligation. When the Lord was thus traveling with His disciples there was much controversy about this. Sometimes it would come to the attention of the disciples that He was being called someone who had been in existence before.

One of the disciples said, "Lord, it is said that you are Elijah. Is it true?" And the Lord said, "Who has said this?" And then He said, "Who say you that I am?" They said, "You are the Son of the living God, and it matters not who you were before, or if you were any of these who have gone before."

So the controversy about who the Lord was before was never settled, Biblically or otherwise. There have been speculations among contemporary men, scholars, that the Lord was the Buddha reborn. There are many speculations. So this cannot be handled as a text without great controversy.

The disciples said unto their master, unto the Lord, when He was healing a blind man, "Who sinned? Did this man sin that he is blind, or did his parents or other ancestors sin?" And the Lord said, "Neither sinned, but this man is blind that the glory of God may be demonstrated." What did this mean? It meant that this man's blindness was placed in the way of the Lord that He may demonstrate the great power of God as manifest through Him.

So you might say that the blind man appeared to give service to the Lord so that he may be a perfect demonstration of the inflow of the power of God for the healing. There was no consequence involved. He gave a service. He martyred himself to be blind long enough for the Christ to heal him. And in so doing he stepped up his own evolution.

Everything that exists upon the Earth is not necessarily explained away through the law of consequence. For instance, man may become a great soul of Light and come into a dark jungle area in order to serve a whole tribe of people. He may be hundreds of degrees ahead of those people. He does not do that because he is being punished, he comes to give a service.

***Student:* Why are so many kingdoms scattered throughout the universe, and what determines whether one goes to this kingdom or to another?**

Let us take for example, a cylinder, and fill the cylinder with small pearls, and each pearl in the cylinder, let us say, represents a conscious life as a part of God. They are all in a cylinder like a cone, a funnel, and at the bottom is an opening. This cone is suspended in the universe and is spinning. It is creating. And now the hole opens up and all these pearls drop down into space. They drift and they scatter. Why do some drift here and some there and all about? Why do they not fall altogether? Why does the law of attraction work differently upon all these units which are the same? They are the same in appearance, the same in size, the same in shape, but they are not precisely identical in every respect. Inwardly they are endowed with the same potential. They have come from the same origin. They always were as all others always were. Would that not make them the same? No.

The Law of Attraction attracts the individual consciousness according to that individuality. If, for example, a pearl of consciousness is attracted in one direction, there must be within its makeup the component parts which are magnetically attracted to only this direction and none other. Now, when from the great funnel of creativity all the seeds are scattered in the universe, the law of consequence, of birth and rebirth, begins.

The Father has but one life, it is taught. This one life is made up and composed of hundreds upon thousands, millions of lives, but it is one life. The one life is expressed in millions of accumulated lives. Each life, as a conscious part of God, is to learn one thing, awareness, so that it may consciously stand forth and say, "Yes, I and my Father are one."

It is the difference between emotionally saying, "I love God," and intellectually saying, "I am one with God." There is a vast difference, for the emotion knows and responds by instinct, intuition and desire, whereas the intellect and the awareness does not respond by emotion but by conscious understanding of that principle.

That is the goal of each of those pearls of consciousness, that they may stand forth and consciously proclaim their Godhood, their heritage. In the process of acclaiming his heritage on the road, there are placed on man burdens, many hurdles, to tempt and to deter him. There is one direction to go, one clear, straight path, but as you progress it is like going through a maze. Before you can arrive at the end you must explore the entire maze, for every avenue is also a part of the whole. And when it is completed and the Godhood is recognized, back it goes into the funnel once more.

However now it is grown in size. It is no longer a small pearl but a large pearl. The pearl was seed-like, now it is a large pearl. It is then refunneled back through the All once again, and it drops now as a mighty lord or a mighty god into a different universe, into a different set of conditions far above in consciousness from its earlier day.

Now its second day begins, and the second day is the day of godhood where that great pearl now becomes a god in the universe, and it is attracted, by the same principle of attraction as before, to the area of the universe where it will serve. As a God-state there are many burdens placed upon its consciousness to be overcome, just as the burdens upon the Earth must be overcome by the Lord of the Earth, for He is responsible. And just as the Lord of the Earth and the Lords of all the other planets are responsible, the One God is responsible for all of the planets in Its domain.

There are endless cycles in the God-state. When each cycle is complete, the pearl of God-realized consciousness becomes greater and mightier, and it also reunites into the All. So when once more it emerges into the mighty All, greater and vaster becomes the power.

You may say to yourselves, "But what is the ultimate? What is the infinite? What is the end? How much further do I go?"

No one knows, not the mightiest god, the highest lord, the greatest logi, for in this great universe of our Father the end has never been reached, nor can it ever be reached. But this you may know—you will complete and you will end the struggle, problems and difficulties of this plane and all of its lessons, only when you cling to service, education and self-betterment in all avenues.

When you have each on the inner plane, consciously, in full recognition, declared yourself eligible for discipleship, available for service, your life will completely change. Above all, when you have denied and given up self and have said to the powers-that-be, "May each of my lives hence forward be devoted to the betterment of mankind, not the self," a whole new dimension will open to you.

Throughout your successive incarnations and their consequences, the self is set aside and you shall continue to motivate always in all areas of esoteric teachings. You shall have struggles, yes, but you will be fully entrenched upon the path. This means SERVICE FIRST, SELF LAST.

That is the key—Service First, Self Last. This is the motivating power in the coming incarnations. For the service is well plotted, the chart is well laid out. You may trace throughout all of your lives, even now to your earliest memory, and you will find that somehow, some way, you served. However, you may at any time consciously say, "Close the door. I do not desire to serve any longer." That is up to you.

It is advisable that you now build strong steps to your temple by your daily devotion, your daily study and your daily giving over to those states of mind which wait patiently for you to come and capture them. *It is the state of mind that is important.* When that is mastered everything else will fall into place.

All things parallel, all things repeat. This present life you have is a repetition of your past life, only it is progressed a notch higher; nevertheless, it is a repetition. It is what you would call, musically, a variation on the same theme. There are key points or highlights from life to life which parallel each other. There are peaks, and those peaks are predominantly the same in time, ratio and condition from life to life.

Man arrives at a position in life where he can look around himself and say, "What have I accomplished?" And when he finds what he has accomplished, it is manifest in what would appear to be the smallest of ways, the most insignificant, the most anonymous. And those small things, to the man who has earned his place in the universe, are the greatest and the most important. In all of your searchings in life, the greatest wisdoms, the greatest Truths, the greatest problems to be solved in the world of man and science, are the simplest, most uncomplex of all things. Man is so busy being lost in equations, in evaluations, in reasoning, in emotion, in philosophizing, that he misses the one basic value of all things—simplicity.

Always seek simplicity. The greatest simplicity is silence. How else can one learn in meditation, unless through silence?

Before the perfect temple, the perfect mind, and the perfect body may be manifest and maintained, the approach toward life must be made more harmonious. It is one more asset besides the mental, spiritual, and physical. It is the quietude, the quietude of quiescence. It is where the mind, the body, and the soul remain at a state of quiescence. This quiescence is missed by many students upon the path. Those who study, who desire to improve themselves spiritually, often do not approach the wisdoms with the quiescence of mind which brings one ultimately to the point of selflessness.

How do you practice quiescence? True quiescence is where, through disciplined, harmonic breath control, you relax the entire physical body and mental body, wherein your mind has ceased to be active. There ceases to be an abstract thought and there ceases to be a physical thought to move you. Your mind must become, as it were, blank, void, an abyss, but this abyss must be an endless, harmonious, warm-flowing stream of peace. It is in this abyss, this peace, in this quiescence, that one reaches a state of spiritual being.

You have within you the capacity for this. You have the mental approach to discipline your body and your mind. Try to sustain this experience through a fifteen-minute cycle twice a day. Let the world be shut away from you. Above all, it is absolutely paramount that you bring into your chamber not one thought or disturbance of your physical condition. When you enter your chamber of meditation, affirm at the threshold that you leave your physical condition outside of yourself. As you enter the temple for prayer, enter saying, "I am a pure channel of wisdom and harmony in the universe, therefore, all things within me are in harmony and peace."

No matter how your body may ache or how severe a pain you may have, you must cease to recognize this as a physical condition. Simply state that within your universe there exists a conflict, and by bringing your vortex of spirituality to the Father in prayer this disturbance or conflict shall be appeased and shall be set at rest. That, then, is the perfect preparation for your prayer and meditation.

In meditation, recline and begin to breathe slowly and deeply. Prolong the breath, control the breath. Be the master of the beat of your heart and the intake of your air into your lungs. Become conscious of your breath. Breathe like a great respirator, slowly and rhythmatically, and as each breath is drawn into your body, hold it for a second or so. As you are holding it, envision before you a brilliant light, emanating and radiating from your solar plexus, your center of atunement for that purpose, to stimulate the solar plexus, and to stimulate all the other chakras.

The teachers have what is called "a mirror of reflection." It is comparable to your television or cinematic screen and can be attuned according to each student's vibration, to his image. This image is, in turn, reflected upon the screen in full auric color and dimension, so that teachers are able to study every degree of progress in the student's nature. They are able to study every center and every organ of the body.

The first thing is to enter the quiescence. Do not strive consciously to produce positive thoughts, for when you attempt to produce a positive thought by eliminating the negative thought, often you reproduce negativity. That is, if you have thought negatively of an individual and then you say, "I will now think positively. I love her, love him, love the condition, even though it was rotten," the negative still remains.

It is difficult to release, so by using will force to eliminate the condition you merely push it back, and back it comes into your aura again. So the first thing is to cease to have a conscious thought of any condition.

First cease to have a conscious thought of your body. It is restful. It settles down, becomes quiet. That is the primary thought. Your condition matters not. If you have fifteen severe pains per day, what, in the infinite sense, does it matter? True, on the physical plane it is most disconcerting. True, on the physical plane you have to contend with this. And yet, if this exists on the physical plane, is it not true that on the spiritual plane you have the same soul power to transmute the physical disturbance and to arrive at the inner state of mind where you say, "What does it matter, for if our Lord could walk the way of the cross bearing a burden of great weight, so can I."

Think of His pain, and you may be sure your own pain will cease to mean a thing to you. In the quiescence you will state this fact, "It matters not." By the controlling of your breathing, consciously, you will ease from your mind all external thoughts. If the doorbell should chime, if the telephone should ring, it should not concern you. Day by day discipline your mind, your body, and your soul to enter the quiescence. Do not merely lie down, say the Lord's Prayer, and drift off to sleep. That is not enough.

Cease to think. Enter into the great stillness of the universe, wherein the Empyrean choir sings its hymn of universal peace, wherein the great harps of wisdom vibrate their strands of music throughout your whole soul system. Every cell, every atom of your body, shall be quickened by the vibratory communion, the great symphony of music in the silence, and the peace and the Light which is beyond comprehension. Every speck of energy within you, your whole fortress of energy, shall revolve and rotate at great rapid speed, and the light of the candles of your chakras shall glow brightly on the altar of your temple. And when you once more emerge into consciousness you will be filled with greater power, greater determination, greater strength, than you have yet experienced in all the years of your physical breath.

These things which are given to you are not beyond your depth of understanding. These things are so. They wait for you. You must ask. You must do. For all things in the universe require work. There is nothing idle, there is nothing still. There is only activity, and the greatest activity of the physical dimension is prayer, or the quiescence. Though the body is in repose, the soul is active, and then the true self becomes dynamic and the body is rejuvenated.

Each day that you surrender your spirituality and give in to materiality, material thoughts, material desires, frustrations, anxieties, you surrender more and more of your greater universe. And each day, consequently, your body, your temple, your manifested movable vehicle, decays and becomes more and more confused. War shall break out in your body, just as war breaks out on Earth, the physical planet. You read daily of uprisings, of confusions, of small revolutions. This is only the greater reflection of man's combined negativity. If each one upon the path would consciously enter the quiescence and cease to think, there would be less of this confusion.

Do fifteen minutes at mid-morning, and in the hours at night when the world is asleep, do it longer. Before you go into the quiescence bathe your body in pure water. Let the cleansing be a symbol. As the water flows upon the body, affirm that as the living waters of God pour upon this body, it washes away down the whirlpool, into the drain, all negative physical conditions and all negative conditions of the mind. When you enter the meditative chamber you enter in physical cleanness, mental purity and spiritual oneness. You enter like a babe to receive the milk from your Mother's breast, to receive the love from your Father's smile.

We understand the difficulty in the depths of density that you all live in. Yet, it must be, for how could you understand the other aspects of God unless you were shut off and sent to school without visible support. The angels are about you. They hear, they see, and they know. Your every thought is registered and understood.

Your teachers represent the cross, and you represent the crucifixion, for they take unto themselves what is called esoterically the soul rejuvenation of the individual. Each of you represents to the teachers the breath that is needed in your body. Each of you represent to the teachers the beat of the heart that your body needs to flow the blood through your universe.

If you suffer, your teacher suffers. If you have a need, your teacher knows your need, and if you suffer through that need, your teacher suffers with you. If you would not suffer, he would reach you. He would be able to impart to you and share with you the cosmic joys so that you would not suffer. However, your suffering and his suffering are far different in degree, You may suffer mental torture. Your teacher would not suffer mental torture; he would only suffer a pang that he did not fulfill his duty to the best of his capacity. To him it is like the sharp pierce of a needle through the heart of his soul. Then he resolves he must work harder, he must give more.

If you only knew, if you had any comprehension of the degree of power you each wield in your mind, you would cease this very second to think of anything other than God and positivity. If you knew the power you hold, the staff and the rod and the scepter of authority! For when you are upon the path, when you are in the Universal Brotherhood, when you are disciples, great is your responsibility, and it becomes multiplied day by day. Each day you learn a new lesson, each day you open your eyes and you say thank you to God. You become aware as the days drift away how little you know, how ignorant you really are in the face and the reality of the All. Yet you go on and on to absorb the All with the essence of your all-embracing nature.

CONTEMPLATION

Like the great sea at night,
When the breezes are calm
And the moon is golden
On the waves,
May I be.
For peace resides upon me,
And within me,
As I contemplate the sea.
In my moments
Of inner conflict,
May I imagine the depths of the sea,
At peace in the great light of the moon.
And may I be
Deep and powerful,
To resolve all conflict,
And create, of mine own,
The calm of the sea,
The great sea at night.

CHAPTER XII

Image and Likeness of God

You are told in your Scripture that God created man in His image and likeness, yet if you look all about you at all of the variety of the millions of people who populate your Earth, you will not see any two that are an exact image of each other. So how can they be in the image of God? How did God create man in His image and likeness?

Through mind. For God is mind. God is Universal, Cosmic Intelligence. And so, according to the story of creation, He endowed and imbued within every single individual that power of mind to use as he would.

When creation took place, God looked all about at all of His creations. He created this, created that, separated the waters from the land, created the fowl of the air. He saw that He had done all of these things, but something was yet to be created. So, God thought, and through that divine impulse of thought man was given that which God already had, the power to create through mind.

Now, how was this power used? In as many myriad ways as there were humans upon Earth. So the very first endowment which was given unto man was God's universal mind to use as he saw fit.

Man's creative power comes from his fine potentiality for using the gift which God gave him, the gift of mind. *The only way to create is through mind.* Through mind God created the whole cosmos, the complete universal system of your known universe, and systems beyond this system. Man in his own creative orbit through the power of mind is a replica of the mind of the Divine, but he has not yet awakened to his divine potentiality.

In order to awaken to this divine potentiality, he must first accept the gift which God gave him for creative productivity. He must look within his mind and realize, "Oh, it is through mind that I am made in the image and likeness of God. God created all the systems of the universe through His mind. I will create my own system, my own universe, through the power of mind." That is the only creative force which exists for man.

Name one thing in the world of humanity which did not first exist in the mind of an individual or a group of individuals. There is no such thing upon the face of the Earth. It does not exist. God created the systems. God created the Earth. God did this with mind. God endowed man with this power to use as a creative force himself. Acumana has already given techniques for using this mind.

First, contemplate the power of mind and say, "Oh, this is my gift! How am I using it? Am I using it to create a world for myself which I dislike? Am I using this power which is my gift to create a world which is to my liking?" Thus you examine the very world in which you live and decide upon what you wish it to be. Then you begin through the power of true conception to create your world the way you wish it to be.

This is man's creative power. This is the way in which he is made in the image and likeness of God. Man daily creates. In his body he can create destruction or he can create positivity.

Man must recognize that he has his own solar system. You can take any portion of the body or the brain and put it under a microscope and find that the atomic structure is a solar system unto itself. If man has created his solar system to be sickly, to be weak, to be dissipated, then that is his creation. If he has created his solar system, each and every aspect of his physical body, to be strong, capable and immortal, then that is his creation.

He creates this only through the power of mind. So if man has decided, whether consciously or unconsciously, to use his power to be a cripple, he will be a cripple. If he uses his creative power, which is the power of mind, to be an Olympic runner, then he will be an Olympic runner. It is entirely up to him to decide how he will use his power to create his vehicle.

Every diseased body which lies in any hospital was created that way, through the power of mind, or through the absence of the conscious use of the power of mind. Every mental ward throughout all of your institutions contains patients who have in some way misused the power of mind. In the universal scheme of things, those who have misused the power of mind can misuse it over and over again, throughout many lives, until they take it upon themselves to stop the misuse of this power and begin to use it correctly. At any given point the individual may stop the negative creation and create the perfected body for his eternal being.

Acumana now sees much need for students to ask questions. You may now ask before we proceed.

***Student:* Have we individually grown enough spiritually that we can rely on our own thoughts, on our own feelings, when we are completely unemotional about something?**

When you are unemotional, most assuredly, if you trust it.

***Student:* In other words, if we have thought out some things well and unemotionally, we can accept our decision?**

Do not be deceived by the thinking process. Do not let analytical reason kill the intuitive awareness. You must balance the two so that you are given the true answer. That is what you are growing for, to gain the balance within you. Reason will always give you theory, and theory is not proof.

This is what has happened to religion. The moment religion becomes organized, becomes analytical, it turns into theology, and then all the Truths are gone. Christianity has suffered this way. Judaism has suffered. The Buddhists have suffered. The Zoroastrians have suffered. The only ones who have not become theorized are the Truth seekers, because they are not organized. They are not gathering together in a mosque or in a temple. They are more universal in their concept.

Student: Do any of the churches have these Truths that you teach?

The Christian church is the most enlightened of all religions but it must be reborn. Ultimately there will be a gathering together for enlightenment, and what will bring this about will be science. Science will produce it. Philosophy and religion are becoming more and more allied over the last two hundred years. You will find that more highly evolved beings will take up scientific work. They will force science into the higher planes. Orthodox science will have to evolve. Religion and science must become one, for the salvation of the world.

Student: It has been said that everything in nature, whether alive or inert, has its own particular energy pattern. Do you agree with this, Acumana?

What you speak of is a rate of vibration, and all rates of vibration have an energy pattern in the ethers. For example, all gold has the same pattern. Water, pure water, has its same pattern. The base element is always the same.

With man there are different rates of vibration in their reactions to certain physical conditions. You may find some who have the same mental capacity but who are vastly different otherwise. How would one account for two people who have the same level of awareness to be totally different? Here again is individuality, soul awareness, spiritual depth. Like the snowflake, no two crystals ever have been or ever will be alike. Each man is individual, each mineral, each essence, each animal on the whole scale of physical phenomena has a different pattern according to its soul pattern in the universe.

Student: You have stressed the importance of shedding personality and opening ourselves entirely to Divine Will. We realize that this is the ultimate goal of all of us, but certainly it is not feasible or practical for those in our stages of evolution. We all have eons of

time to develop before we reach that stage of soul evolution, so why do you urge us to do it now when it is humanly impossible for us to do at our stage?

It is not humanly impossible. Let Acumana explain. From a technical, analytical point of view, it is so. But remember, when you are upon the path, when you have chosen service to humanity and more spiritual enlightenment, you have in proportion greater responsibilities to your soul growth.

Therefore, if each day you strive more and more consciously to learn the lessons allotted to you, greater becomes your spiritual growth and greater becomes your inner plane growth. There are very few who can reach the point in their present evolvement to be able to fully surrender personality. What they will be able to do is recognize desire and set desire aside, so that their personality becomes a universal personality, so that the ego (let us call this ego) does not scream out like a hawk in the night to hinder their spiritual growth.

In any cloistered order there are those upon the path who daily meditate to surrender personal pleasure, personal desire, personal ambition, and above all, personality. Perhaps from an analytical point of view they are esoterically not at a point in their evolvement to surrender. Yet they are disciplining themselves through prayer. They are taking upon themselves more balance, so when they arrive at the point of surrender it is as easy as taking off a coat. When one arrives at this point of surrender of personality it is not easy, unless you have been prepared upon the path long beforehand, as Acumana and other teachers have been preparing you. This is surrender of all the things you have worked and evolved up to that point.

From the very beginning your soul says, "I must perfect personality." Point by point it must ascend. Imagine the length of time consumed in the developing of all those lessons and growths only to arrive at a point where you must then say, "All this I have done. Now I must set it aside." It is not an easy task, which is why so few are there. By preparing today to eliminate desire and ego your personality becomes more expressive universally. Believe Acumana, it is a great accomplishment and the rewards are great.

***Student:* Are erroneous teachings and individual misinterpretations of basic Truths retained in the subconsciousness until they are replaced by the correct interpretations and understanding of basic Truths at some later date?**

Every individual expresses Truth according to his own level. However, if one expressing Truth according to his own personality level assists another in releasing that person from a condition and opens up his spiritual consciousness, then there is positive value. On the other hand, the same interpretations may create within others fear and doubt. If one tries to force others into their line of thinking, this is in error. Each soul must identify himself with a particular Truth according to his own soul awareness.

Your own nature, spiritual nature, because of where it is on the path, identifies itself either positively or negatively. It is such with most people, cut and dried, to accept Truth as they see, hear, and discern it. Eventually, when their soul consciousness opens like the Lotus, they are able to take in more Light and they will gravitate to the area of perfection closest to their level of consciousness.

***Student:* We know there are seven-year cycles in a person']s life. That seventh year is usually sort of an adjustment, but what determines whether there is a physical or a mental or some other type of adjustment in that seventh year?**

Herein is where astrology would assist. Your particular sign or planetary formation, and the power you are emanating and are attuned to determines the nature of whether there is a physical or a mental strength or weakness. However, know this, that as each cycle comes about the whole physical body is changed. Sometimes there is a completely new mental body. Sometimes there is a new emotional body.

***Student:* Then is that why in the seventh year some people seem to grow older or sort of deteriorate while other people seem to be much better after each seventh year cycle?**

The cause here is in the Law of Mentalism. The amount of mind power they are projecting upon their body and their life determines their amount of deterioration or progress. No one need deteriorate. It is up to the individual.

When you are in a seventh year cycle it is a very appropriate time to make certain physical changes in your patterns. For you will find all physical things within your nature working in balance to assist you. The aura changes too, at this time. Your whole universe within you is completely altered.

***Student:* Well, then, at the end of the astrological time, or birth date, one should sense either being very much better physically or spiritually, shouldn't they, or that something has gone wrong in that seven year cycle that still needs to be adjusted?**

Yes, they should, but often they are not able to discern it. Those who are attuned upon the path are often able to attune to that cycle, and their whole nature will change. However, you may go through the seventh cycle and come into the new one and still continue in the same old patterns of thought, feeling, desire, emotion, and motivation.

***Student:* On another subject, Acumana, if evidence of disease can be seen in the human aura, are we correct in assuming that the aura will reflect the disease before it is shown outwardly in the body through the characteristic physical symptoms and that the healing is first noticed in the aura before all the physical symptoms have disappeared?**

This is absolutely so. Let us consider for a moment the vital body, which is seen as the aura. This is the body where the physical nature is reflected. The two are as closely allied as your blood and your heart are. Each is distinctly different, but they are closely allied. The vital body, or the aura, within each one reveals first hand any physical condition that is beginning to develop. Even before the physical symptom is manifest, the vital body long since has manifested it. Through the law of mind the mental body inflicts the condition upon the physical counterpart.

When the mental body inflicts disease upon the physical body, then the vital body of your aura takes it on and reflects its perfect image. First you must treat the vital body before the physical body can be healed.

There is a law of balance, the first thing to be treated is the mind, the seed of the condition. That mental concept must be repolarized, redirected, to form a new mental body. When you have mentally analyzed (gone into yourself) and cleansed the mental body, then a link is formed between it and the vital body. When the vital body begins to heal, the aura reflects the healing, and, in turn, it is reflected upon the physical body, sustained and maintained by the mental body.

Student: **Can persons of gross material impulses and desires be readily recognized as such through their auras by those on the inner planes?**

Most definitely. Also with the aura there is sound. Often a teacher or a worker on the inner plane can discern such an individual long before he sees his soul light, for they hear the sound vibration emanating from them. If it is one of gross materialism, it has a shrieking, deafening sound of total disharmony and disunity, and it shatters the ethers around them. Color and sound are almost synonymous.

Ultimately you all strive for the perfect tone quality. You each have a soul tone and that soul tone resonates to every tone or vibration in your body. You have one soul tone. Each of the vital centers in your body, and each vital organ, has a sound value. If it is healthy it has one sound, if unhealthy, another sound. And if you are spiritually in tune with yourself, mentally and physically in alignment, the emanation which is heard is harmony.

If you are not in alignment with yourself, if your spirit has been suppressed, your chakras have been inverted and your whole nature is that of materialism, lust and licentiousness, the soul tone is muffled, stifled. Then the gross nature vibrates with a shrieking, deafening, shattering sound. You can see the etheric patterns around the aura like fine crystals shattered all the time. As the ethers and cosmic rays around the individual try to rebuild and form to feed the aura, they are constantly shattered by the emanation of negative sound.

When you are in perfection where your physical and spiritual bodies have become one, you will arrive at a tone of soul emanation and you will become a symphony. All those composers who write great works are attuned to the etheric wave of the soul. They are in resonance with universal sound, soul sound. What they are doing, in reality, is blending their harmony in sympathetic accord with universal harmony. It is like having in your possession a transmitting station which can plug into any frequency or any channel. What they hear in their mind and set down is the music of the ethers. They are hearing etheric soul sound. To combine universal sound takes almost mastery. For in universal sound there is also negative sound, the opposite, which is shattering. They have to combine the perfect balance of both. The great percussions crashing together are not negative and destructive, but are a shattering sound. Yet with the great percussion and cymbals together blended with the strings of the ethers, you have a harmony and a symphony of magnificence.

Student: **In what manner are the emotions of fear, hate, and love reflected in the aura? We know that they have different colors but, for instance, what color does hate assume in the aura?**

You will find that hate, lust and violence are all reflected in the aura in tones of red, deeper and darker in color according to the intensity. They are vital deeds and it is the vitality of the body which projects them. Love, kindness and affection start with the most pure pink and in perfection when there is universal love it blends into the royal purple, on and on into cosmic colors out of your spectrum.

Acumana will tell you how each of you, though not being able to read the aura yet, can intuitively perfect this awareness. You can read the aura of a person by the countenance of his face and his hands. This is an important key. There are three points upon the face and head of a person that any of you can observe which reflects the aura. The first is the brow. The second area is beneath the eyes, the circle around the eyes. And the third area is the mouth. You can tell materialism from spiritualism in these lines. Those who have more materialism, more desire, more hatred, more bitterness within them, will have many lines around the mouth, puckered lines, pulling lines, almost as if the whole face is pulled together.

Around the eyes you will find lines reflecting those who strive to see spiritual things but yet are always pulled by the sight of materialism. There is a constant struggle within them.

It is an inward struggle at all times to hold to the concepts of Truth. The forehead, according to the lines, the main contours and main shape, the amount of tension, will give indications of material frustration. With discernment and practice you can observe and intuitively sense the problem, according to the lines of contour in a person's face. Hands are equally revealing.

The hands, if they are short and stubby with many lines and much thickness, are the hands of materialism. The hand of a spiritual person does not become large and gross in shape. It may be small or it may be long, but it has grace in it.

If a person has a smooth brow and a serene face, it is usually a reflection of inner peace and a depth of spirituality within. They may not be fully aware of their own potential, but they are motivating peace and spirituality.

***Student:* How does intense fear reflect itself in the aura? What color does it manifest?**

Intense fear is not seen as one specific color. It is a pattern that is emanated. Fear sets out geometric patterns of a destructive nature from the aura. Oftentimes fear can be seen like darts emanating from the aura. If the aura is red at that particular time, the darts can be black. Sometimes they can be brown, sometimes dark green. It is seen as patterns from the heart of piercing intensity, like lightning, pointed darts.

***Student:* Are animals sensitive to that, and is that why they will sometimes attack a person who is fearful?**

If an animal's psychic body, vital body, which is very sensitive, is pierced by these projecting patterns in your aura, it may attack. It attacks that which it does not understand.

***Student:* Do the auras of animals vary with the individual animal as do those of the human?**

No. There are many species of animal and yet each individual within a species has the same aura, for they are of a group spirit. However, if an animal is sick, the aura will reflect the condition.

***Student:* That's why other animals will attack it sometimes, isn't it?**

Yes. And sometimes they will leave it, for they sense that it is sick. They see its aura. Also, they see your vital body, whereas you see the physical body. Each species of animal has a different aura, a different light, yet they are all under the guiding light of one group spirit. There is no right and wrong in the animal kingdom. For man to kill another is wrong. For an animal to kill a man is not wrong. They are not subject to the law of consequence, the law of cause and effect, as man is. That they must gain through their evolvement. This is why one should never chastise or severely criticize an animal. What he is doing is instinctive. You can, however, channel him and show him another way through love.

***Student:* I once was exposed to a machine that reflected color from the spoken word. Was that connected with the aura?**

Yes. Word is power, and it penetrates the ethers. Each word has an auric pattern, according to the intensity of the word. Soft words of love, kindness, gentleness, emanate warm, peaceful colors. Piercing words, hatred, lust, anti-words, emanate a dark aura and take on geometric patterns which are destructive in their nature. These emanations go through the ethers and attack the vital bodies of subjects. If you project a criticism, hatred, bitterness toward others, those words, which have a pattern of jaggedness, actually go through the ethers and attack the vital body of the recipient.

***Student:* What reaction does it have on the person himself?**

Eventually it builds strong mental karma. It comes back like the boomerang, in one lump sum.

Student: **Then, the same principle would hold true not only with the spoken word but with a thought, wouldn't it?**

It is so. But the thought is easier to control than the word, for the word carries an emotion. You may have the thought and then you can say, "It is in error of me to think this. I now bless this person." When you do this you have eradicated it. When you have the thought and you speak it and then say, "Oh, I was in error," it has already gone out. Then you have twice the amount of work to do to recall and dissolve that pattern in the ethers.

Student: **So if you've thought something and in the next second you realize it was an injustice and erroneous, you can neutralize it by your blessing of it?**

Yes. Send the opposite, and strive always, whenever you do this, to eliminate that condition within your nature which would cause you to think in such a way.

Student: **We've been told that just before death on the physical plane the aura disappears. Is that correct?**

It is so. The aura disappears a few hours before death.

Student: **We've also been told that a person who can see the aura can determine various physiological conditions, diseased conditions, in certain parts of the body through dark spots in the aura. Is this correct?**

Yes, each organ vibrates, and in its vibration it follows a pattern and an energy that can be measured. When it is distorted or malfunctioning, its rate of vibration, depending on the condition, is higher or lower, and it produces a different color. This, in turn, is reflected as a mirror-image in the aura. Those who have open sight can see in the aura the location and the condition. It is like a carbon copy.

***Student:* Is it true that the higher a person goes in soul evolution, the greater width the aura takes and the further it extends out?**

Yes. For example, Christ's aura spread in circumference around about Him in an area of a thousand yards or more.

***Student:* What does a golden color mean in the aura?**

That is holy, purity, such as the Christ aura. Oftentimes saints and the immaculate ones are depicted with a golden aura.

***Student:* What does the white aura mean?**

A white aura is equally as pure as the golden. White is the sum total of all the colors in perfect balance, perfect blending, when each light has returned to its source and become pure. The gold is also a pure state. Beyond that Acumana could not tell you the color, for there is no word in your English language to explain it. The great Ascended Masters all emanate a golden white aura. There are great bands of gold in it, and sometimes great bands of rose, blue, and purple. They can equally emanate all the prismatic colors in the spectrum as well as those colors which are outside of your spectrum.

***Student:* Can almost anyone who is fairly sensitive eventually train themselves to see auras?**

Oh, yes, you may see auras. If, for example, you focus your physical eye on the pineal gland or the center of the forehead of another and concentrate on that area without blinking your eyes as long as you possibly can, you will see shades of the aura outlined around the individual. It will give the illusion of being like a cut glass in an outline. You will see how far their aura extends. The more proficient you become, the more you concentrate and direct your attention over a period of time, the more you will cultivate the sense or the quality of the aura and also be able to discern the colors in the aura. Usually the first color perceived is green, which is of the Earth.

Everything is reflected in the aura. It is a perfect carbon copy of the whole physical, mental, emotional and spiritual nature of man. You can also tell in a higher capacity what a man has eaten for dinner in his aura. When you reach a point of great inner discernment you can even tell what the man has thought five minutes previously.

Your teachers, your masters, your enlightened ones who work with you, have your archetypal image. Do you understand the archetypal image?

***Student:* Yes. We've been told that it is on the left side of the head. Is that correct?**

Yes, it is so. Through your archetypal image your teachers have a carbon copy of you in their inner abode. There is a replica of you in auric form with your teacher at all times. With every beat of your heart the image changes. It changes its health aura, it changes its mental aura, and it changes its spiritual vibration.

***Student:* Can one look at a person and determine from his aura whether or not he is being possessed by a disincarnate soul?**

Oh, yes, most assuredly, for it is in the aura that they first attach themselves. Like a viper they attach and hold on and they begin to suck vital force from it. But the aura is in a weakened condition to begin with or they could not enter it.

***Student:* Aren't the etheric bodies weakened through excessive drinking or eating or other excessive outlets?**

Through weaknesses of any capacity, yes, the auric nature becomes weakened. The aura is a deep, deep study. It is little understood by many, and those who do understand it guard their knowledge. We will go into the unfoldment of the aura from an inner esoteric point of view. You will see how it fits into the universal scheme of evolution. Even your Earth has an aura, and the other planets in your solar system have auras and etheric bodies. Everything in nature has an aura. Anything in the universe that vibrates has an aura. That vibration is its aura. Man will one day be able to measure the vibration of the aura, and he will also be able to measure each of the vibrations of the seven spiritual bodies.

***Student:* Acumana, tell us something of the soul note.**

When Acumana long ago was a student, Acumana would run to the teacher and would oftentimes speak out of turn. Then Acumana learned the art of speaking only when being addressed. Acumana learned that what one believes is not established in the communion of words but rather the idea behind what one believes. So, it is very important to have resonance or tonality in the communion of words. When you speak, you set forth a vibration, a tone. That is your soul tone.

Your soul tone is in the resonance of all your words, the sound that you emanate, be it, "Good morning, good evening, how are you?" Whatever one says, be it useful or useless, the sound alone is important, not so much the words. For even in the incoherent babblings of a maniac there is great Truth, great depth. There is a part of the brain which receives the sound waves, the vibrations. Each of the vibrations, if you have a graph, has ups and downs. They have long and short and sometimes they have twisting movements like serpents.

Now, carried on that image is an idea, and that idea takes symbolic form and is registered in the brain through the membrane of the ear. And the place it goes to is the part of the brain which instantaneously receives what you are saying, whether it is emotional, intellectual, or whatever the image behind the sound is. So the brain has a great capacity to understand.

When you hear something which is emotional, the brain automatically understands this is emotional. And it is through the intuitional faculties that the interpretation of emotion is arrived at, so that one can say, "Therein is one who is caught in an emotional fever." If what one says is very cold, analytical and intellectual, devoid of emotions, then automatically the intuitional processes within your brain interpret and send to your conscious mind the complete analyzation that this is cold, calculating intellectualism.

You do not necessarily have to hear sound in order to interpret a man's level of understanding. A person's whole countenance, his whole deportment in life, gives off an auric vibration in two capacities. There is the auric emanation that is the light and then there is the auric vibration. The two are different but alike. The auric emanation is the light and the greater the person's capacity, the greater the auric light, the emanation. The auric vibration is something different. The auric vibration is what you feel in the presence of another. Emanations and vibrations are similar but different.

In the fine etheric structure of man's aura there are membranes. There is a membrane body around and about you and that membrane body is the intelligence of your aura. These sensitive membranes are like fine film. It is different than the intellect of your mind. The aura has an intelligence and that intelligence has the capacity to receive or reject vibrations which are helpful or alien to the well-being of your overall existence.

The membrane which is the intelligence of your aura is a living essence all of its own. It begins to form when you are approximately seven years old. Its intelligence begins to function at that time. It is a shell around you in the womb and is born with you. And that shell in the womb receives or repels and protects the living embryo.

Esoterically or mystically, the invisible shell begins to grow upon birth so that instinct alone, survival alone, protects the infant. That is, when the infant is stung by a mosquito or irritation comes to the body, the body begins to break out because the membrane has not become strong enough yet. That is why infants oftentimes are prone to all kinds of strange maladies of the skin and of the atmosphere. The membrane of their aura has not yet developed. It takes the first seven years for it to be developed.

Now, when you are in the presence of someone very negative, very hateful, very downtrodden, you feel this presence. And it can pull you down. You do not even have to see their face, you can feel it in the whole room. That is the membrane of your aura, that is the intelligence of your aura directing to your spiritual centers knowledge, awareness, insight. And if you are aware enough, you can determine what it is about the person that is disturbing to your own well-being. Sometimes you must leave the room right away.

With people who are physically oriented, that is, their physical senses are predominant, as in an alcoholic, or those who are addicted through a narcotic form of sensuality, the membrane becomes clouded over. The membrane does not function adequately. Physically oriented people, people of licentious living, gratification of the senses, who give forth great emotionalism, shatter this membrane. They destroy it, like alcohol destroys the physical brain. Giving in to their weakness destroys the tissue's structure. And they, in turn, feel no such sensitivity about another person.

In the spiritual development of mankind, if he is developing his inward capacities of self-awareness, as well as trying to maintain and balance his outer life in the world of chaos, he will begin to develop a finer body. So understanding this membrane is very important. All of you have the capacity of building this membrane but not all of you develop the capacity. It is developed up to the age of seven. Then if it is not cultivated properly by parental influence, by schooling, by habits, by karma, or growth, by the time one is twenty-seven years old that membrane begins to become perforated. The perforation indicates leakage wherein external influences of a mundane level begin to seep through the perforation. It is like a great screen, it cannot hold water, and what leaks through becomes an outside stimulation. The intelligence of the aura cannot distinguish or disseminate intuition from logic and reason. It cannot disseminate reality with illusion. Therein is the biggest trap—illusion and reality.

So what happens is through these perforations the lesions begin to welt. The lesions are cultivated and find a resting place because the membrane of the outer aura has become perforated by external conditioning. This is brought about by free will within mankind. First of all, to be emotionally involved in anything, you must give permission to yourself to be emotionally involved. For example, if you are prone to fly off the handle because you do not have your way, whether this is karmic or voluntary, you have to give yourself permission to do it. Then in the very beginning when this weakness indicates itself a perforation begins in the outer aura.

If you begin to explore the avenues of sensation, to find escapism through sensations, you give yourself permission for this and a perforation in the outer aura develops. Eventually this fine tissue membrane, which surrounds your outer aura and emanation, becomes so perforated through distortion that all of the mundane influences, like water through the screen, seep through to your consciousness and they distort your true picture of reality. One imagines a tree to be a house. One imagines a castle on the beach to be one's home. One imagines the presence of another to be the presence of God. This outer membrane which Acumana speaks of has other names in other languages. It is misunderstood by many and often not even acknowledged.

Esoteric growth brings what you might call grafting together. You endeavor to labor consciously, to patch up the perforations in the membrane of your outer aura to prevent Caesar's legions from possessing your being.

Some people are born with certain karmic tendencies which make for a stronger development of this membrane around and about them. This is an indication that many consecutive lives have been geared toward conscious perfection of their vehicle. Those who have not consciously perfected their vehicle do not have as strong an outer membrane. There are many perforations yet, which before this life is over, one hopes can be blended together. The esoteric growth process is like grafting.

In order to graft, you must take something from one place and put it in another place. The grafting symbolically represents the labels you take from your mind through your intuition and apply in life to patch up the perforations. It is a perfect balance of skill. In other words, in the early life, when man is running like a carefree child in the fields of life, he permits himself all kinds of promiscuous thinking and living. He is thus perforating the membrane of his outer aura. Later on in life he must go back and consciously labor with his intellect to develop his mind. He must labor to graft over these perforations. Many do not do this at all from life to life. They simply add more perforations upon those already existing.

So those who are on the path of inner development are in the process of building and rebuilding their outer vehicle so that they may have a stronger contact with their spiritual self, their soul self. This comes about through the development of one's inner life.

Student: **Acumana, you have indicated in the past that we come into the physical plane for a given period of time in each incarnation. If this is so, then obviously it is futile to pray for release to**

the inner planes when sickness, pain or incurable maladies afflict the body. Is this not so?

Not fully. You have a certain given period of time; yes, however, according to your freedom of choice, and according to your application, that time is lengthened or shortened. If, for example, you walk outside and deliberately fall down a hill and injure yourself, you shorten your days. This does not mean it is written that you must walk down the hill, trip on purpose, and shorten your days. It is always beneficial to pray, but it is better to pray for renewed life than to pray for release.

Student: **Suppose someone had an incurable cancer and he was in terrible pain. Suppose his allotted time accorded before he came into this incarnation was not going to be up for two more years, so he would have a long prolonged two-year period of pain. Could he pray for release to shorten the time of his transition?**

No.

Student: **He has to suffer?**

He must pray that as long as he remains, according to the will of the Father, whatever the time may be, he will serve. He must not pray for release, for to pray for release is to deny your physical existence, and if you deny your physical existence you deny the manifestation of creativity.

The power which emanates within the individual knows how and when to release, and it will be done according to Divine Law. It is fine to pray that he not have suffering, that the degree of suffering be lessened. Always continue to pray for healing, for that continuous prayer for healing has a calming effect upon the soul. But never pray for release.

Student: **Acumana, does cremation facilitate the complete severance of the psychic cord?**

After seventy-two hours of complete silence, yes. The shell must be placed in a room of complete silence for seventy-two hours to allow the spiritual bodies to leave according to their own time. Then cremation eliminates any possibility of any degree of attachment to the Earth plane.

***Student:* Then it is desirable to have cremation?**

Yes, it is so. Yet this is a choice.

***Student:* Does cremation cause too much of a shock to the soul?**

Only if it has been done before the seventy-two hour period.

***Student:* How may we help someone who is ill through prayer?**

Conjure up in Christ-Light the perfect image of the one in need. With your soul power, as you pray, extend your hands and envision the figure in need before you. With your eyes closed to conserve your energy and power, imagine waves of healing energy streaming forth from your fingers and directed to the one in need. See those waves covering the body, soothing the body, and going by the very law of attraction to whatever the condition is and correcting it. Try this. It is called absent magnetic healing.

***Student:* I wish I could direct some of that power to my own decrepit carcass.**

First there must be mental transmutation, and when the mental transmutation is complete you will no longer say, "I wish I could direct it to my decrepit carcass," for when you say "my decrepit carcass" you have written a commandment. Your own soul power has said, "My body is decrepit." By the spiritual and mental laws of your being you must arrive at a point where self-criticism, condemnation or critical destruction of the body is completely eliminated. It can be done. You have the power. It is just reconditioning. The minds of even great men sometimes become lax in some things. You are not yet masters but daily you grow toward that Light. Daily each one must have a little more mastery over his own being.

It is not beyond the realm of possibility for you to live to be two hundred or three hundred years of age, but it means altering your entire life mentally, physically, and spiritually. There is no reason for a man to make his transition at such an early time. The ancients lived for many, many years.

How old do you think Moses was? He was between six hundred and seven hundred years of age. The accurate number is vague. Renewing the physical body is a challenge. If you aspire toward it you must daily live the concepts of Truth. Forget yourself and be in service, and before you know it much time will have gone by and you will find you have lived a long while.

If each student is sincere in his meditation and asks of the Infinite forgiveness for the weaknesses within himself and tries daily to strive to eliminate those weaknesses, many things are possible.

Any condition within your own consciousness which is an enemy or a foreign agent to your development of higher consciousness can be alleviated if you ask. For what does your Scripture say? "Ask. Knock." Ask your teachers and the Hierarchy to assist you, to lend their power to your power.

Forgiveness is only a word which means to *transcend from.*

Peace now be unto you. May the golden radiance of Christ Light and wisdom enfold you. In its broad arms of peace, may the blanket of warmth protect you in the chill of the night. Like the great mother of all wisdom, God shall enfold you in His heart, for you shall know that you are not motherless and you are not fatherless in the great universe of all things. You shall return to your home, the Father, in peace and counsel.

SANDALS

My feet
Housed in sandals
Carry me forward
Toward the Light.
My sandals,
Symbols of progress,
Symbols of ascension,
Walk with surefootedness,
Up the great mountain
Of awareness,
Of wisdom and light.
I thank Thee,
Oh, my Father,
For my feet,
Housed in sandals,
Carrying me forward
Toward the Light.

CHAPTER XIII

Esoteric Healing

Acumana now will give you a lesson of esoteric healing. The purpose shall be to unfold within your own soul consciousness the great power for healing, transmutation of all conditions, mental and physical, thereby enabling you as a disciple and initiate upon the path to proceed through life with purpose and a mission.

We want each one to be a brighter light. Each one must hold in his hand a candle, and as you progress down the avenues of evolvement you shall be likened unto Liberty carrying your torch. You, the Olympian runners, shall light the way for others to follow. All those who are in thirst, in hunger, and who are without clothing, spiritual clothing, will find consolence in the radiance of your spiritual light. Before this becomes possible there are certain disciplinary processes that must be unfolded which are latent in the individual. It is the purpose here to unfold and unleash spiritual, cosmic radiation within you.

You will reach a point as we proceed in your silence and meditation where a state of self-success is completely realized by your consciousness. As we unfold the teachings we shall unleash the Divine Mind concept within each, that you may become healers by the projection of Divine Mind.

Before we proceed, bear these points in mind. It is essential in a meditative state that the body be placed in complete repose. Become so calm within your physical nature that you are unconscious of the physical body.

Each limb becomes devoid of attachment to your mind. Sit in the most comfortable position for this purpose. Thus you proceed into the silence.

Before we go to the healing of world conditions, first learn how to treat someone near to you. State in your mind the condition and name the recipient, the person you desire to work with. Above all it is important that you contemplate only the positive aspects of your recipient for the divine healing. Healing is of the mind, body and soul, not just the physical condition. If you are, for example, healing one who has need of prosperity, abundance, it is still a healing.

Contemplate for a moment someone you know who is the picture of prosperity, according to your concept, a person who reflects as an outer manifestation in life, abundance and prosperity. Conjure up in your mind an image of this person before you. See him or her in the midst of prosperous endeavors. Bless the person in those endeavors. Surround him or her in your mind with more radiance. If you see an abundance of prosperity, bless the person and send some more prosperity. Then send to this person prosperity of the soul. Prosperity of the soul is gained, recognized, and manifested only by becoming prosperity conscious in your own subconscious state. Before any of those who are upon the path may shed the burden and shackles of limitation they must first cease to think and function within the self. They must turn their attention, their radiance, toward others to bless them.

Now proceed into the silence. This, then, is the procedure. Envision before you, in your mind's eye, the name of the individual who is the picture of prosperity, according to your concept. See that one surrounded with the golden radiance of Christ Light. See that Christ Light as you see the lotus. It is the same. You may use the lotus or the Christ Light. See the person in the heart of the lotus, surrounded by the golden aura of divine supply. Bless him. Bless her. Do not, above all, concern yourself with the why and the wherefore. Do not involve yourself emotionally in your meditation. You must forget self and become a divine channel. It is there within each of you to do this.

When you have envisioned the golden aura of prosperity and supply, Christ protection, surrounding the companion, go into the heart of the lotus. Allow yourself to be released from the physical vibration and let your own spirit soar to the Olympian heights. Let your soul glory in the

Light of the universe. Go into the heart of Sanat Kumara. Let the teachers and brothers of Light work with you. Continue consciously to send radiance to your companion. See this person in full radiance, doing good, benefiting, being receptive to more abundance.

Now we shall endeavor to release from your subconscious mind all bondage, all limitation, that you may become attuned to the frequency of prosperity in the universe. That is our endeavor for now. When you are able to treat an individual consistently, without attachment, without personality, then we shall proceed to other forms of healing. For there are multitudes to be treated. There are nations to be healed. There are forces of the universe to unite. There is much of the universe to unite before the great golden door to the temple of esoteric knowledge may be opened to admit a ray of wisdom. We must climb the ladder slowly, step by step.

Patience is the first key. The second key is non-attachment. The third key is revelation. Hold these three keys, these three primary thoughts, in your mind. Patience, non-attachment to personality and inner revelation.

As you are in the silence be also attuned that your inner ear and your inner eye may perceive the Light and the wonder of the universe. Hear the silence with its echoing celestial sounds. Become one with that sound. Breathe in natural order. Keep your eyes closed and relax. Your aura is protected with radiant Christ Light surrounding your inner temple.

Go very slowly, step by step, just as an infant at birth must grow day by day. Each day his body grows, his mind opens up and unfolds, as the spirit is brought more and more into consciousness. When it is necessary for the young child to learn how to walk, he first learns to take one step at a time. This takes coordination and discipline.

Prayer is a science of coordination and discipline. For there is no effect to all the prayers, all the treatments you do, if your mind wanders undisciplined like a young pup through the fields, or if it wanders like a young child at play from one toy to the next. There is then no action, no cause, no direction.

You are the captain of your own ship in your own sea. You have charted your own course. You are the captain and the navigator working in coordination. And as you coordinate your spiritual, your psychic and your physical faculties, you must learn discipline of mind and body, to keep the body still at all times so that any affliction of the body becomes undiscernible, unrecognizable by you. You may be stung by the bee in the field but you shall not feel the sting in your body. That is how still and silent you must be. You must become totally unaware of your own nature, your own evolvement. This takes time and practice. Above all, it takes patience with yourself, patience to sustain one thought, one thought only.

These things may only be unfolded through a steady process, step by step. Treatments may be short in duration, yet they are effective. If you remain too long with one condition the treatment becomes ineffective. The mind has a tendency to wander, to amble off in other directions. Then you lose contact with the object of desire, your sole desire. Then you begin to take away the substance you have lent to that desire.

Now, Acumana will give you a key, an esoteric secret used by all ancient teachers, used by all illumined ones upon the path, for treatment. Henceforth you shall use this concept in all your endeavors for treatment for any condition which you approach.

When in the process of healing another, contacting another positively, it is important to remember that first of all in your mind's eye focus your inner eye upon their eyes. It is said that the eyes are the windows of the soul, and so they are. For the physical eye is the entrance to the spiritual reflection, the spiritual nature. All you need to do is gaze into the eyes of another person and you are instantly met with the power of his soul, the sincerity of his love and the purpose of his nature.

As you proceed, envision your eyes meeting their eyes. Stare into the heart of their eyes as you treat them. Hold their gaze esoterically. Hold their attention. You have contacted their soul vibration reflected through their eyes. Then they can receive the benefit of your work.

In your prayers, your meditations, when you are working with another and you are unable to imagine the color of their eyes, it is unimportant. What is important is that you concentrate all your power upon focusing in the heart of their eyes. And then, through your third eye, into their eyes, direct all the God power, the cosmic radiation, flowing through you. See it reflected in their eyes. A happy person reflects the joy of his inner contemplation through his eyes, just as a sad man reflects the melancholy through his eyes. Watch the reflection of his eyes, as you treat the condition. The reflection will change according to the intensity of your own power.

Always remember, your needs are known by the Father. Your wants are fed by the Father. Your desires are appeased by the Father. You are one with divine substance, you are one with Divine Mind. You are made in the likeness and reflection of God. You have no want, you have no desire. Your brother has much need, for he is in dormancy, he is unaware of his identity. You have stated in the trinity your own name; therefore, you know your own soul's self. Your wants are unimportant in comparison to your neighbor's.

That, therefore, is the primary thought you must bring with you into the silence. And as you go deeper and deeper into the silence, you must even become unconscious of the self, saying it has no want. Sit in utter, profound silence, body still, breath still. Breathe as if the stillness of the universe permeates your soul. Become aware of the beat of your heart as the beat of the heart of the universe. And let the heartbeat of the universe fill and reverberate in the hearts of all mankind. Thus you become that one heart, that one mind, that one soul radiating its love, its wisdom and its power throughout the universe.

Who is to receive this healing? Go to your telephone book. Pick a name. You know not the person and it matters not. Each night for one week treat that name as you have been taught. Spend fifteen minutes in disciplined concentration. Still the mind, still the body, still all thoughts coming in. Sit in silence. Contact the eyes of that person. State their name. See them perfect. See them whole. Bless them. See them enfolded in the loving arms of God. See them nursing upon the milk of Mother Nature, that their bodies, their minds and their souls are filled with the golden elixir of divine consciousness. See them as a young child in the arms of their mother, with their Father protecting them with the radiance of His strength.

Now, repeat seven times the Lord's Prayer, or any prayer of power of your choice. As you say each word slowly, concentrate upon that word and imagine the great radiance of power in words gathered like seeds upon the world to all places in need, to all people in need.

MEDITATION

Mine heart is likened unto
The young hummingbird,
Who upon his wings does light
Upon a rose,
Upon a lily,
Upon a sweet vine,
And doest the nectar suck of life.
Thus knowing,
Thus free,
Doest fly
From one to Thee.

CHAPTER XIV

Entering the Silence

What is the Silence and why must one enter the Silence? First, silence is that state or condition manifested through mind, Divine Mind where soul and spirit live in eternity. Silence is the whispering of eternity throughout all ages. Silence is the inner temple within man wherein all things are made whole.

Silence is that aspect of which Christ said these words, "The kingdom of heaven is within." When in your studies you learn the concept of the great microcosm and the macrocosm, you learn, in essence, that you are but a reflection of the greater All. And what is the greater All? The manifestation of Divine, Infinite Intelligence, God supremely All. You, as the microcosm in this great reflected universe, have many aspects, many natures. Each of these natures must be shed like an onion before the heart, the core, the seed, the purity, the Truth may be recognized and revealed.

The only way this is possible is through the silence. So the silence is the great sentinel, mighty and powerful, dynamic in force, which guards the gates of eternity, wherein dwells all knowledge, all peace, all Light, all oneness.

Why the silence? Silence identifies you, the threefold man, the body, mind and soul, with its object, God. Silence identifies you in mind with your soul and your body. The silence identifies the body with the mind and the soul. And lastly, the silence identifies the soul with the mind and the body, all three becoming one. The mind and the body must become like unto two lovers who meet. And the body becomes subdued in its animal tendencies. The natures inherent in it from the days of Eve become dormant. The mind and the body act as one, and the soul is at power acting through the mind and the body. Then you become one concept, one being, one mind.

The silence enables you to journey deep into the depths of yourself. And the deeper you journey into the depths of yourself, the deeper, the broader and the greater is your understanding of the infinite universe. It is only through the great silence that the doors will be opened to admit the splendor and the Light wherein is rooted the great flower of everlasting love blooming, wherein is rooted the great heart and soul of the Christ principle. This is only possible through silence.

Throughout all ages, the mystics, the sages, the prophets, have all taught man one thing—prayer, and how one may enter prayer. It is for this purpose, now, that we unite. For it is said that where two or three are gathered together, there are thousands upon thousands of Lights, Powers, united.

Silence is the most difficult of all things to control, to enter. Above all, have patience with yourself. Remember, you have been conditioned throughout years of your work-a-day world of activity, to the world of struggle, to the world of strife. And before you may set aside these worldly states of mind you must first quiet the mind, quiet the body, so that your soul may begin to ring its keynote throughout your nature.

Many have attempted silence only to find that they have no patience. They have attempted to enter the silence and have assumed that they have had profound depth in their prayers and their contemplations only to find that they have deluded their mind into thinking that this state has existed. True silence, true profound depth, exists, and may be reached only through persistence. It takes persistent efforts to master the mind, to master the body, to displace from your consciousness all disturbing thoughts, all disturbing conditions, past, present and future.

You must displace from your material mind all the states and conditions which produce disturbance. You must become oblivious to all states and conditions which produce within you the faculty of thought and reason. You must become oblivious. You must cease to care. Cease to think in your mind of these states or conditions which produce disturbance.

The quickest, most powerful way this is brought about is by affirmation that you are in the heart of the cosmic flower. Think for a moment of the cosmic flower, the cosmic flower of all things, the great golden Light, and rooted in the heart of this great cosmic flower is the Christ consciousness. In your mind's eye conjure up an image before you of radiant, resplendent Light in the center of a cosmic flower, a lotus. Imagine this Light in its radiance spreading broader and broader, its golden Light embracing you as you gaze upon the heart of the cosmic flower.

Hold that thought in your mind. If another thought of external conditions enters your mind challenge it. Say instantly, *"This is the hour of prayer, wait in patience, my friend, and we shall meet."* Set aside that thought.

Concentrate your whole being. Do not sit merely in a relaxed position and allow the mind to drift aimlessly about. This is futile. Nothing is accomplished under this state. Focus your mind with your whole attention on one condition—the cosmic flower, wherein is rooted the heart of Christ, Christ consciousness. Hold it before you in your all-seeing eye. Imagine this great, golden glorious Light engulfing and embracing you. Go deeper into this Light, but remain awake, do not fall into the arms of Morpheus. Remain conscious. Know that the body is still there, that the body still functions, and yet the body becomes light, lighter and lighter.

Now, as you go deeper and deeper into the heart of the cosmic flower, become aware that surrounding you is great Light, great warmth. Think no thought now as you proceed. Your mind must remain in a total state of non-thinking. The only thought in your mind is the thought of this great cosmic flower, the lotus and its golden Light, and you diving into the heart of its golden oneness. Then, once you are surrounded in this great Light, ask, while you are in this Light, that all things may be made whole.

The body must remain still. Hold your head straight. Sit erect, put your hands relaxed upon your lap. Let the palms be facing upward in thanksgiving. Try to keep your spine in one line in order that the vital force may enter through your chakras and up on into the crown of awareness.

Now, place the golden Light of Christ protectiveness around you.

Remember that it is a struggle to quiet the mind. It is a struggle, but proceed, constantly affirming your identity with the Christ and the cosmic flower. Now, remain relaxed, remain composed and in a state of peace.

As you now have discerned, to truly enter silence is not an easy task. To acquire mental, physical and spiritual discipline your body must be totally relaxed, your mind totally dormant. You are in a receptive state of consciousness now. Your vibration is greatly elevated.

Now, do not pray for yourself. Instead, pray for your neighbor. For our next journey into infinite mind it is desirable for you to bring to mind the name of one most in need. Repeat the name in the silence three times to yourself. Then conjure up in your mind's eye focalization upon his eyes. In other words, imagine your eyes meeting his eyes. And as you repeat his name in the silence, steadying your glare in consciousness into his eyes, see God, see Christ, see perfection. Enter into the silence repeating his name over and over. As you repeat his name, concentrate upon his eyes and project God. After you have said his name nine times continue to concentrate upon his eyes as you go deeper into the silence. And as you see his eyes before you, direct golden Christ Light to those eyes. Envision a beam of great, golden Christ Light descending and penetrating through those eyes, permeating his entire nature. Repeat the name audibly, do seven sacred OMs, and envision this golden Light, this vibratory power, emanating through his consciousness.

Now we will proceed to work, in our great silence, upon world affairs. Regardless of what your political beliefs may be, those who are in charge of the outward manifestation of governmental affairs for your country need power and assistance from all on the inner and all those on the outer planes. So now direct your attention to the Great White Lodge. Lend your power to their power for world peace. Envision the great veil of blue mist of the east. Imagine yourself suspended above the Earth and beneath you suspended in space and rotating on its axis, is the world. See the Great White Lodge, and you are a part of that great white band. Envision a mist of blue ether surrounding the Earth emanating from this white band. This blue mist is peace, tranquility and goodness. Envision it falling like rain to all places in the world where it is needed.

Your moments into the silence may seem short of duration, but remember, you must proceed cautiously and slowly at first. Through the persistence and the application that you put forth it will improve, it will increase, and, indeed, give you many great treasures.

Prayer is truly a science little understood by the world of theology. Now you must begin to learn how to mark time in prayer so that even in the physical ethers you may have constant repetition of a beat, a beat penetrating the physical ethers. And yet, that beat shall hold your attention to one thought—God, God, God.

Begin to discipline the conscious faculties which constantly, within your human nature, interfere so that you cannot enter through that gate. There is a time, a rhythm, a cadence to prayer. Just as you have discerned in the hymns, the sacred OMs, the chanting. In all things there is a rhythm, a cadence. You will begin to learn rhythm, the rhythm in the universe, the swing forward and backwards, the pendulum, back and forth, to and fro.

You will begin to understand now the rhythm of prayer in relationship to the rhythm of your own nature. Your heartbeat has a rhythm to it, it has a beat, a cadence. Your blood, your vital force as it flows through your body, has a rhythm and a cadence. You walk about with a rhythm and a cadence. Your breath is in a rhythm and a cadence. So the universe in its endless chain and cycle has a rhythm and a cadence. You must become a part of that greater rhythm and cadence. This is done through prayer.

Now, if you desire, you may ask Acumana questions pertaining to prayer.

> ***Student:*** **Why is it that even when you are well rested there is a great temptation to lose consciousness into sleep when you are in a state of meditation or prayer?**

It is the bodily nature, the animal nature. The mind and body do not desire the spirit or the soul to have liberty. Therefore, the mind induces a state of sleep upon the body. The soul or the spirit still soars out, however, by the conscious control of the body. And the mind and the soul is then consciously able to enter all the greater realms and to therefore benefit.

So, in direct answer to your question, it is the body and the mind of the material, mundane plane keeping back the spirit from its true goal. Continue to assert the will in discipline over the body and the mind.

Assert the will over and over.

Sleep is a time of bodily rejuvenation when the spirit and soul ascend from the body. Meditation and prayer are something entirely different. You are gathering together all of your mental, physical and spiritual thoughts and energies, and focusing them in one direction, pinpointing them to one goal, one object. That gathering together, like the harvest, identifies the mind, the body and the soul with its true nature, God. The body is rejuvenated as in sleep, but it has a greater rejuvenation power through the conscious directing of the will and the soul and the body to one object. Sleep is only an escape into the endless avenues, and it must be conquered during meditation.

> ***Student:* When you are in a state of prayer and suddenly a truant thought comes in and you realize that your prayer has been interrupted by this truant thought, is the whole concept destroyed? What is the best thing to do after that?**

The whole concept is not destroyed. When this challenging thought enters your mind you must immediately, with the force of your will, dismiss it. Constantly continue to reaffirm the object of your prayer. Refocus, repolarize, holding to that one object. It is comparable to a man in a great wind storm, a hurricane. He walks down the road. He has an objective, a goal. The winds come, the rains come, they buffet him about. If he is true to his goal and true to his object, as in prayer and meditation, he will crawl if necessary to get to his object, to shelter. If, however, he becomes fearful and begins to fight the wind, he fights a losing battle. And he shall truly be picked up by the wind and carried away by the storm.

But by focalizing his mind, his soul and his spirit to the objective before him, his goal, no matter how fierce the winds are, he still stands erect and moves forward like a great charging dynamo of spiritual energy. This is what you must do in prayer and meditation, charge forward, constantly holding your objective before you, regardless of what these alien thoughts may be.

Now remember, in the beginning you will have more alien thoughts than you have during your conscious awareness. For the body and the material mind, that which is rooted to the Earth, the mundane plane in you, does not desire for your spirit to have liberty. There are two forces fighting for survival within, the animal nature and the spiritual nature. It is the eternal struggle.

Many thoughts will assail you in your ascent toward illumination. Your own strength and your own spiritual power determine how rapidly you shall surmount these obstacles. It is why you are here on the Earth, to evolve and grow, to learn lessons. But before you can truly become ascended, before you can truly reach masterhood, you must return and return and learn all of Earth's lessons over and over, body after body. To master self, the mind, body and soul. When you have done this and you are consciously able to master the forces of nature in the universe you may go on to the greater realms beyond.

***Student:* Is it best when the state of sleep imposes itself to get up, stand up, do something physical?**

Yes, if it is necessary. However, it is a matter of vibration. If it becomes so profound a state of sleep, so strong then you may, in truth, do something to revibrate your nature. Do whatever is needed—knee-bends, stretches—to recirculate and restimulate the vibration within you to counteract the inducement of sleep.

***Student:* Acumana, may I ask a question about sleep? Sometimes I awaken from sleep and the bottom of my feet are burning. I feel like I have been running. Do you know what causes this?**

You *have* been running. You have been doing too much astral travel and not enough going into the higher dimensions. When you run along the astral clouds sometimes it can cause the sensation of burning on the physical feet. Acumana will give you an exercise for going further out of the body in sleep. Out beyond the astral.

This is also a way to go into a deeper state of sleep in your nighttime hours. First select any prayer which is comfortable to you. A good prayer for use of this type is the Twenty-Third Psalm. Or take any prayer that you have placed into your memory. No matter what your last act is, before time to go into slumber, begin to repeat that prayer and spin of it a thread of light that takes you out and out.

Repeat it as many times as needed until you fall into a deep sleep. It is preferable when you do this to be lying on either the right side or the back, not upon the left side. Lying upon the left side, places some restrictions upon the heart area, not heavy, but if it is done habitually it could be less beneficial.

So you spin the prayer, like the spider spinning the thread, you spin of the prayer a thread of light, and you go in your inner being out upon that thread of light, leaving your body in perfect repose to slumber as it will. You will have much different experiences in sleep if you will do this.

***Student:* Acumana, how does a dream occur?**

Divine Mind has freedom of expression. It knows no limitation. Sometimes it sees that which will come to pass because it travels to a great place where these things are set up to be done. Sometimes a dream is your creative mind creating. However, all things that come to you in dreams do not exist in the great cosmic. Many dreams are given to you because your mind has reached the point where it is ready to receive. Any vision which comes to you which is memorable, write down, so that it can be useful to you. Some dreams are revelations. Your mind knows no limit of growth and expression in repose. It travels to far, far places where great beings speak to you. It is all a part of your preparation.

***Student:* You have told us how to get past the astral level by the prayer on the beam of light. I am interested in the sleep process itself. It seems to me that when I awaken in the morning where I've been has a lot to do with my attitude or my feeling on many things of the day. Could you tell me a little more about this? First of all, I'm not quite sure where the astral level is.**

The so-called astral is immediately after your physical world. It is the immediate, first level outside of the physical body. The body upon the astral seems as physical as does your physical body on the physical level, but it is not. It is not as dense. It is forever a complete, perfect counterpart of your physical body, including replicas, with most people, of the whole internal system. Acumana is speaking now of the astral body when it leaves the physical body for travel.

Acumana will tell you a very amusing thing. On a certain astral area, people are even provided with toiletry facilities. The whole thing is like a complete counterpart of the physical, only in a thinner form.

Then the next level is a level of much confusion, which is called the lower astral. It is where many, many discarnates roam, and where all kinds of confusion exist. So on the first level out you have an exact replica of the physical. The next level out drops a certain appearance, and it can take any shape the creature wants. So if it is an evil creature it can take the shape of an unusual form. Let us say it is a one who died of extreme alcoholism and does not see its way through to higher regions. Then it can take the form of a gargoyle, gargantuan evil appearance, although it is harmless, or it can take the form of anything it shapes in its own mind. Or it can be a zombie of the same general structure as the physical. That is the lower astral. It does not mean higher-lower, meaning height. It means lower elementals, less consciousness, less dimension of realization of its own capacity for perfection, a lower vibration. It has nothing to do with up and down.

***Student:* What about reincarnation, then? Do they come back the same as others do?**

There comes a time when they go through a purification process. They go through chambers of clarification, equivalent to your rehabilitation centers, and finally they are allowed to re-enter. Sometimes they re-enter by grabbing a body that has the same weaknesses or tendencies which they have. This is where obsessions come in. Sometimes they grab a little infant body and enter in place of the spirit which was preparing the body. That does not happen often, but it can happen. Most often they migrate in groups to different areas of great confusion where there is much, much birthing taking place, such as in Oriental countries. Much birthing is taking place because they think they will overwhelm the world through multiplying. They might well do so, except that they do not live as long. There is the balancing of all things in the great plan.

Student: **What would the next level after the astral be?**

This is called the etheric realm. There are many dimensions of the etheric realm. The word *etheric* comes from the word *ether*, place of ether, fineness, and the higher you go in these realms, once again having nothing to do with higher or lower, up or down, the higher you go in consciousness the less you have of the physical counterpart. Finally you become in the highest of the etheric realm a pure spark of Light, pure energy, a pure pinpoint of Light which is capable of great expansion or of being a tiny, minute pinpoint of Light.

Student: **Does one go to the astral before getting to the etheric?**

You have no reason to ever stop on the astral. You simply follow the beam of light, and you are in the etheric realms. You do not need to go on the astral. Sometimes it so happens, when people do not put themselves across the beam of light into the ether realms, that they do have astral world experiences in their sleep. Many people do, and they come back and call them dreams. They say, "I had a nightmare last night."

There are many kinds of dream. Some dreams are psychological, having to do with the previous day's activities. Some dreams are astral dreams. There are dreams of a prophetic nature.

There are many kinds of dreams. Psychological dreams are for the purpose of cleansing the mind of the trivia, the stresses, which got stored there during the day. Those who do what is called retrospective meditation, looking back before retiring from the last moment to the very first moment of the morning, seeing any areas in which they could have had better experience, revising the experience in the mind, will have better sleep.

In reference to the emotional nature, say that sometime during the course of the day you have a heated argument with some one. Flaring of tempers takes place between the two of you, and the event is not closed satisfactorily but it is closed with animosity. If at the end of the day you had done what is called retrospective meditation, contemplation, when you got back to that experience in your mental awareness revised the experience, heard it as a warm, wonderful tone going between the two of you, sent blessings, love and light to the person, you would have completely changed the nature of the experience. You would have cleansed it and you would not have to go through the dream at night for purification.

***Student:* Sometimes we hang onto emotional thoughts, reliving them. This is harmful isn't it?**

You are only holding a thought form which some day will have to be purged out. It might as well be done now. You can do retrospection on your whole life. In fact, at the time of death to the physical, a person sometimes thinks he is drowning or dying in some other way, and then he comes back and says, "I saw my whole life flash before me." So you can take your life and you can do a journal entry upon each phase of it which you found to be less than satisfactory, and go through the mental awareness process with great, deep feeling of sincerity, and cleanse that area. Go through forgiveness of self and others, go through understanding, go through blessing those involved and releasing them; and most of all, release yourself from whatever grudges or discordant attitudes you held toward yourself. Then it is cleansed and you save yourself having to do that at a later time. You save yourself the stress of carrying the experience into your sleep. You save yourself having the condition stored in your emotional nature.

The only time to achieve your mastery is now. If each one of you would only do this each night of your life, especially when you are living predominantly in the emotional body, you would soon cease to live predominantly in the emotional body and live more in the body of pure feeling and the mental body. For the more you do the retrospective contemplation, the less likely you are on the morrow to make the same mistakes. You will instead have the thought, "Oh, I had better not do this because I will have to go through retrospection on it if I do."

***Student:* Can one bring with them from another lifetime to this life certain negative feelings, confused emotions?**

Sometimes they are brought with you. Sometimes they are built by the attitudes of the people around you and your reactions to them.

You are responsible for all your thoughts, all your deeds, all your attitudes, all of your convictions, after the age of eleven. Prior to that time your parents are responsible. From eleven years on you are responsible.

Eleven is the magic number of taking full responsibility. Every child should be reared so that from the age of eleven on he or she can be totally responsible when the circumstance calls for it. But how many parents do that? Not that they are thrown out at that time, but they have been taught the sense of total self-responsibility, including responsibility for their own attitudes, their own deeds, their own actions, and their own physical well-being. You are responsible for your own actions back to the age of eleven, so you can do retrospection as far back as you can remember.

Now let us go back to night sleep. You fall asleep by building the ray of light. You lie however you lie, and you see in your inner vision a light going out, upward, a beam of light which can be like a ladder. And you allow your consciousness to go up on that light. Your teachers meet you sometimes. Sometimes you go to a great library. Sometimes you go to a gentle resting place, lie upon a lovely hillside, and listen to great harmonic music. Sometimes you go into the dome of rejuvenation. There is so much to experience in the etheric realms. It is filled with blessings.

You are the wayfarer who goes out on the great boat. You say, "Wonder where I will be going this trip!" Sometimes the wayfarer knows his destination, but most often when he goes into reincarnation he says, "There is this port and this port and this port I would like to go into, but I wonder what else is in store for me?" And he gives over to the process.

Now let us go back into the silence once more, and as you go into the silence you may each take your own condition this time. One condition that you have to be transmuted. Mentally project into the ethers that it is right and it is perfect. Then together say seven times, as you did before, the Prayer of our Lord. Then come back into consciousness.

Remember, always use the Christ protection in all things.

RETROSPECTION

As I go into retrospection
at this hour, all words, deeds and
thoughts contrary to the will of my Father
are disintegrated. In this period of elimination
of worldly cares, the period just before
sleep, I now enshroud myself with
radiant light, that I may in purity greet
God, my Father, and the hosts of Light.
May I, upon awakening, have remembrance
of the joys of paradise, and may I have
completely forgotten those unradiant contents
of the day past. Thank you, oh God,
my Father, for allowing
me the privilege of retrospection which
purifies my being. I give myself into
Thy care and keeping.

CHAPTER XV

The Pyramids and Atlantis

Often students ask, "What of the pyramids? Why were they built? How were they built and what is their purpose?" Acumana will tell you something of the pyramid.

The pyramid in symbolism represents the full trinity of man. It represents the trinity of the cosmos, the Father, the Son and the Holy Spirit. It is the perfect triangle, only it has four sides. It is the four corners of the endless universe. It is facing in a perfect direct compass direction, north, east, west and south. The four corners represent the four Buddhas of evolution or the four lords of creativity, the Lord of the North, the East, the West and the South, who hold the reins of evolution in the universal scale of evolution that you are in.

There are four mighty Maitreyas, great hierarchies, great gods of each direction. The pyramid has to do with evolution, the four lords of evolution, the four corners of the universe. These great Maitreyas are in charge of the full hierarchical scale in your plane, including its cosmic scale. The pyramid pays homage to this. It is composed of an exact number of stones which are set in an exact position.

Inside the great pyramid is a temple of initiation where Christ took his master initiation. There are passages and subterranean tunnels beneath the pyramid which go down deep into the Earth. There many mysteries are concealed, including the mysteries of Atlantis and its heritage. Many of the mysteries of periods even earlier than Atlantis and Lemuria are concealed there.

It is here where Hermes, the thrice-great, conceived of the Hermetic philosophy. Only a master could enter these temples. It was here where John the Baptist and Jesus, the Christ, took their inner initiation. It was here that Moses was able to cross the threshold of the inner temple by walking through the walls. Zoroaster also took his initiation in the Great Pyramid.

The secret chamber of this inner temple has been concealed since the last golden days of Egypt. All the great lords and masters in Egypt, the sages, the priests who knew all these laws, who knew much more than you are capable of understanding now, could foresee every event for ten thousand years ahead. They deemed it necessary to close the pyramid. They sealed off its esoteric chamber so that it could not be found for many thousands of years. It shall be found in the coming future by those of the inner Light, for there is an entrance to it.

Buried beneath are the ruins of an ancient city, a civilization great and mighty. It is in a perfect state of preservation in the inner chambers of the great pyramid of Egypt. There can be found there effigies of men and women of Atlantis. They are gilded, mummified in a perfect state of preservation, each being approximately eight feet to nine and one-half feet tall. There will also be found blueprints of the most advanced type of atomic and cosmic energy and machinery yet conceived of. There will be found documents of civilizations long since gone by.

The records of the universe will be found concealed in the pyramid. These records are like a looking glass. In them all knowledge is known and retained. Only a master could possibly have the developed consciousness to retain this wisdom. It was of this that Christ spoke in His great prayer, when He stated, "Our Father which art in heaven, hallowed be Thy name." For when you gaze into this recorded reflection of the universe and you see the countless ages past, the millions of years gone by, when you see civilizations that have come and gone, when you recognize and see the plan of evolution, you can only utter "Hallowed be Thy name."

There also you will find documented, detailed to the finest degree, plans to build machinery and flying craft the likes of which your generation and the next fifteen generations will not have.

There will be found the means at your disposal on how to harness the cosmic energies from the sun. Also are documented all the ways and means of harnessing human energy, the energy within the cell, how that energy within the cell, combined with the cosmic energy of the body, may be transmuted into a different type of energy in order that the body may be levitated at any moment and carried through space in a cone, in a cocoon.

One of these plans tells how you may harness your body heat, how you may take that body heat and harness it through combining it with cosmic radiation. It is a simple device. The plans tell how you can build around yourself a force field, an energy field, that becomes a pulsating, radiating light, visible to the eye. This light solidifies into a crystallized form, like in a test tube, and you become dimensionless within that force field. You are not subject to the law of gravity, for that force field breaks the law of gravity and you are able to travel anywhere you choose.

The pyramid is considered to be the archives of all esoteric wisdom. And yet the burial chambers are empty, for they were used for a purpose. They represent the king's chamber and the queen's chamber, which is the father principle and the mother principle. The chambers also represent stages of initiation. There are seven levels, seven subterranean passages, beneath the pyramid wherein these great things are documented and kept in a perfect state of preservation.

Why the pyramid? All these mysteries are placed there as a reminder to man throughout the ages that with combined effort, oneness of mind and purpose, man is capable of building a pyramid. For the pyramid represents the ascent toward perfection.

And what of the capstone? You know the capstone is gone from the pyramid. The capstone represents perfection and perfection can never be experienced in this universe. The capstone was created in solid gold. It was removed by the high lord, the high priest of that dynasty, as a reminder that perfection must always be striven for but never reached. You keep striving for it. For if you remove the capstone, is there not another capstone on the capstone? Remove the capstone, which is a triangle, a pyramid. Remove that and you have a smaller pyramid, do you not? Then you have another capstone. And another, ad infinitum. So you can never have perfection. It just keeps breaking down into smaller and smaller fragments.

The gold capstone is concealed in the heart of the pyramid. It is solid gold, made by the collective power of mind of one of the high Maitreyas who transmuted, concentrated, focalized his cosmic power and created the capstone in solid gold. It is a different gold than is ored from the ground. It is a universal gold and its brilliance is what illuminates the whole pyramid and its chambers. It is likened unto radium in its power. It is concealed deep within the ground.

The stone was mined from various places throughout Egypt and even outside of Egypt. However, much of the great work was done by levitation, contrary to what is believed historically where it was said that thousands of slaves were whipped and beaten. True, thousands of slaves were used, and they were beaten. But also, in the inner temple, where no slave could see, those stones were placed by levitation. For generations and generations archeologists have looked and sought, but they find nothing of importance.

***Student:* Is it true that there are more or less traps where…**

What they call plunderer's pits? Yes, indeed. When and if the true passage to the temple is discovered, they will find it is operated on leverage or balance. Simply by pressing upon a stone it counterbalances another stone, and the whole wall shifts. They will have to dig a great deal before this is discovered. There are seven plunderer's pits before the golden door of the temple can be reached. Only the ones who are permitted to enter will know of the plunderer's pits, which is all foretold on the stone which operates the counterbalance.

***Student:* Everything that you have defined is in existence in that pyramid in physical form, not in etheric form?**

Yes, in physical form. The air is dry, and everything is in a state of perfect preservation.

Student: **They put the stones in place, you say, partly by levitation and partly by slaves?**

The levitation was done by the priests of the inner temple. The stones were placed nearby, but they could not be placed in their proper positions because no lowly one was permitted into the hallowed temple. The priests placed them there by levitation.

Student: **Could you explain how the slaves got the big outer stones in place? They were of tremendous weight.**

They used balances and counterbalances. They had a system of logging, wherein thousands upon thousands of logs were hewn and rolled. They were put down like a runway and they rolled the stones over them. Hemp was placed many times around these huge symmetrical stones, and slaves would pull the stones over the logs.

Now, what of lifting perhaps a hundred thousand tons of rock up to great heights? This was ingeniously done. A slick surface, like a runway, ran the full length of the pyramid. When the stone reached the point where it had to be taken upward, huge hemps were stretched over to the opposite side. Then somewhere between fifteen to twenty thousand slaves would pull on these numerous cords.

Imagine the strength of the cords! They were oftentimes as big around in circumference as a man's arm. They were wrapped around the stones and the slaves would pull in rhythm and lift the stone up.

The driver of each group of slaves had a whip and he wore a leather cap with cuts in the eye which covered his face. He wore thongs around his legs. He would lash the whip, and the crack of the whip was a beat. This beat was given to the whipper by someone standing on a platform at a distance. Progress was made by relays. The relay man would watch the progress of the stone as it ascended up the shaft and would then relay a signal to another man who, in turn, would relay it to the whipper in order to tell him whether to pull faster, slower or more steadily.

The runway was like what you call your slippery slide. A very slick surface was used. Great trees were severed in half and floated down the Nile. Then they were brought to the base of the pyramid and were split and smoothed. Then platforms were built and were added as each level of the pyramid became higher.

***Student:* What was the time, approximately, in history when it was built?**

The great pyramid goes back to Amenhotep, thousands of years before Christ. The Pyramid of Giza was built according to specifications of the great pyramid in Atlantis, which was five times bigger. The pyramid in Atlantis, where the great esoteric temple was, stood high upon a hill overlooking the capital of Atlantis, with a road that ascended up to it. The whole city was built around this pyramid. It was covered with pearl, or what you call alabaster. It was like the lining of a sea shell. Imagine, a pearl-white temple! It was a stepped pyramid of perfect symmetry.

The capstone was solid gold, approximately eighty feet square. Imagine the size of the base. It was as tall as, perhaps comparable to a forty story building. This capstone conducted solar energy, cosmic radiation. This was brought through gold tubes down through the center of the pyramid, down deep beneath it where generating power was distributed to the populace of Atlantis. Acumana has told this to students before. Please forgive the reiteration, but it is good for you to hear once more to refresh your memory.

The pyramid stood upon a plateau facing the ocean, with a ramp which ran from the entrance of the temple. The golden doors of the temple were immense. There was a walkade around the top. On each corner of the plateau were huge effigies representing the four Buddhas of Creativity. They were white and carried golden lights in their hands, torches of creativity that burned all the time.

The ramp came from the doors down into the sea. At the sea level was the grandest port in the universe. Ships of all sizes, power and dimension would dock there. Hand carved marble docks of the most exquisite design. The pilings which sank into the water were carved like grape arbors of black marble. The whole city, the capital of Atlantis, was built around the pyramid. The population of the whole continent of Atlantis was approximately twenty-four million people. The capital would be comparable to a large city such as Los Angeles.

Now Acumana also will explain how scientists of their day taught their students in the temple. Also there were scientific laboratories on the mountainsides. The mountains were carved away. Today engineers come with big machines and move mountains away, yes? What did they say in Jesus' day? "If ye have faith, ye may move mountains." All you need today is a bulldozer and you may move a mountain, but it is through faith nevertheless.

Recently Acumana heard of a new word for bulldozer. Acumana's friend says, "Here is one for you, oh teacher. What of the caterpillar?" And Acumana says, "A caterpillar is a small creature." And he says, "No, teacher, look," and he shows Acumana a picture of a caterpillar (tractor) and Acumana says, "Will wonders never cease, my Father." See, when Acumana was a young boy, oftentimes a caterpillar would crawl upon the arm. Now Acumana understands the caterpillar can roll over the whole carcass!

In Atlantis it became necessary to move mountains, to level them, to build shrines, to build universities. Sometimes the mountain was carved on levels, steps. There were residences where people would live as you have here, very often, in your community. In the scientific universities in Atlantis they were learning how to build a force field around the human body whereby by studying and knowing the laws a person would be able to harness his own solar energy.

You are a composite of millions of atoms and cells are you not? Think for a moment the radiant energy going on in your universal system. If you are the sum total of millions of atoms within one cubic inch, and you all know in nuclear physics that one atom has great power, think of the power degree in radiation to one square inch of your being. Now multiply it by your whole dimension. Think of the power stored within you.

Now imagine that if you could tap the resources of your own inner essence, the energy within you, and build a force field around your body so impenetrable that nothing of this world could penetrate it. It would be liken unto the most solid steel imaginable, and yet it would be a rate of vibration. It would be like a tube of light around you and within that force field you would be solidified. You could teleport yourself anywhere, for within that force field around you, rotating, would set up certain physics laws contrary to the normal laws of physics.

This is all done under the control of the mind. At first it is controlled from a central control station by the rate of vibration. There were those who observed the progress of the community, similar to your police force, only they were not called police, they were observers. There was a central board where there were machines which knew the rate of vibration of each force field created around the individual. And as that force field was created by this central board, its rate of vibration increased and at will, as in the Law of Magnetic Attraction, they could repel or attract the individual in the force field.

For example, you would be suspended above. The rate of the vibration of your force field would be attuned to the central control board. Now according to the Law of Magnetic Attraction you would be drawn to wherever you were to be brought. Then simply by reversing the laws of polarity, you would be placed in another place. Each place had a degree of vibration. Each city had a rate of vibration. There were relay centers or stations which gave off rates of vibration, and these observers would be directed by remote control within their own force field, their own flying machine, to observe and protect that which was going on. Also, they had instant communications.

It is a similar process to what you have today in television. Their force field acted as a reflective mirror. It reflected the vibration of whatever it was in contact with and that reflection was beamed back to the central control board. Then its image was reoriented into the image as it happened, similar to television. You are using television only in its most meager capacity.

Many times they observed the workings underneath the sea by television. They would have beams going down deep into the sea. By using solar energy they could direct radiant light. One solar bulb could give off extremely high wattage when operating on solar energy.

The Governor, or one like the Governor, the ruling Lord of Atlantis lived in the Spun Crystal Palace. It was built of solid crystal in different shades of pink, blue, green. All the colors of the spectrum were taken and crystallized. The light energy was taken by these master architects in Atlantis, and they were crystallized. Some of the walls were as thin as paper or thread, and were solid crystal.

There were, for example, thousands of threads of crystal which hung great lengths. Amber crystals. They formed a curtain in the great throne room. And thousands more were of another color, so that the whole curtain represented the whole color spectrum, in crystal.

This curtain or backdrop vibrated at all times. It gave off symphonic vibrations, for it was attuned to the ethers. When you entered the chamber and stood there, and looked upon this crystal background, you saw the colors of the spectrum reflecting its radiance. And it gave off the most perfect harmony or blend of sounds of each color that it vibrated. It filled the great oval chamber with beautiful sound and vibration.

The throne was of one solid crystal, the most pure crystal quartz ever found in the world. It was a huge throne and it was carved in the most delicate design of all. It was carved to represent creation in its greatest sense by some of the greatest artists of your world, who have long since gone into great Light.

Many of the great artists in your time were creators, architects and designers in Atlantis. And they have recreated for you once more, some of their great works to leave to you which they had done in Atlantis.

This Spun Crystal Palace was made by great master artists. It was the crowning glory of the golden age of Atlantis, where man could take the known elements and create an edifice worthy of a Lord. It stood upon a plateau overlooking the whole city.

It had a central spiral staircase which went up without any support. The staircase was built of solid blocks of pure rose crystal quartz that were set one upon another all the way up. They were supported by counter-balance, balance upon counter-balance. This went up to the various levels. There were many rooms. Created within this great crystal palace were some of the finest sculptures in the world. Some of it even yet has not been duplicated.

Solar energy radiated the whole city so that there was light at all times. There were networks of underground systems, underground transportation. They were like pressure tubes whereby one could step into a cylinder and travel hundreds of miles, from one community to the next.

All this was done with solar energy which cost the citizens nothing. Water was piped in from deep out in the sea. It was piped into great reservoirs and converted into pure water. And the energy in converting it was used for other things. Nothing was ever lost or wasted on Atlantis. Atlantis, indeed, knew the golden age. It produced the finest fruits, finest vegetables, finest foods. Most of the Atlanteans were pure vegetarians.

Now you may ask a few question of Atlantis if you desire.

***Student:* Is it still standing at the bottom of the sea?**

No, it has crumbled.

***Student:* Were all of the records of Atlantis destroyed?**

No, they were brought out by great Lords of Light. Many have been placed in different esoteric temples, one being in the pyramid of Giza. There are other places. There are records of Atlantis in Shamballa. There are many records in the Himalayan mountains and some in Lhasa, way beneath Lhasa. They have been placed in various centers throughout the world.

The buildings of the Mayans were based very much upon Atlantean influence, only you will find there more of the peasant Atlantean influence rather than the aristocratic influence.

The great temple of Atlantis was an adoration of the seven-fold God principle. It was a temple of the cosmic fire. Imagine when the sun hit this temple of pearl in the valley! This great capital of Atlantis was surrounded by high mountains covered with snow. The climate was semitropical all of the time.

***Student:* Acumana, have we all been on Atlantis?**

You have all been on Atlantis, yes.

***Student:* Were there other people living on the Earth at that time?**

Yes. There were other populations. They were newer and younger souls of different races and tribes going through different stages of evolution.

***Student:* Is this what America is building to?**

Yes.

***Student:* What about their ordinary modes of transportation?**

It was no problem, there were wide thoroughfares. One did not have to walk if one did not choose to. Although it was recognized and taught that the exercise of the human body was, indeed, very important. So walking was engaged in often. When it became necessary to move more rapidly, one simply stepped upon one's tray of transportation or utilized the force field.

***Student:* They could all work this force field?**

Not all of them. The average man could not work it. The average man had a tray of transportation, like a small magic carpet. He would step upon his magic carpet and say, "Away, oh, magic carpet." (And Aesop flew away into the heart of all the Arabian Nights.) Much of the mystery of Atlantis is concealed in the Arabian Nights.

***Student:* Well, then that individual did not direct and control his so-called magic carpet but it was done by a central control?**

No. The individual who had his own, directed it and controlled it through his own mind power.

***Student:* Was it propelled by solar energy?**

Yes.

***Student:* Then the Atlanteans must have built the pyramid in Egypt.**

They were responsible for the pyramid in Egypt, yes. For the great master architects such as Amenhotep, who built the great cities such as Memphis and the pyramids, were Atlantean architects who recaptured once more the mysteries and concealed them beneath the Great Pyramid.

***Student:* The Egyptians didn't build them then?**

Yes. They were Egyptian then, but they were Atlantean in origin.

***Student:* If the Atlanteans were so advanced, what happened to their civilization?**

Lust and selfishness. Over a long period of time Atlantean man became aware of the creativity that he was producing. He would sit back and look at his work and he would say, "My, what fine work I have done." The "I" became very self-conscious. The teachers would say, "Oh, workers of Atlantis, it is God within thee that does this. You are only the tool, the instrument for the Divine Plan. It is God who manifests it through you." And he would say, "It is not so, teacher. My hands have carved this edifice. It is with the sweat of my brow, it is from my mind that I produced and created." The teachers and wise ones would say, "Oh, no. It is Divine Essence. It is God that does this. Jehovah."

And as time progressed, more and more the human began to take over. Man began to express different desires. Then man began to eat of the flesh. And he began to take on more fleshly things. The exiles from the mountains, the woods, would partake of the desires of the flesh of the woods, and some of them infiltrated down into the communities. And they told them of the newer things they had found in the woods and the wilderness.

It took a long time, but the tribes began to move in, the lower degree of evolvement. And they would seduce the higher Atlanteans into their ways. And some of the Atlanteans produced offspring of the two dimensions, the dual consciousness, that of the mundane and that of the spiritual. For the true Atlantean lived in the etheric and the dense body. He lived in and out. He was conscious of all worlds working together. He was conscious of the law of correspondence. For all things correspond and he could live within all levels of vibration in those planes.

Then when the flesh became so important, flesh meaning the desire senses, animal senses, he became more conscious of the Id, the ego, and he forgot the God. And then the darker tribes moved in. This was all promulgated by the darker tribes. Soon Atlantis was covered with a black shroud of negation, selfishness.

Suddenly man decided that he was better capable of ruling. It became similar to that which you have in Communism. They tried to subjugate the masses. Those who had more intelligence tried to convince the masses that there was no such thing as gods and the lords, even though they walked among them. Then those gods and lords began to ascend rapidly from Atlantis. Many of them took off in great accelerations of Light and left the Atlanteans alone to work out their own problems, to see if they could overcome negation in their own way.

It became worse and worse over a long period of time. Those who had remained true to the cosmic principles continued to hold to the Truth they knew. Then men began to commit brutality upon one another. They would try to force their opinions by beating and torturing the body. Then they produced death. They would slay another as vengeance. And the decadence and downfall began.

Warnings were sent over and over. But the warnings were not heeded. The great angels of Light would descend in great shafts of Light and say, "Oh, people of Atlantis, have you forgotten the great golden days of glory and Light when you had no want, when you had no need, when you trusted and had faith? Can you not recapture, rekindle, that flame of cosmic love and understanding in your souls once more? Listen not to the words of Satan. Listen not to the whisper of Lucifer."

And the Atlanteans would be torn. And they would say, "Yes, we remember the days." And once more they would look about them and they would say, "But we see with our eyes what we see. And we know with our heart what we know."

And they would turn from the Light. And they would say, "How may we have trust and faith in that which has deserted us and abandoned us? If it is true Light, then it will, indeed, eliminate the conditions that have produced this negation!"

The great heavenly hosts, the Hierarchy, the Archangels, said, "Yes, it shall be done. For it is all written in the Book of Life. Conflict arises, and out of conflict is produced chaos. And from chaos is produced new birth and resurrection." And down Atlantis went in chaos, for new birth to grow upon in a new way.

There were great cataclysmic explosions, volcanoes. One of the highest peaks of the mountain ranges literally blew off, shooting fire and lava high into the air. Molten rock poured down in sheets upon the people. The ground shook and trembled. Huge balls of fire came hurling from the heavens plunging into the city.

A tremendous ball of fire struck the Great Temple and blew it to bits. From the energy stored in the Temple that explosion alone practically split the whole core of Atlantis. Great tidal waves began to descend upon the city. Fire ushered from the bowels of the Earth through great geysers. Thousands upon thousands died. It lasted for many, many days. The whole foundation beneath Atlantis, the mountain it was built upon, became a molten heap of lava. It shook and vibrated and set loose the whole foundation beneath it.

The whole chain of islands connected with Atlantis had literally blown to bits, and started great tidal waves. Some of them, hundreds of feet high, came crashing upon Atlantis from all sides, sinking, drowning thousands of people. The ground opened up in great geysers. Great fire ushered up, and then finally, like charcoal, smoking, the sea swallowed it up and engulfed it. The waters smoothed it over, put out the fire and subdued it. And there it has remained, in its grave of ashes and salt.

***Student:* What was it physically on the Earth that caused that? I mean, did the Earth tip?**

There was a great meteor which hit the Earth. A great meteor hit what is now called the North American continent, which changed the polarity of the Earth. It tipped it from its original axis, and started a whole new chain reaction. New mountains, changes.

***Student:* Well, that was the Ice Age then.**

Yes, it brought about the Ice Age in the North American continent and produced great cataclysmic changes here. The meteor was sent by the Lords of Destruction, and when it hit it changed the Earth's whole polarity, shifted it from its axis. It is why you have two north poles, the true magnetic north, and the other north. The true magnetic north is not at the north pole. That was the original pole when it was on its axis.

Student: **Before the cataclysms took place were there then many different levels of consciousness on Earth? Were the Atlanteans the highest?**

Yes, and their purpose was to colonize and educate all of the world to the glory that they had. But the Atlanteans recognized that there were many tribes, many races of man in the world who could never comprehend nor utilize, to the best of their advantage, the knowledge that they had in Atlantis. They would never force their way. They only tried to persuade and show them.

Student: **They were truly God-like?**

Yes, truly God-like. They became like a myth to some of the more hostile races, some of the more savage peoples in the world. When the Atlanteans would come in their great ships to bring them teachings and benefits, those people could not comprehend the Atlanteans being in the physical body and they made myths and legends about them. They said they came like great beings from the sky. Many of the North American Indians in their legends say, "Great beacons of light descended." These were Atlanteans, the true golden Atlanteans, who came to share. They came in their great dynamic powers of light to help colonize, to help build up the race.

Student: **Then who were the exiles that you spoke of that were around the area?**

Those who could not conform. They were asked to leave. If they would not leave then they were expelled. The exiles were those who could not and would not conform to the God-like pattern.

Student: **Then they were just physically isolated?**

Isolated, yes, in the wilderness, in the forests.

***Student:* There must have been an exodus from Atlantis by those who knew of the end.**

Yes, there was a great exodus. For hundreds of years the sinking of Atlantis had been prophesied, by the teachers, the seers and the mystics. They prepared their students, just as you are being prepared. They were prepared. Their students were told, *"Seek ye first the kingdom of God, hold not to the ways of the world. No matter what the material world offers you, hold first to the ways of God."*

Those who were constantly being prepared, re-vibrated and re-focalized and held to the principles, regardless, were the ones who were spared, who escaped. Some of them, not all of them. Even though they remained true to the very end, some went down to comfort the others. They were martyrs. They said, we will stay through all the destruction and help the others who have not been lifted out. There were many who volunteered to stay, the teachers, the mystics, the channels. You had channels similar to this who taught in the temples.

***Student:* Where do the darker forces that express constantly come from?**

They are in the astral. Remember, there is a Lord of Evil. There is what you call Lucifer. Lucifer is not evil but was named to be evil. There is light and there is dark, and there is the eternal struggle, the endless eternal struggle, for the supremacy of Light. Light will always win.

If you have darkness on one side you have to have light on the other. Otherwise the law is erroneous; and you know the law is correct. Out of free will, evil as such created itself. God, the Supreme Creator, will ultimately bring all to the Light.

Humanity must be balanced. Think of the scale. Scales symbolize the balance of humanity. How many will join the right-hand side, or how many will join the left-hand side?

Free will is the determining factor. For remember, God favors not one or the other. Eventually it will all be absorbed. However, you are promised nothing in the left, but promised all in the right. That must mean something. That is a prophecy.

It is said, *"Let the right hand know not what the left hand is doing."* This means that you should be so much in control of your own self, so much in mastery, that you are only going in one direction, to the right. For all life points in that direction. All prophesies lead in that direction. Why have the great Prophets come over and over? Why has Zoroaster come? Buddha, Confucius, Mohammed, Christ? Why do they always come and teach the same thing?

Who has been sent from Lucifer's army? He dares not send one disciple, for so false and so erroneous are his claims to power that if he sent a disciple the truths and claims which he predicts would crumble as ashes. He is a coward. What he does send is false prophets.

The important thing to remember is that you must go in one direction only. When a student says to his teacher, after contemplation, "Well, teacher, if it is inevitable what the consequence is, then what does it matter if I decide to go the other way? It will all be all right in the end anyway." Many a student has said this. What do you think the teacher says? He says, "Student, that is true. However, we do not know for sure that our Father will decide to create once more. Then where will you be? You will still be in that abyss. If you have dropped down the ladder to begin anew, maybe you have dropped down the last time that He decides to create, and you won't have a chance. Then where are you?" So that has indeed stopped many a student where he is.

Blessings unto you and peace. Remember, you are being prepared for the coming of the morrow and the morrow after that. And each day brings more Light to your soul, more peace to your mind, and more strength to your being. Walk in the knowingness that you walk with cosmic beings of understanding and power. Blessings in the name of the Father and of the Son and of the Holy Spirit.

ASCENSION

The great flight of ascending stairs
Is before me.
I ascend, standing erect,
Confident and trustworthy of Truth.
I know that I approach the great door,
The Door of Knowing;
And as this door opens,
And as I pass through to the light,
All of the greatness of God's universe
Will be revealed unto me,
Will give me confidence
That I shall always ascend
In the knowingness
Of the light of God.
I shall never slip or fall backwards.
I know Truth.
Truth has proven itself to me.
I am steadfast in all I do.
The great flight of ascending stairs
Is before me.
I ascend, standing erect,
Confident and trustworthy of Truth.

CHAPTER XVI

The Temple Beautiful

Acumana is most pleased as once more we meet in the valley of understanding, for we have for you a special surprise. We shall take you into a place of initiation on the etheric, The Temple Beautiful. You may not, as yet, have the ability to completely comprehend the initiations, but you will have a vivid awareness of these things Acumana will describe.

The Temple Beautiful is a great, magnificent temple of the teachings of Truth. In it all the Truths are taught. Art, which is the highest expression of man, is taught in the temple. Love of all things, oneness, and above all, concentration of power is taught. Many things are done in The Temple Beautiful, many arts, many chants. There are many systems of creativity. There are many performances which help man to awaken within himself the glories which dwell within him. Exercises similar to what you call yoga are taught. These are performed in a different degree than in your physical world, but the same purpose is accomplished.

Concentration is taught to the little ones at a very early age. When one is able to concentrate, then the Great Within is released. In The Temple Beautiful creations of beauty are made through the expression of man. In ancient times there were many in The Temple Beautiful who had the creative gifts of sight and profound beauty of expression. Many things were produced, things of beauty and purpose, through the power of concentration. Even now communion is received from higher areas, and from what you call the dead, as a matter of course. All work together, in magnificent rooms and halls of creativity. There is a hum of creativity filling the atmosphere.

In ancient times there was an art called the sewing of buttons. This was a great service that was done. As a student passed the various stages of initiation in The Temple Beautiful, from one degree to another, he wore a robe which was indicative of his degree. On these robes were the beaded buttons. There were only a few who were chosen to create the buttons. When a student passed, for instance, a certain degree, say open sight, he would wear a particular button, and in that button there would be created a design which symbolized that degree. This was called the "sewing on of the button."

There is much creativity and activity in The Temple Beautiful. The most sacred activities are the initiations. Now Acumana will give you a description of what happens in the adjoining chambers and their purpose. Some things we cannot give you but we will give you those which you are permitted to have.

For one moment close your eyes and listen to Acumana's words.

Now there is emptiness before you. See before you a nothingness of space, endless, endless, on and on. Time ceases to exist. There is neither you nor your fellow man, only a vast void of nothingness. A long way off in the distance before you is a pin-point of light, a tiny pin-point of light. Now it moves toward you, and you move toward it, and it becomes larger and larger. There is no air, no wind, no sound. All there is is this tiny light moving closer and closer and closer. Now you are suspended! The light moves toward you, and now you are a part of this light!

Now, observe and listen. It is night. The heavens above you have not been seen before as you know them in your existence now. The planets and constellations are not the same as you observe them in your world. It is a warm evening. Look upon it as you would look upon a picture in a gallery. Now there is sound. There is the rustle of the wind upon the dunes. The etheric land of the sweet-flowing Nile is where you are now. You look in the distance. Many bright torches are burning before you. As we proceed, we see that we are approaching a temple of worship. We become aware of the architecture, of the landscape. We are aware of its total existence. You now see every stone. You feel your feet upon the steps. This, my children, is The Temple Beautiful!

You hear singing within. This is the great chorus of the Temple chanting and singing. They are in contact with the gods of their existence. This is the ceremony of Fruitility! Now you stand within and you see before you, in this oval hall of beautiful illumination, bright candle torches such as you have not seen before. You see before you robed priests, completely void of hair, robed in beautiful attire. Large buttons are seen on some and small on others.

There are seven musicians there in the circle down below the steps. There are three levels of steps all the way around. On the steps are dancers void of all clothing. They dance "The Dance of Fruitility" of life. The chorus chants for the fruitility of the country, the soil, the crop. This is a worship not of selfishness but of fruitility of the earth.

In the center of the dancers stands a man of gigantic size and strength. He represents, in this dance, the strength and power of all mankind, and around him dance the women. They move and sway their bodies, writhing, sliding, making gestures. All the movements you see are filled with a great flooding of emotion, of feeling, of meaning.

There is one who reaches her arms high, symbolic of all that grows. The chorus sings its chant. The priests bow their heads in prayer. The sweet smell of incense and perfume fills the hall. Another dancer stands and then falls and crawls upon her knees, swaying in beautiful motion. Then there is another who is clad in a thin veil. She stands tall, erect and beautiful, magnificent in strength. She represents mankind as you know it in woman.

There are nine dancers. They all bend toward the center. The man standing tall and powerful represents fruitfulness. He is the seed of all life. Now you see they all come together and it is symbolically the fruition of each one of these women. They are all being seeded with the fruition of life.

Your Western world would not permit this. Each one of these women has now become a part with the strength of the man. The peak has been reached and the music has reached its climax. The purpose of fruitility has been achieved. All stops. There is silence. Statue-like everyone stands in silence bowing their heads before the earth. For the seeds have thus been planted. Then there is a hum, a soft rolling hum. It spreads over the entire land. Power has thus been raised and sent forth. Then they all leave the hall. Dancers return, priests return, musicians return. The scene fades. Now we are going into another phase.

It is impossible for you to find these things in any other place. In this great and magnificent temple there are many chambers for many things. This ritual was not done from the point of gratification, lust. It was all of deep significance, for all produced. This did exist and it did work. For those who were in the temple were deep students of the occult and of the mystical, and their power did spread over the Earth.

Now we will take you into the chamber of the first initiation. The first one is a paramount one, which is the confronting of one's ego entity, the beast. The discovery and the confronting of the mirror of your own beast nature. Now, this is very difficult for man to face. It is a terrifying experience. There is a hidden chamber in the temple. In this chamber is the Pool of Reflection. One goes down a magnificently carved passageway where the stonework is so perfectly fit together that one could hardly put a hair between the two stones. They are painted very bright colors, vivid pinks, and what you would call morning yellows. The walls are covered with hieroglyphics, the dead language, early Chaldean, Sanskrit and languages which man has long since forgotten.

As you move through this corridor, you see that it is illuminated, but not from any known source of light. It is illuminated by the consciousness of the masters which you call hierophant, the masters of this temple, who hold in their mind's eye the illumination. They illuminate it with conscious thought. And one gradually descends this corridor. Passing through you see one being prepared, bathed and anointed. You must descend into what is called, *the all together, nothingness.* At the bottom is a circular dome-like room. It is like an arena. There are musicians and there enter the priests. Steps lead down to the center of the room.

Look closely on the steps. There are objects on the steps. The Initiate comes into the room and the musicians play. Singing begins. The Initiate is wearing nothing. He has given himself over to himself. He says, *"I give myself completely to whatever comes."* He must follow the steps down to get to the center of the room. When he steps down he steps upon a row of thorns and proclaims a cry of pain. He must sit upon the step to take the thorns out. But when he sits, he sits upon a bed of thorns. How he does bleed! On each step are things of pain and discomfort. When he reaches the last step, there in the center of the room is a pool of water. The water is illuminated from above, from the dome. Now there is stillness. The water is like glass. It is green, very lovely green water like the water of Earth. It is the symbol of the Earth, a circular pool. The Initiate is to learn through his inner senses, his inner psychic, that the descent symbolizes his descent from the kingdom within, heaven if you like, down the passageway, down the uterine passage into the pool of life, into birth on Earth. It is birth, the birth of spiritual essence, the Atman. The initiate's intuitional faculties must be attuned to dramatizing and experiencing this descent.

He circles the pool, and as he looks into the pool he sees his reflection. But what he sees is not himself, it is not his pretty self. He sees the beast. He sees what life he has evolved from, the slime of the Earth and the depths of the seas. He sees himself as a beast, hideous to behold.

Acumana will describe for you, if you like, what he looks like, this beast. He sees on his face a beak, like that of a hawk, and he sees where there is hair, this is not hair, but feathers pulled straight back. They are very close to the head, to the beak. The eyes are dark, deep hollows. And the eyes are flaming torches of red embers. And he sees moles upon his face. He sees that his hands are like the hands of a beast who climbs about, with fingers covered with hair. And he sees that his breast was covered with scales, like the belly of a serpent. And he sees that he has talons upon him, and his fingers grow long, like talons on an eagle. And he sees that his feet are the feet of a vulture. He sees that the lovely serpentine, angular projection of the spine is like that of a great dinosaur, with great arches, great overlying blades of heavy armor of blackened flesh. He sees the beast. He sees his mouth, the long tongue of the serpent. And blood drips from his mouth.

A very horrible sight to see, because he has seen the beast of his dual nature. He is the perfection of the infinite creation God made manifest in duality. On the other side of the pool stands the perfected man, the beautiful image of God in man, in evolved form. And in the reflection is the hidden nature, the personality, the beast, that which he had evolved from. Both are fighting and struggling to control the very essence which operates him, the beat of his heart, his breath, the life, the spirit, which is invisible.

His purpose, in this first initiation, is to simply see the reflection with non-horror, but amazement. And say, "Ah, this is me. This is the perfection of the universe. The good and the evil as one, wholeness, completion. The way before me, though it be hard and strange and painful, must be walked, and at the end I must not give up but I must extend myself before God and say, '*Father, I have come.*' "

Some cannot even go beyond the first great descent, so horrible is the sight of what they have evolved from. But it is not horrible at all, it is evolution. Some fall away in a swoon, and seemingly are consumed. They fall into the pool. That is the symbol that they are consumed by their own personality. And others stand back, see what they see, and they face it. They say, "This is I. I am this. This is what life is about." They want to see it. Others turn away in disgust, not wanting to look at the mirror of who they are. Those are the three faces of that initiation: the beast, the self, and the Divine.

It is *THE ACCEPTANCE.* It is the total accepting of the nature of life. It is seeing the magnitude of the oneness of life. That is the symbolism of that particular inner sanction, that inner temple. That is the first stage, the confronting, the mirroring and confronting of one's total nature.

You have all heard of the two-faced nature. You know this in a great magnificent epic written by a very remarkable saintly man, by the name of Goethe. He wrote Faustus. In Faustus' great drama was this hidden side of his nature, the beast, the devil, the dark force, which is all part of the Infinite Being. It is what you call the yin and the yang. It is part of the balance. Faustus battled with it and won. And this is the same type of drama, so it is an accepting of one's divinity by seeing it, recognizing it, not being horror stricken by it or by all those thoughts, all those feelings of where you have come from. You see, in the acceptance of this, seeing it for what it is, one understands the wholeness of life.

***Student:* Could that be when humor was started? When one could laugh at oneself?**

Quite so. When one could look at himself, the utter frivolity of that life. After all, this is the nature of the beast. So when one is able to laugh at this state, not turn in horror, suddenly the reflection in the pool changes. There is no longer a beast, there is the loveliness of the face of Infinite Being shining through. Then one has pulled off the mask of comedy and tragedy, and the real performer is seen, Infinite Being. That is the final phase of that initiation.

Now we go to the second room, the second stage of initiation. It is a nice, pleasant room. It is a beautiful blue room. It is very comfortable, is it not? Peaceful and nicely decorated, not richly but pleasantly. Now in this second room, through an arch comes our Initiate. Is it you? Who comes with you? No one! No musician, no priests, no dancers, no one. And yet the room has a presence about it. You wander about the room. What do you do? You sit down on an inviting place for relaxation, a divan for relaxation. It is designed for the candidate to relax in complete comfort. The room has much pleasantry in it. You are all alone here. Interesting what you are doing. You are becoming aware of the room, observing this and that. Now look what you do in the center of the room. You meditate! You have observed the room and you go to the center and meditate. You sit on your haunches and meditate. In this room, in the midst of physical comfort, there is no spiritual opening. There is the comfortable piece of furniture. There are other pleasantries.

The purpose of this room is to make use of *IDLENESS,* to always fill every moment with a productive state of consciousness. Idleness does not mean you have to do something with the body every minute. It is the mind, the idleness of the mind into darkened passageways which leads one no place. Wondering, the confusion, the if-this, the if-that, the worries, fears, anxieties, frustrations, this is idleness. And that idleness, in that mental capacity, begins to destroy what is the most vital center in man, his imaginative, creative faculties. So the lesson here is to take that idleness and with a single-pointed purpose of being or mind, change it into an imagined, creative state. Let the energies pour forth to fill the mind with joy, thanksgiving, wonderment, so that the mind is not idle, so that the mind is renewed, resurrected. This room of initiation is most meaningful.

Now we proceed to the third room, the third stage of initiation. We enter a large room with a high ceiling. There are many bouquets of flowers. There is a wonderful magic scent. And there before you is a banquet with generous platters and bowls of food of many descriptions and much color. We observe as we go through the door that there is another door up above on the high steps. Through that now has entered one priest.

The dancers come in also. There are three women and five men. And here comes our Initiate. Look how he is dressed. In a burlap sack! The women dance around him and needle him to come down into the bottom of the room that is filled with food and wine. More priests enter and stand all around. The women take many strange positions to tempt him. One is wining him, another is offering him fruit, grapes. Another is daring him. Another is caressing him. He is strangely puzzled. They dance about him more and they make many suggestions. All are tempting him, bringing his appetite to more than just food. The priests glare at him. Now comes the test. What must he do if he desires to go into the next room? He rises and casts aside the appetites, ascends and goes out the door.

He could have had anything he desired. But in order to go on to the next phase of initiation he must leave the room of plenty and temptations and not willfully partake of it. This room is very hard for some initiates to get through.

Now Acumana will tell you something. If the Initiate of ancient times did not pass a test he was never permitted to return to his outside world. He had already seen too much. He was put in a special place and he was required to go to work in the house of death. He was told all of this by his teacher before he began the tests. He knew that if he did not get beyond the third or fourth room he could not return to the world. The rest of his life he stood working over big vats burying the dead. This was not cruel, not wrong. For if he did not have the strength to proceed, if he had any doubt, he should not have entered the initiation.

First the candidates are taught to know themselves. If an initiate knows that his weakness, for instance, is for wine, then he knows he cannot go through the test until he is completely cleansed of this weakness. Because of the conditioning of present day man, certain practices engaged in then seem today to be archaic and barbarous, but at the time they were not. Whether they were priests or scribes or humble peasants, they conformed to certain principles simply as a means of the preservation of the esoteric arts. Speech from the mouth of man was forbidden that he may not give of the inner teachings.

This initiation then was the *CASTING ASIDE of the APPETITES.* Casting aside of the appetites is something greatly misunderstood. There are certain aesthetics, (the philosophy of art and beauty) there is the aesthetic path that one might trod. It serves a great purpose.

There is the path of renunciation. It serves a purpose, but the appetites here are of a different nature. These appetites are those of compulsions, where one becomes an utter slave to the gratification of what he desires. It could be any kind of an appetite. It could be the appetite of affection, of food, of drink, of sex, of friendship. Whatever one begins to become utterly absorbed in, the destructive emanations of it, rather than being passive to it.

Man, today, lives in the third room. Many do not do anything with moderation. This is the story of mankind. This is the beast there in the pool. That is his lust. That is what tantalizes one. We're not saying here that you must not do this, and you must not do that, and you must do this. We are simply saying, moderation, discretion, balance.

Abstinence can become a passion too, you know. It is not wrong to desire what you desire, or to express what you wish to express, only do everything in moderation.

The fourth symbol is in a very interesting room. Acumana will take you there. Here you are confronted with a door, an arch. This is made from one solid piece of stone, carved, and in the center is what you call the *crux ansata.*

You know what the crux ansata is? It is the symbol of eternal life, the circle of the cross. The symbol of eternal life is hewn out of the center of the doorway. You are led to the door. The high priest says to the Initiate, "Now open the door."

This is the beginning of the symbol, that you must labor. He gives you a rod, which is very much like a crowbar. You must wedge this bar into the stone door. You must work and labor, hour after hour, to remove the stone from the arch, to open the door. It takes a very long time. It is very exhausting, because you are working hard. It is the symbol there of the work you do with yourself in life. So you are laboring to open the door, and finally it opens. What do you think? What do you expect to see? Darkness! You enter the darkness of the unknown. It is so dark, that it is dark upon dark, and there is a rush of wind. So you enter. You've labored, sweated, worked, and you have opened it. You remove the stone by working just on yourself. And now you enter the most darkened chamber the mind's eye can possibly conceive. There is a rush of wind. And there is a profound silence, so silent that it is hollow.

You step into this room into the vastness of nothing. Now you are complete. You look at the hands, your feet, and they glow like a lamplight, like a light in the lamp stand. You are the Light! You are a solar system, you are a sun! You are a Light in the darkness. Where do you go? You turn around and the door is closed, and there you are. You are Light in the infinite universe, to create, to go anywhere you wish, for the universe is yours. You and the universe are one. That is completion, and that is the end of the fourth initiation.

It is the complete mastery over all things which speak of the death of the soul. Over all things which are the denial of the life-regenerating forces. In other words, complete resurrection where death, which is darkness, the absence of light, no longer exists. The Atman, the eternal man, is born. The Christ, which is an ancient symbol, has resurrected. *Thou art the Christ.* "Thou Art" has overcome death. You have resurrected from the grave of your own making and *CAST ASIDE ALL PREVIOUS CONCEPTS,* theories and notions about life, death, and the afterlife. All such misconceptions are burned up in the fire of life, which is the symbol of the heart.

Now you love life and all of its expressions, the totality of mankind, including the beast. When one becomes consumed by the totality of the essence of life, you see, then nothing can destroy the temple, which is the body, of the living God, of the Atman. You are invincible. You are an eternal man, the One, the Body of God, Spirit. The temple, which is the symbol of the great pyramid, is the eternal foundation which nothing can destroy, not time, not wind, not man. So that you do not die, you live eternally.

Now the fifth room opens before you for the fifth stage of initiation. It is a large room, almost round in shape. It is as cheerful as a stone room can be. Through the arch you see a deep pit. You see the arch at the end of the room. You go through the arch, then through a small opening like a tunnel. Two priests enter first. Then in walk five more high priests. And here comes the Initiate. Now, observe. As he walks in, look at his attire. What is written upon him? Observe his body. It is painted a bright color. It represents gaiety. It represents worldly things which are cheerful, bright. He is led to an opening through the arch and told to enter. He sees nothing. One priest picks up a stone and hurls it through the opening and nothing is heard. The Initiate is told he must enter. He is told how he must walk through this tunnel, for in this tunnel are many pitfalls. This is where the word *"pitfall"* is derived from.

In this tunnel is a deep crevice and you must walk cautiously to get around the pitfalls. Our Initiate comes to a fork in the tunnel. To the left is a tiny light, to the right nothing. Which way should he go? How should he proceed through the tunnel of darkness? These Initiates must become sages of the universe. They know they must go on. They have reached the time of evolvement and have gone through similar experiences. So the candidate proceeds into the darkness, and he falls into the pit of the cobra. One time he trips on a wire and a large stone comes down the shaft. He knows that he must remain calm at all times and still go on. After a time he emerges into the light.

This room represents the *ABSENCE OF FEAR.* The inner voice speaks: *"Though the way is strange and dark, proceed."* Remain calm and stand straight and you cannot err. He desires to become a priest. He knows that he would not be called to have his life taken, so he forces himself to remain calm. Now we close the vision of this room.

What really distresses man is this unknown. The unknown is always fearful. That fear of the unknown is always there to be worked with. Is the Light bright enough? Where do I go? What will I do now? What will be the outcome? Wonder what that will be? The unknown is the symbol of an external fear, a trepidation. It is always there to be worked with, *as you,* that beam of Light, that marvelous glow of Light in a darkened universe. Wherever the soul goes it brings Light, and it goes on into more of an unknown.

Now Acumana is not permitted to give the Sixth and Seventh initiations. The seventh is of a final nature, the ultimate. When everything of the beast nature has been completely conquered and understood through love, and everything is finally cast off, totally, one becomes the greatest sacrifice in the world, which is to give your Light wherever it is needed. You have overcome the final ultimate, the quest of all quests, death and life. You are one in the cosmos, yet you sustain life. So you give your Light, or your life, that more life might be lived. And, of course, it is yours automatically. So it cannot be extinguished.

The Sixth Acumana cannot tell you nor can he give you. Both of these are deep secrets of the occult.

Now we will go into the eighth initiation. We shall visit the eighth chamber. It opens up before you and becomes another room, not as large as the others, and darker. This room, as you notice, is shaped in a perfect rectangle. It is very narrow. Suspended on the wall on chains are odd-shaped urns, many urns. They go around half of the whole wall. There is a door at the far end of this room, a very small door. The door opens and in come the priests once again. They line up along the wall. Now comes in the Initiate. This is the eighth stage and he still has to go to the ninth. He stands in the center of the room. He is wearing a very festive robe. He is very proud of his robe.

Now the priests have gone all around the room and in comes the high priest. He comes up to the Initiate. Now do we see what the priest does? He strikes him to the floor! Priests come and clean his robe. Now they hurl insults upon this man and his robe. They tear his robe from him until he stands naked before them. They ridicule him. They reach up and get ashes from the urns and hurl them upon him. Now they go back to their corners, and he digs himself out of all this mire and stands up again.

Perhaps he desires to defend himself, to protect himself, but he knows that he must face all things. Now comes the high priest with a long sharp stone, and he shames the pubic region of him. The man has nothing. He has gone through mortification. Now they leave him alone. Two monks come in and take him gently to another room. Now what would this represent? This is the *CASTING OFF OF THE PERSONAL EGO.*

This casting off would occur after the individual recognized the seven deadly sins of man, which have been given throughout all the ages of man. Those individual personality characteristics, or the seven deadly sins of man are cast off completely by the discovery of their latent sucking of your energies. They are like parasites. They are hidden. They are like mice behind the wall. You think the household of your being looks quite good, but inside there are things running about. So one goes on an extermination hunt. You have to have a guide to take you there. You can't go on your own, lest you fall into the plunderer's pit. You have to have a teacher. It is paramount.

Now we will take you into the ninth chamber, the Chamber of Anointing. The anointing with holy oils is most powerful. This great art is lost to antiquity except by a few. Now in the chamber of the holy anointing, observe as you enter, on the walls, a painting of a large body of water. In one section you see a bright shining star. It is called the North Star and you see also over here the sun. This mural of water painting is on the walls all around the room. In the center of the room there is a large hole. This hole has within it a liquid the color of green. Many holy oils are in this hole. Many priests stand about. Through the door comes the one to be anointed. Over on the other side are musicians. They play different notes this time. Priests chant. There is one other priest who has not been seen before in the other rooms. He is a slight man and wears the golden robe of Light. He is the high priest who performs the anointment.

Now comes the Initiate. He wears a tarnished gown. It looks as if it is not clean. It is symbolic that it is not pure yet but it will be. He is being led by two priests up to this pool. Now he is being elevated by two more priests and is being lowered into this oil. A wonderful fragrance comes up. Priests chant an intonation. Each one has its specific effect on the spiritual centers. Now the Initiate is submerged and held by the root of his hair. All priests now push down. He is submerged. He is lifted, and his gown is gone. He is once again submerged, and once again lifted. Musicians play a different note. Great power builds in the room. Thrice he is submerged. Then he is brought out.

Now the man is in a state of coma. He is placed upon a stone slab. The priests all surround him. They hold a cloth that is made special and rub him down. They clean the oil off. Not one portion of his physical being is free of oil. He is wiped down. He is lifted and carried to a separate room and wrapped in linen. In one hand he holds a stalk of herb, a well-known household item. It is cinnamon. There he will remain until consciousness has returned. He is able from then on to participate in the higher teachings of the Temple. He has passed all nine phases of cleanliness, the last one being desire for breath. Now before him are greater things, for this is only the first portion of his initiation. Now the priests fade away, the musicians fade away. The scent fades away. Again it is gone. The scene is complete.

So the ninth stage of initiation is the *OVERCOMING THE DESIRE OF BREATH.* When you have not even one treasure to hold onto as a possession, not the ownership of anything, even your own life, when you are willing to surrender everything because you realize that you have nothing, you are nothing, you are one with God.

What does God need? That is the necessary, essential point here. If you are one with your All, what could God possibly need? So it is the discovery of that Oneness, that you need nothing, your lack means nothing. You surrender everything because you need nothing. You are all of it. You are the totality, the infinite creation.

Acumana has given you these various rooms of progress in The Temple Beautiful, the nine initiations, the nine cardinal errors of man, to overcome. Nine basic elementary cardinal errors of man to reach perfection in.

There is more in The Temple Beautiful. There is health, abundance of many things, rain, worship, all symbolized together by the priests. And all these things have been proven. There are rooms of rejuvenation, halls of great art, and sculpture. There are grand rooms of dance, of music, of sound, and of rhythm. There are halls of learning where you may hear the Great Ones teach. There are also temples of worship and sanctuaries for meditation. Around the Temple there are exquisite gardens, with birds and sky creatures such as you have never seen. Guardians of the Temple stroll through the gardens engulfed in the beauty of radiant rainbow skies. Students who have come from the earth plane in their etheric bodies, freely move through the gardens, greeted by the Great Ones who reside there. In your night sleep ask to go to the Temple Beautiful for rejuvenation and inspiration. There are many such temples in the ancient lands. All accomplish the same thing. India has its temples of initiation, Egypt has its temples, Atlantis had them, too. They all accomplish the same thing—the perfection of man over all things.

Now, become that great center of Light, become that glowing ember of purity and perfection. And as that great glowing ember grows and swells and expands in the perfection of the universe, take unto you in that glow and that perfection, peace, serenity and cosmic awareness. This is your destiny. Let that glow and that Light radiate and permeate your nature. And may you radiate and shine on the external as well as the internal. And may your glow and your Light permeate all who come in your aura. And may your aura emanate healing perfection, wisdom perfection and divine protection to all in your orbit, by the power and wisdom of God, our Father. Amen.

THE STEEPER PATH

Oh God, my Father,
As the path of awareness
Grows steeper before me
In the endless evolvement of time,
Greater are my tasks
To stay within the beam of awareness.
This I gladly accept, oh Father,
For how else may I become one with Thee?
Even through hardship, I give my thanks.
Even in struggle, I praise Thee.
May my heart beat only in
The purest flow of awareness.
Through my veins, oh God, my Father, may vitality flow
To stimulate my being
To oneness with the All.
Quicken my consciousness to the tasks at hand.
May my feet, though they be rooted to the earth,
Move only in the direction of light.
May I walk willingly and eagerly
Upon the steeper path.
This I ask not for my mortal self, oh God,
But for that part of me which is Thee.